THE CONTROL
OF INVESTMENT
IN NEW
MANUFACTURING FACILITIES

The control of investment

E. A. STALLWORTHY

in new

manufacturing facilities

Gower Press

First published in Great Britain by Gower Press Limited
Epping, Essex
1973

ISBN 0 7161 0101 7

Computerised origination by Autoset, Brentwood, Essex

Contents

Illustrations

Preface

Management is concerned not only with the operation of plant installations to make a profit on the product, but also with the provision of extensions to existing, or new, installations in the expectation that these, too, will show a profit. They have to be concerned not only with the economic operation of existing assets, but also with the economic construction of new assets. The larger manufacturers and the major engineering contractors maintain staff with specialised knowledge and experience, but there are many smaller companies who only occasionally become involved in major new investment and who could not afford, therefore, to maintain the necessary facilities.

The purpose of this book is to set out a method of approach which should ensure that all the more common mistakes are avoided. Further, an approach to project management is outlined to ensure that the plant is eventually built within the estimate. Whilst many of the techniques discussed are applicable to the chemical industry, these techniques can be applied to other industries once the underlying principles are appreciated.

The scope of this book has been set largely by the need for detailed guidance both in the approach to investment in new manufacturing facilities and the control of costs. It is necessary, therefore, to begin at the beginning, because only if the initial approach is correctly established will it be possible to institute control. It is in no way an exaggeration to describe this as a real problem in terms of control. There are many firms who have, perhaps, only one major extension in ten years. This could mean that the managerial staff may be confronted with the problem for the first time. Therefore, there would be *no* previous experience available and the venture would appear to be a 'leap in the dark'.

Part One outlines the problem in some detail and defines the attitudes which have to be adopted for its successful solution. Part One goes on to discuss project evaluation in the particular context of the eventual control of the costs of the project. The project evaluation process establishes the objectives that have to be met in relation to any particular project, so now there is but one problem left—achieve that target!

Part Two discusses the organisational framework to be established to enable costs to be controlled with any degree of success. With most companies this organisational framework will exist at least in part, but it is often the presence of an existing system which creates many of the problems. The objective here is to demonstrate the very real differences that exist between an organisation designed for the control of manufacturing operations, and an organisation required for the control of new capital projects. These differences need to be fully appreciated.

Part Three deals with estimating techniques and is, in effect, an outline of the 'tools' to be used for the purposes of cost control, the basic tool being the estimate itself.

Part Four outlines the implementation of the procedures to be adopted for targets to be achieved. Whilst it is true that targets have been met in the past without the use of techniques comparable to those outlined in Part Four, my comment is that this has been far more by luck than judgement. Knowing that there are engineering contractors and consultants for whom the subject of this book is their day-to-day business and who are, therefore, continuously involved in the building of new plants, I realise that I may be thought to be stating the obvious. But what is obvious to the eye of experience can be hidden from those with no real experience. There are a large number of companies whose capital investment programmes are such, that they inevitably lack the opportunity to gain experience in this field. They can be in sore need of guidance and advice in relation to the potential pitfalls that await the unwary. It is for the benefit of those that this book has been written and it is hoped that even those for whom cost control is their daily business, there may be certain techniques which have some element of novelty.

Although simplified equations, graphs, and various 'short-cut' methods are demonstrated, every effort has been made to indicate either the underlying principles, or the philosophy, behind a particular approach. The true value of the data presented will not be found by taking numbers and slotting them into the equations or graphs used to illustrate the text, and thus find a specific answer to a specific problem. No, the true value will only be found when there is an appreciation of the method of approach. This appreciation will give the manager or engineer the confidence and the necessary skill to proceed on his own when encountering problems for which a predetermined approach cannot be established from the data given in this book. The importance of this cannot be over-emphasised. The reader must make every effort to understand the assumptions made and the application of empirical data derived from past experience to new situations. He should never allow himself to fall into the easy habit of number substitution, or even form substitution.

There is, indeed, no substitute for the reader developing his own data, his own forms and his own techniques, using the principles outlined. Only in this way can we have confidence in its application and appreciate its limitations.

Acknowledgements

I am indebted to the numerous people who have influenced my views on the topics covered in this book and have helped me, by advice and criticism, to set them down.

I am also indebted to a number of industrial firms and business associates who have supplied information and illustrations, and reference is made to these in the text where appropriate. In addition, special reference must be made to Courtaulds Engineering Limited, of Coventry, England, in whose employ I was at the time when this book was first drafted. My thanks are due, therefore, to Courtaulds Engineering Limited, its Directors, and my colleagues in that company, for the help given in the early stages, and for permission to reproduce certain standard forms and reports employed by them in their business.

I must confess to a lack of patience in attention to detail and I wish, therefore, to express my appreciation of the services of Mr H.v.d. Doel, of Oude Tonge, in the Netherlands, who spent many hours translating rough sketches and crude diagrams into neat and legible drawings.

E. A. STALLWORTHY
Breda, February 1972.

PART ONE

BASIC CONCEPTS

1

Planning the Investment

Management in general, whether concerned with research, production or marketing, is sometimes confronted with the need to expand production. This expansion then takes either one of two major routes:

1 The expansion or improvement of existing production facilities

2 The establishment of entirely new production facilities

Once expansion is contemplated, management becomes involved in development, design and construction activities which are, at least to a degree, outside of and sometimes widely removed from its normal activities. In the early stages of the development of a production facility, a wide variety of activities will be required. There may be a need for fundamental process research, market analysis, the design development of specific items of equipment, plant location (site) surveys, or investigation into any one of the variety of problems encountered as the project develops.

These activities will be designed to provide answers to a number of leading questions which are always posed at this time:

1 Will it show a profit?
2 What will it cost?
3 Where will it take place?
4 When will the development take place?
5 How will we implement it?

Answers to all these questions and many more, will have to be provided before a firm decision can be taken to proceed, but they all revolve around making effective use of the capital which is going to be invested in the proposed facility, and hence 'fixed'. It is one thing to strive to make the most effective use of available capital in this way: it can well be quite another to clearly demonstrate that effective use is going to be made of the capital, and yet another to ensure that the promises made are in fact fulfilled. The approach adopted will vary from one company to another, and most will already have certain established procedures evolved over a number of years. These procedures will be tailored to the needs of the particular company, and the type of procedure adopted is often dependent upon the size of the company.

Whatever the context, and whether the company is publicly or privately owned, it will be subject to certain legal requirements and its management will be responsible for the optimum operation of the available facilities for the benefit of the shareholders. It must be further assumed that it is a basic policy of that management that it is committed to long-range growth, and could utilise internally generated funds or generate further new capital from the shareholders and loan funds. The possible use of loan funds, in particular, imposes a certain minimum requirement in relation to the ability to employ the available cash resources successfully.

In order to satisfy these needs, it is always necessary in the end to evaluate the 'return on the investment'. All such evaluations have to recognise the time value of money and time is ultimately found to have an importance equal to money or, to use a well-known expression, *time is money.*

Basic Objective

The objective of the proposed investment will be a manufacturing plant which is an economic success. Economic success, in this particular context, will be ultimately measured by the magnitude of the return actually achieved on the investment made. This objective, therefore, must always be to the fore. A variety of people and a range of talents may contribute to the attainment of the objective, and as a result may lose sight of the goal. The research engineer and the chemist will be looking for a perfect process, the works engineer's ambition will be to minimise maintenance costs, whilst the salesman longs for a product without equal on the market. These several objectives, whilst admirable in themselves, are not the stated objective. The design could, in theory, be perfect, the plant on completion could operate precisely as predicted, the product could be the best of its kind, but all this will be to no avail if it is impossible to make a profit. The plant can be a technical triumph in these circumstances, but not necessarily an economic success. Thus it has to be recognised that applied economics have both an integral and essential role to play in the development of a manufacturing plant.

Economic factors

Economics, we are told, is *the science that investigates the conditions and laws affecting the production, distribution and consumption of wealth.* The primary task of management seeking to increase existing production, or to enter new fields, is to apply these principles and thereby ensure that some of this *wealth* attaches to the company to whom it is responsible. Thus, all involved in the development of the project, from the day it was a 'gleam in somebody's eye' to the day when it is in full production must make their decisions with a proper regard to costs in relation to both the potential investment and the return on the investment.

The problem is made more complex because the company will only have limited capital resources at its command, and may be presented with a variety of investment opportunities between which it has to choose. New products and processes will be vying for capital with potential plant expansion, the replacement of obsolete facilities and perhaps with pending acquisitions and mergers. Management is, therefore, faced not only with the task of appraising the economic feasibility of a particular project, but also with the much more critical task of singling out, from a number of possible alternatives, those investments with the greatest potential earning power. A biased presentation of one particular project can cause more worthwhile projects to be abandoned or deferred. Management has a variety of methods to aid it in the selection of projects, designed to ensure that a choice is made which will offer the best profit potential. The various methods which are adopted all have the same objective—the reduction of a complicated proposal to a simple expression of its profitability. Profit can be assessed in terms of the pay-back period, the return on the original investment, the return on the average investment, the yield and net present value. The latter two employ what are known as *discounted cash flow* techniques for the calculation of the figures.

But, any assessment is only as valid as the various estimates which have contributed to its calculation. Consideration has to be given to sales forecasts, fixed and variable production costs, overheads, working capital and the fixed capital investment. These various elements have to be considered in relation to both cost and time. Before we can consider profitability we need to know not only *how much* money will be required but also *when* that money will be required. This is the kernel of the matter and whatever the industry and whatever the manufacturing process, there are a number of factors which will have to be considered in detail if the objective is to be achieved. These factors may be summarised as:

1 Physical
2 Chemical
3 Mechanical
4 Practical
5 Economic

All these factors influence, and sometimes one of them will control, the situation. Every effort must be made to minimise the capital invested in the facility, whilst at the same time, maximising the profit to be made from it; but none of the factors stated above can be ignored.

The Problem Confronting Management

Management, when proposing to initiate expansion, has to make a sound assessment of the various factors involved. Where the management is not of a size to justify its own project organisation, its basic problem is a lack of relevant experience when contemplating investment in new projects. Management expertise will have been directed to the efficient operation of the existing installation. This experience is relevant, indeed indispensable, to a sound evaluation of any new development, but unfortunately it is not enough by itself. There is no doubt that, of the various imponderables with which management would be confronted at this point, the capital cost is usually the most difficult to assess. At the end of the day, it can be the most accurate figure in a series of estimates, but at the beginning the necessary background information can be completely absent. When it comes to assessing the market, evaluating product cost, and estimating a possible selling price, the techniques are familiar even if the figures which result are extremely speculative on occasion. But the preparation of an estimate of capital cost involves a range of techniques which relate to construction, rather than production, and so lie outside the normal field of experience of those considering the new development in its early stages.

The problem is often intensified by the need to establish the possible capital cost of the proposed project at a very early stage. Such an assessment is usually vital to an appraisal of feasibility, and essential to a decision as to the value of continuing work on the development. There is also the problem of alternatives. There could be two or more processes available and the respective merits of the alternatives have to be evaluated. In any such evaluation the capital cost, the sum to be invested, will inevitably play an important role.

It is possible to transfer these problems to a consultant or contractor and this will be discussed in detail later. But there could be a number of reasons, including that of secrecy, which could inhibit this course of action at least in the early stages. It is true that when the viability of the project is under study, an accurate estimate of capital cost is not essential to a sound appraisal. The capital cost—or rather the annual depreciation charges attributable to the investment—rarely figures significantly in the profitability calculations. At a later stage, of course, the actual amount of capital called for can be critical in determining the ability of the company to proceed. If the total capital required is greater than the resources available, then the project *cannot* proceed, however profitable it may be.

This fact is a demanding reason for knowing the order of magnitude of capital cost at the earliest stage. If a company's resources are measured in hundreds of thousands of pounds, it is useless to contemplate a project that will cost millions. This is another reason for seeking to ensure that *all* the factors have been properly considered—not only the direct process requirements, but all the ancillary requirements. The theme of this book is control. Only if *all* the relevant factors *have* been considered will control be possible and it is for this reason that detailed consideration will be given to establishing the scope of the problem.

One other matter deserves mention in this context—the reliability of the data used. Management must realise and accept that it is dealing with a series of estimates, to which one must inevitably attach a *margin of error.* Further, most problems will be complex, with the result that there may be more than one valid answer to the problem. This constant possibility of alternative answers, each of which has its associated margin of error, means that there is invariably something which has to be left to the mercy of 'horse sense'. Often there is obvious conflict as, for instance, between capital cost and operating efficiency, so that the final proposals are quite likely to be the result of a series of judicious compromises. Every care must be taken to avoid a hasty decision, and due consideration must be given to each factor in its turn. The human element must also be taken into account. People tend to have fixed ideas, sometimes amounting to obsessions, and these must be controlled. The late Professor Percy (of chemical engineering fame) once remarked that there were some civil engineers who would make an umbrella of cement. Personal idiosyncrasies need restraint. National characteristics also need to be recognised. In Britain, there is unfortunately, a tendency to 'worry through', believing that all will work out right in the end. But the whole tenor of this book is to encourage the full development of all the necessary preliminaries even if that involves delay, since only by doing so will inefficiency be avoided and costs kept to a minimum.

2

Standard Approach

The approach of manufacturing companies and related organisations, when meeting their problems and overcoming them will be governed to a very large extent by their resources. The several factors already enumerated will call upon a range of disciplines, such as:

1 Engineering
2 Estimating
3 Accounting
4 Planning
5 Purchasing

These disciplines are directly involved in creating the new manufacturing facility. There are other disciplines, such as sales and marketing, that will have to provide data to establish the nature and the viability of the project, but these disciplines will be continuing their normal function. The disciplines outlined above, however, even if available in the manufacturing organisation, will be required to perform tasks so radically different from those they normally undertake as to require an entirely new approach. In large organisations and manufacturing groups, these disciplines may be concentrated in a department dealing with the process development and viability of all new major projects. In such circumstances the central department may, either see each project through to a conclusion or, hand over to local management once the project has been approved for construction. Usually, it is this local management which will thereafter commission and operate the plant in the actual event. All this is related to organisations which, by virtue of their size and needs, maintain technical staff who have specialised knowledge of the problems involved. Such staff will have accumulated data over the years and have available the fruits of many years of continuous experience in design, procurement and construction of manufacturing installations in the industry in which they are engaged.

This book, however, is intended to provide guidance and data for managements who do not maintain such resources, usually because the need is only intermittent and it would not be economic to maintain staff to meet, what would be, infrequent calls upon its services. In such circumstances, the best possible use must be made of the resources which *are* available.

It has to be recognised that the term 'manufacturing' covers a very wide area. The industries involved are as diverse as food manufacturing and processing, textiles, the chemicals industry and metals manufacturing and processing. Within each such group there is further diversity to be coped with in relation to these various disciplines, since the features to be evaluated are concerned not with the product, but with the plant which produces it. For instance, using the chemicals industry as an example, plants for the production of pharmaceuticals are very different, both in type and size, from the average plant unit in the petrochemical field, whilst the manufacture of fertilizers or plastics—processes demanding mechanical handling equipment rather than pumps and pipework for the movement of materials—is different again. Some plants are operated in the open air, whilst others must be housed in buildings.

Initial Stages

The possibilities in relation to the type of manufacturing installation required are too diverse for enumeration. The type of organisation requiring the facility is equally variable, but the most common background to the development of a new project is an existing manufacturing company, and the approach used in this book assumes that the company exists and is considering further investment. This means that the company will have a history of growth and performance established by a series of investment decisions made over the years. The new development will then take one of three major forms:

1 The development of a new process for the manufacture of an existing product

2 The development of a new process for the manufacture of a new product
3 An extension of existing facilities to manufacture an existing product

The technical and cost data already existing in the company will be of value in each of these possible situations, therefore, its resources will probably be most extended when it is dealing with a new process and a new product. It is of value to consider the successive stages that will have to be followed through in such a development. The other alternatives will employ only some of these stages, dependent upon the degree of novelty in the proposed development. It must be recognised that the simplest of the three alternatives, an extension to existing facilities, will still involve a degree of novelty. An extension built without novelty would be a standing condemnation of the management responsible for its building, since there must always by the possibility of improvements based on operating experience. There is rarely any substantial excuse for ignoring such possibility of improvement, although the 'play safe' mentality does tend to inhibit progress of this sort.

The first step in the development of any new process or new product is the basic idea. This may be spontaneous, or it may be the result of some research programme. If the idea seems promising then it has to be studied. Study may require a research programme, which must involve a survey of both the technical and economic aspects. This can lead to preliminary market surveys, laboratory-scale experiments and the production of samples of the final product. If this preliminary work is promising, then the next stage might well be the construction of a pilot plant, or some other semi-commercial installation, to provide production experience and basic data for the development of the full scale project. At this stage, more detailed market analysis will be possible, the sales potential can be investigated, and potential cost and selling prices established. It is at this time that the first capital cost estimate is prepared in detail and a preliminary cost/profit analysis of the project developed.

If the economic evaluation remains favourable, then further development work has to be carried out. It is at this stage that many companies, particularly those with limited design resources, call in a consultant or a contractor to develop further the design to a stage when a realistic estimate of the probable capital investment and profitability of the project can be made. Assuming this more detailed appraisal to be acceptable, then the project is implemented, a complete design is developed, orders placed, the plant built, tested and commissioned.

All the foregoing takes time, and at every stage the economic feasibility of the project is being evaluated. Up to the pilot plant stage, the magnitude of the potential capital investment will not play too significant a role, but once it has been decided that the full scale project is to be developed, its accuracy becomes much more critical.

Earlier it was mentioned that a number of people could contribute to the successful completion of a project and that all must work to one common end, namely, the ultimate economic viability of the project. But, whilst this objective may be achieved and the project becomes an economic proposition, the question can still remain 'Is it making the *maximum possible* contribution to profit?' The requirement is not merely *a* contribution, but the *maximum possible* in the circumstances. It is all too possible to be deceived in this, and company policy can often create a situation in which all are misled.

The possibilities in this context are best illustrated by considering an efficient manufacturing company, which over the years, has improved its profitability by reducing direct labour costs, making more efficient use of raw materials, and reducing down-time on the plant to a minimum. This background experience has *conditioned* management, who study the operating reports and watch for any deterioration in the position they have laboured to establish. Those from management who are commissioned to develop, design, and build the new plant will be fully aware of this particular orientation of management. There is no doubt, therefore, that they will seek to build a plant that will have the minimum direct labour operating costs, minimum maintenance costs and the minimum of shutdowns. In the course of securing these several objectives, it is very likely that over-capacity will be built into the design. Over-capacity takes care of errors in judgement in the original design, will contribute to achieving the minimum targets already stated, and also looks to be a far-sighted, prudent approach in the event that subsequent increases in production are required. All this can be achieved at a cost. The capital investment will be higher than it otherwise would be, but the completed installation could still show a profit—perhaps quite a handsome profit.

Considerations such as those outlined above, lead to the conclusion that the building of a plant for the minimum economic cost—that is, at a capital cost which will maximise profit—requires a very different approach from the one just outlined. Minimum operating cost, minimum maintenance cost, minimum shutdown time, will lead to an increase in capital cost. On the other hand, minimum capital cost may maximise those other costs. So the search must be for an optimum solution. An approach must be adopted which weighs the various alternatives, one against the other, and indicates which course will actually maximise profit. This is a process of optimisation, which these days is often referred to as 'value analysis'.

The Role of the Accountant

Up to the moment, only the engineering and estimating aspects of project development have been considered. But, it was said that accounting had its part to play. Certain features of project development are considered to be the particular sphere of the accountant. Typical of these are:

1 Fixed charges, such as depreciation, local government taxes, rent and insurance.
2 Financing charges, including interest on loans and the return of the investment.
3 Income tax and corporation tax liability.
4 Governmental fiscal policy, the incidence of government grants and similar matters.
5 Value of existing assets.

There is a need with item 5 to distinguish between the 'book value' (the depreciated original cost), the market value (value as a going asset), the replacement value (cost of replacement at today's prices) and the salvage value (scrap value less dismantling costs).

All the foregoing are matters which are relevant to the company as a producing unit and are matters with which the accountant has to deal as a matter of routine. When investment in new production facilities is planned not only the accountant, but others, such as the engineers and the estimator, have to be aware of the impact of the financial principles and procedures involved. The end of the matter will be the provision of a new *fixed asset.* But what is a fixed asset? There is also the need to distinguish between *capital* and *revenue.* Rules in these matters will vary from one company to another, but the following definition of capital expenditure, and hence that which constitutes a *fixed asset,* is widely accepted:

1 Expenditure incurred in the purchase or creation of tangible assets having an expected life of more than one year, intended for use within the business and not for resale. This applies both to the replacement of existing assets and to the outright addition of assets.

2 Expenditure incurred in extensions to existing assets as defined in (1) above, but excluding any expenditure incurred in preparing for the increase in the extent of the asset.

3 Expenditure on existing assets where an element of improvement is involved, but limited to the cost of the improved parts, no account being taken of the cost of installation or prior dismantling for their provision.

Another distinction of interest to accountants, and through them to various local and government bodies, is the difference between *buildings* and *plant.* This distinction appears simple enough on the surface, but can, in fact, be quite complicated. In general, the cost of an item of plant is taken to include not only the purchase and direct cost of the item itself, but also related work essential to, and special to, that plant item. A typical list is given by Figure 2:1, but to assist in understanding the extent of such items it is best to consider the effect of the removal of the item of plant concerned. Is what is left re-usable as it stands for a different installation? If not, then it is treated as plant, integral with the item installed.

Cost analysis

These requirements from an accounting point of view lead to the conclusion that a fairly careful analysis of the costs incurred in developing a project will be necessary. It will be demonstrated later that, in any event, such an analysis is vital to the control of expenditure. The immediate point to be appreciated is that such a cost analysis must reconcile with the requirements of the accountant.

Development expenditure

Consideration of capital expenditure and its analysis would not be complete without some reference being made to development expenditure. This type of expenditure usually occurs in the early stages of an investigation into a project, being related to items such as the building of a pilot plant or an experimental production machine. There may be a number of stages in the development, operation and improvement of such plant and there will be an attempt to ensure that the end result in an operable item of plant or machinery. It is important, therefore, to ensure that the costs are analysed in such a way that only that expenditure which results in a durable asset of a tangible nature is finally capitalised. All other expenditure can, and should, be written

PLANT ANCILLARY WORKS

1 Plinths to machines
2 Stanchions for pipework and cables
3 Pits for conveyors and presses
4 Concrete cooling towers
5 Apertures for the passage of pipes and cables
6 Steel guard rails
7 Platforms essential to the operation of specific items of plant, and not for general access

Figure 2:1 Typical building works that can be classified as 'plant' for accounting purposes.

off as development expenditure. It is usually related to a research account, and treated as revenue.

One of the problems associated with the control of such expenditure is the impracticality of indicating in precise terms the probable total cost. Nor is it usually possible to define with any real certainty the anticipated asset that will result. This question of possible cost is usually brought to the estimator, who is thus presented with a real problem. The normal method of solution, however, is to place a ceiling on the allowable expenditure, recognising from the start that the expenditure may, or may not, yield a result of value. The expenditure actually incurred is then treated as capital expenditure in the first instance and included in that sense in the profitability calculations being made at that time, relative to the project as a whole. Later, when the actual cost is available, it should be possible to analyse the cost and determine to what extent the physical items available are usable, and hence an asset. Then a value can be placed on these items. But this value must be carefully limited to the actual cost of the materials and components incorporated in the equipment, together with the cost of the erection of those materials. All other expenditure should be written off.

Planning and Purchasing

Every manufacturing organisation has its planning and purchasing facilities. The production of the factory has to be planned and the flow of materials, in and out, has to be organised in relation to both time and space. The maintenance of the facilities will be similarly planned, whilst the purchasing organisation will be responsible for securing all the necessary materials. When a capital construction project is initiated, the same facilities are required, but their application can be and usually is so different, as to demand an entirely different approach. It is very important, therefore, that this difference is appreciated and recognised.

In the field of planning, it is vital to realise that so far as management is concerned, to know what *is* has extremely limited value, the main relevance is in relation to what *will be.* The problem of planning can be considered under three main headings:

1 Short-term concepts
2 Medium-term decision-making
3 Long-term studies

All three are relevant, both to manufacturing and the capital construction project. So far as the short-term concept is concerned, this relates to a period which averages some eighteen months, the estimated life of the project from authorisation to commissioning.

Short-term planning

Short-term planning in relation to manufacturing operations almost invariably centres around repetitive operations whereby duration can be precisely established. Project planning, however, centres around a large number of diverse operations where the duration is indeterminate. These operations are largely interdependant, and various techniques have been developed over the years for their control. An early, and still valuable concept, was the Gantt chart, is illustrated in Figure 2:2. It is very difficult to establish inter-dependence on such a chart, so the technique of the *network* is now used, so that the interrelationship between the various activities, in terms of time, can be indicated, and the *critical path,* or sequence of events that controls the overall time taken, can be seen. A typical example is shown by Figure 2:3.

Medium-term studies

Project development also calls for medium-term studies. It is usually considered necessary to forecast up to five years ahead in terms of potential markets for the proposed products, but this is an activity

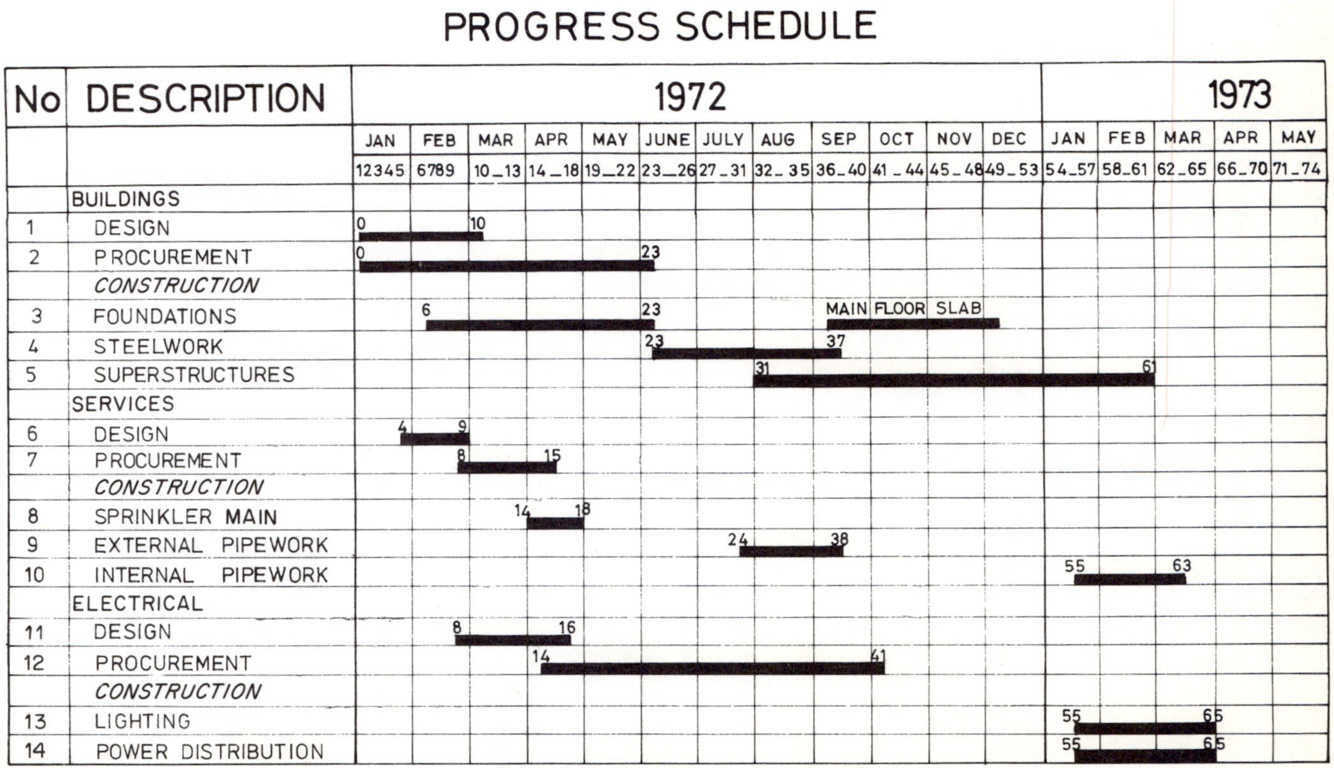

Figure 2:2 The Gantt chart. This is a very direct, simple illustration of the 'bar-line' approach to project planning, giving a clear presentation of the principles involved. The project is a new factory building, and this chart can be compared directly with Figure 2:3, since it relates to the same project.

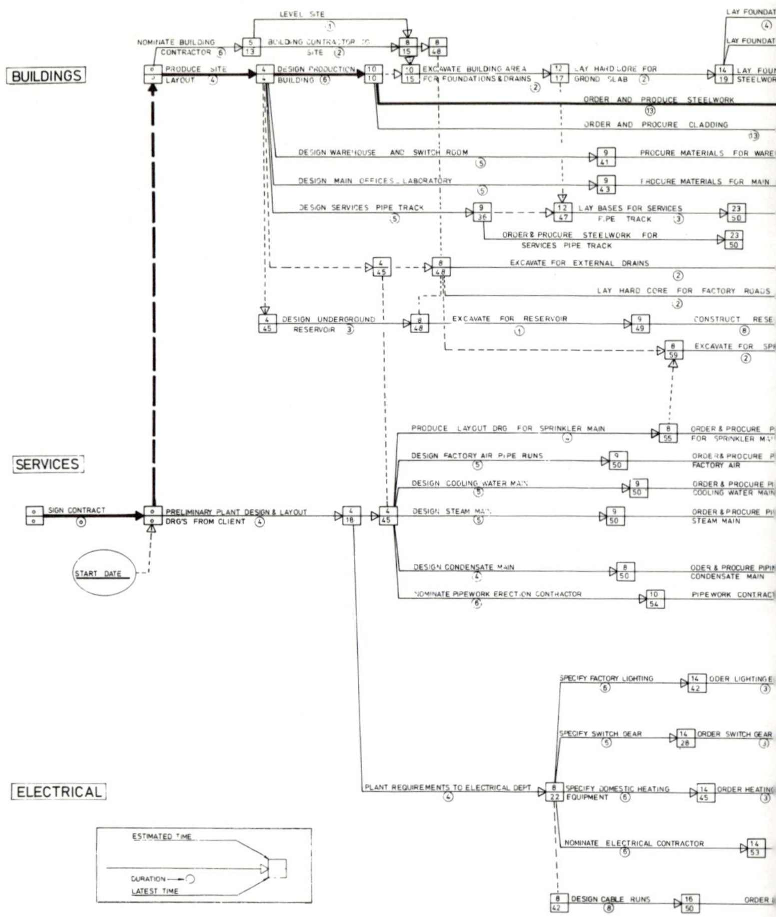

Figure 2:3 A typical network. By contrast with Figure 2:2 this is a network diagram for a new factory building, covering all aspects from design to completion

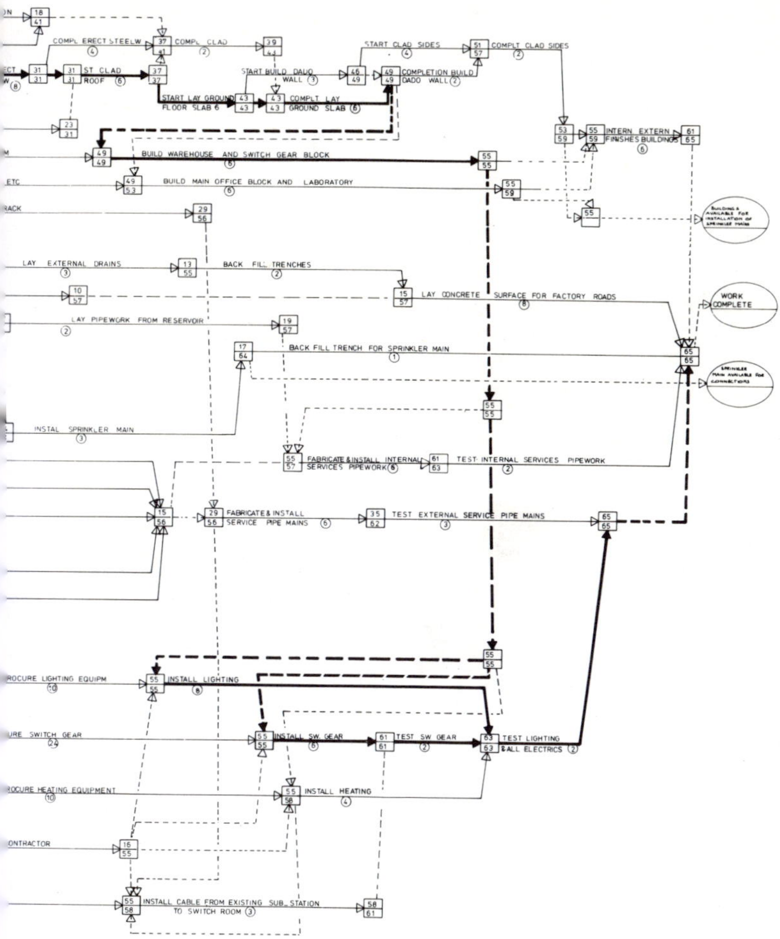

of erection in considerable detail. Despite the complexity, the critical path (heavy line) is readily ascertained.

more relevant to production. The difference lies in the impact of optimism, or pessimism, in the objective in view, particularly since the period requiring analysis is much longer than is demanded for production. Factory production may be planned for three to twelve months ahead, depending on the process or the nature of the product, but a new factory can take some two years to build, and it is the market at the *end* of that period that is going to establish the profitibility of the project—the market in terms of both volume and possible selling price. There are obvious risks in such forecasts, and *risk* is a subject discussed later in detail.

Long-term studies

Long-term studies have relevance in so far as they affect the judgements that may be made with respect to potential markets for the product. These are the economic forecasts that are made and which usually involve projections over twenty-five years.

Purchasing

Purchasing is the remaining discipline to be considered. Once again, it is the differences that are important when one comes to purchasing for capital projects. Normal factory purchasing applies largely, although perhaps not exclusively, to goods. Project purchasing, however, usually involves a large element of services as well as goods. Sometimes these services are purchased together with the goods to which they relate—services such as erection and commissioning. Sometimes the services have to be purchased as an entity in themselves—consultancy and design are typical of this.

The purchase of services calls for very different techniques to those which are proper and adequate for the purchase of goods. The difference has to be recognised if purchasing is to play a full role in the cost of the project. At this stage in the review of requirements, it is the approach to the problem that is under consideration. The requirements have to be seen and provided for. It is sufficient for the moment, therefore, to recognise that there is a differing requirement. The purchase department within the manufacturing organisation will *also* need to learn new procedures if it is to be an effective partner in its new role. The relevant purchase procedures are discussed in detail later in Chapter 9.

3

Developing the Project

Planning is programming for change, and business planning is designed to guide management in the exercise of its discretionary powers in relation to the making of decisions. It has been said that to plan is to invent the future. If it is assumed that satisfactory answers have been found to the questions posed (see Chapter 1) at the beginning, then a decision will be taken to proceed. All the experiments, the prototype work, the pilot plant studies, the market research will have been done and the decision made to build the facility. The plan is laid, the future is forecast, a profit is in prospect. How can success be assured? Let us begin by realising that success never can be 'assured'—there is always risk. The risk can be assessed and methods of evaluating the degree of risk will be explained in due course. The purpose, once steps are taken to implement the project, will be to minimise the risk and this will only be achieved if there is continuous comparison between the planned effort and the actual performance.

The Role of the Capital Cost Estimate

The economic viability of a project will be reassessed at intervals during its development both before, and after, the project has been approved. At each reassessment, an estimate will be made of the fixed capital investment in plant and buildings—an estimate referred to as the *capital cost estimate.*

This is not only the channel along which money will have to be invested in the project. Another possible fixed investment is in land,

and money will also be tied up in working capital. Working capital is the term used to cover the cost of the purchase of raw materials, materials in process, stocks of the finished product and other cash requirements that can fluctuate from time to time, according to the manner in which the plant is operated and its products disposed of.

Fixed costs are, to a large extent, dependent upon the capital invested in plant and buildings. Total operating costs and production costs are always subject to intense scrutiny. Every effort is made to minimise costs, but there is little that can be done about those fixed costs which are a function of the plant and building investment, once that investment has been made. There is much that can be done, however, to prevent unnecessary fixed capital costs being incurred, and the basic requirement for such prevention is control. Practical and effective control of the capital cost is necessary throughout the life of the project, even after it has been physically completed and commissioned. Throughout all this time, the capital cost estimate serves as the standard of reference, the basis for comparison, turning eventually into the completed cost of the project.

The investment in plant and buildings is by far the greater part of the total investment made in any project, and much of the other investment, in particular the working capital, is dependent to a degree on the design of the plant and buildings. Lower investment in fixed capital usually results in lower investment in working capital, but not necessarily in lower operating or maintenance costs. This fixed element is not only the largest element in the total investment but also the most important element because once the commitment has been made, there is no going back. Within limits, land can be sold and working capital can be adjusted, but the plant and often the buildings have been designed to one end only. Indeed, even if it becomes apparent, as the project develops, that the expenditure is going to be substantially greater than was first envisaged, it can be extremely difficult to avoid the extra expenditure. If the money is not spent, there is the danger of being left with a partly completed installation, of no real value to anybody. This possibility emphasises the importance of adequate cost control, so that once the decision has been taken to create the asset, there must be a confident anticipation that it will not cost more than was envisaged when the decision was taken.

The capital cost estimate is of critical importance in this context, and subsequent chapters will demonstrate its role in the development and construction of manufacturing facilities, and the manner in which the cost estimate, if properly prepared, can contribute to the control of costs during the construction phase.

Figure 3:1 Great Coates Works, Grimsby (Courtaulds Limited)

Figure 3:2 Section of a biological plant (Boots Pure Drug Co. Ltd, Nottingham)

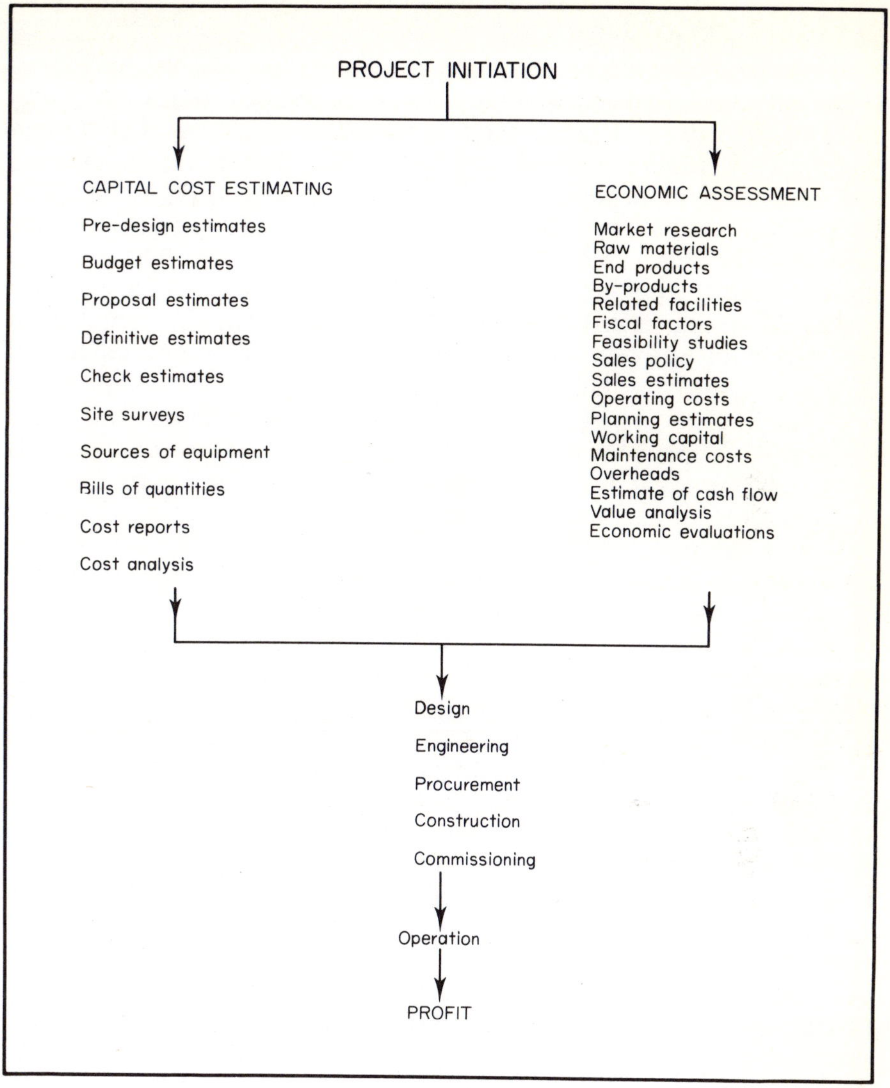

Figure 3:3 The contribution of the estimating function in relation to other economic factors.

The Need for Experience

It has been said, in discussing the role of the capital cost estimate, that *an estimate will be made of the fixed capital investment in plant and buildings.* A fundamental requirement in this context is experience, and the range of experience required can be very wide indeed. The installation pictured in Figure 3:1, a factory which has grown over the years unit by unit, can be less of an estimating problem that the plant illustrated in Figure 3:2, which is a small batch plant. The demand on estimating data will be very similar in both cases, but the very scale of the major installation (Figure 3:2) justifies the employment of specialist estimating engineers, whereas the smaller unit can be the responsibility of a project engineer who would estimate and build without such specialist assistance. But whether the project is large or small the same range of activities will have to be covered in the estimating field, and these are quite extensive. How extensive can be seen by reference to Figure 3:3, where the contribution made by the estimating function is set against the various other aspects of the project that have to be examined if the economics of the project are to be properly surveyed and a profit made.

All the aspects detailed are of general application. These are matters which will always demand study and whatever the industry the approach will always be the same in principle. This is true even of the development of data for estimating purposes. The process technology that happens to be involved is not of great importance of this context. All plants, however complex, can be broken down into recognisable and similar units. This means that the estimating techniques discussed later (Part 3) are of very general, almost universal application. Identical techniques can be used and have been used, for estimating the capital cost of the two very diverse plants illustrated (Figures 3:1 and 3:2), even though one plant manufactures textile fibres and the other a pharmaceutical product. The same techniques can be applied to food processing, the chemical industry, and metals manufacturing and processing.

Cost Control Function

Any project of substance, if it is to be effectively controlled, requires a project organisation with a good leadership, which has the full confidence of the management to whom it is responsible. The organisation requires a leader, often referred to as the project manager. Although an individual may be nominated as responsible, it is probable that many of the people who assist are not directly responsible in an administrative sense. The project manager will give functional guidance, and will organise so that all who are involved in the project, both inside and outside the company, acknowledge and accept his leadership despite his lack of direct authority over them.

For the project manager to exercise cost control of a project a clear understanding of the end in view is required. It must be recognised that for cost control to be effective it must continue throughout, until that end is achieved. Further, each and every one engaged in the project must be *cost conscious,* realising above all that the saving of costs in one area could easily lead to the spending of more money in another. To assist the project manager, a comprehensive and objective valuation is required of all phases of the project. Records must not be 'manipulated'. They must be accurate, impartial, clearly reflecting scope, costs, related conditions and variations in a concise and comprehensive manner. This demands method, systematic tabulation and forms which set out the relevant data clearly. These practical aspects will be developed in detail later, in Part 4. For the moment, let us recognise that 'prevention is better than cure'. Unnecessary restraints can impose serious burdens on project management and impair the efficiency of the operation, so a proper balance must be maintained between a freedom to 'get on with the job' and the necessity of reporting on what is happening. It has to be recognised that cost factors cannot be paramount. Safety, operability, quality, capacity and time are all important factors and their relative importance has to be assessed in relation to cost.

It is also important to realise that cost reporting is not cost control and that for effective cost control certain basic principles are axiomatic, namely:

1 Real cost control will only be achieved by sound management of the project.
2 Those directly concerned with the costs, such as the accountant, cannot control them. Their reports. however, will assist the project management to do so.
3 The effort to control costs must be exerted throughout the life of the project from the beginning to the end.
4 Effective cost control depends almost entirely on the cost-consciousness of all involved in the project.
5 The initial cost targets set are seen as a challenge to be beaten.
6 Recognition of the fact that control is far too late if it is only initiated once the costs come in.

A study of these several points should bring with it an appreciation of the fact that the ability to control costs diminishes rapidly as the project proceeds. This can be shown graphically, as in Figure 3:4. As the project progresses, the number and detail of the cost control reports increases in inverse ratio to the effect that such reports will have on the cost of the project. When the project is complete, the most detailed cost analysis can be made, but the money has been spent and the time when one can influence cost is long gone.

Variations. The biggest single problem throughout the life of a project will be the changes that are made for a variety of reasons. Here again, self-deception is the single biggest danger. A term in common use is 'frozen flowsheets', but in all his experience the writer has never yet been given a frozen flowsheet to work to which was not later altered in some way. The changes are often alleged to be minor, trivial, insignificant—'they will not alter anything' is the common comment. But this is never true. The smallest change costs money, and sometimes costs are incurred far beyond the benefit that would be gained from the alteration, particularly when changes are made towards the end of the project.

It has to be recognised, of course, that changes are inevitable—the important thing is to exercise control of changes so that there are no unnecessary or unjustifiable changes. For the effective control of variations it is most necessary to record every change, whatever its magnitude, and make an estimate of the cost of the change at the earliest possible moment. Internal changes—that is, changes within the overall scope of the project need this detailed control just as much as those changes in scope which have to be reported to management. If each change is assessed in terms of time, and its total impact on cost evaluated *before* the change is made, then very often the proposed change can be seen to be unnecessary.

The necessity for change being recognised, all change should be directed towards improvement in the overall profitability of the project. This is the function of a study technique which has come to be called 'value analysis'.

Value Analysis

The problem of making decisions regarding investment in plant and equipment, and the related costs inevitably associated with them, is intimately bound up with the economic design not only of the whole

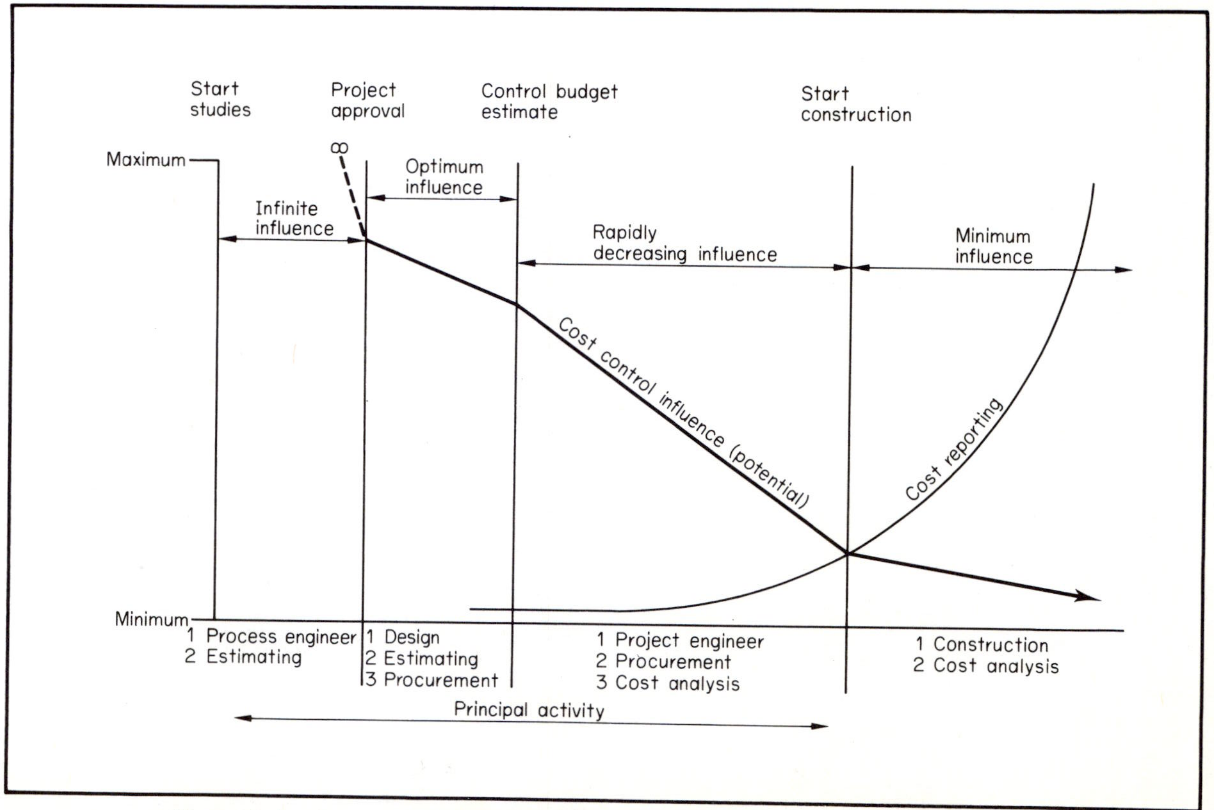

Figure 3:4 *Cost control potential.* The ability to control costs diminishes rapidly over the life of the project, as the volume and number of cost control reports increases. (Reproduced from a paper 'Owners can control costs', included in the 1969 Transactions of the American Association of Cost Engineers, by permission of the author, Mr G. Azud)

plant, but also the design of each specific item of equipment. To maximise profit overall it is necessary not only to select the best investment in terms of the overall concept, but also in terms of the specific content of each component of the preferred alternative. This detailed study, not only of processes, but also of items of equipment in terms of their economic viability, as well as their mechanical or process capability, has developed as a separate discipline over the last ten to fifteen years, and 'value engineers' are now a distinct branch on the engineering 'tree'.

The underlying principle in value engineering is that any assessment of the engineering practibility of an item of equipment or a complete plant must take account of the relevant economic factors. The principle is, of course, long established in relation to *complete plants.* The objective has always been to make a profit from the entity. But to study the individual items making up the entity—that is the novelty in the approach of the value engineer.

In this context, value engineering can be seen as a technique for relating, in a scientific manner, product worth to product cost, and the term 'value' must have the meaning attributed to it when one speaks of 'value for money'. The key process in the technique is simplification. Complexities in the concept, the item being studied, have to be eliminated where they are excessive. The normal approach to any project is to build upon past experience. New projects are almost invariably developments from past history and, in the end, the result of a number of such developments. So we have a step-by-step process, and the tendancy is to examine only the last step, the one just being made, in any detail. This is the route by which complexity enters—value analysis seeks to eliminate it by taking a comprehensive co-ordinated view.

It has to be accepted that value cannot be judged in terms of the capital investment alone. There are certain basic performance criteria such as capacity and product quality that must always be achieved. Further, these performance criteria must be met continuously throughout the life of the plant, which introduces the concept of reliability. Once these basic criteria in relation to performance and reliability have been satisfied then value analysis can be adopted to minimise the investment cost. But let us be sure that the criteria established are the ones we really need. Do not ask for 24 hours a day, 168 hours a week reliability, if the process is not wholly continuous, and products can be stored. Do not ask for 99 per cent purity if the market is equally happy with 98.5 per cent purity. Do not introduce unnecessary 'margins of safety' in estimates of product volume, product diversity and so on.

Value analysis, as such, does not scrutinise such requirements. It goes on from there, accepting these criteria as basic, and examines the process with a view to proposing changes which improve the return on the capital investment without endangering the criteria laid down.

There are, of course, hidden fallacies in the approach, often hidden under a wealth of technical phrases, such as the 'role of probability', and 'decision theory'. The basic objective already referred to must be kept in mind—maximum profit at minimum cost. The fallacy in using value analysis to achieve this obective is that, once analysed, it must be recognised that the objective as such does not exist. Maximum profit, says the value engineer, is infinitely large, whilst minimum cost is zero. All that can be done—and this limitation must be recognised—is to study a few alternatives from among the multitude that are no doubt open for consideration, the few being those that we have the time and the skill to consider. Value analysis is no panacea, any more than is cost control or any of the other techniques that are employed in project development and management. All such techniques have their limitations. The basic and continuing limitation is the frailty and the weakness of the human resource upon which it all depends.

Before leaving the subject of value analysis, perhaps it is important to emphasise that, like almost everything else in project development, it should be carried out as early as possible in the development of any new project. This means that value analysis should come to the fore once the screening evaluations have been carried out and the path is clear in terms of product and capacity. Value analysis can then highlight the proposed investment cost and specify guidelines that should lead to the minimum investment compatible with the declared objectives.

Cost Reality

When the decision has been taken to go ahead with the project, an individual or a team will be given the responsibility of seeing that the objectives embodied in the project are achieved. Whatever the individual, or individuals, were before, the leader now becomes the project manager or project engineer, and is supported by a project team where the size of the project warrants this. The project engineer (the descriptive term which will be used from now on) may, or may not, have been involved in the prior studies and calculations that will have led to the decision to build, but it is almost inevitable that the decision will have been taken on the basis of an estimate of capital cost which no-one really trusts. So the project engineer is immediately under pressure to review and revise this estimate, and to improve its accuracy. So the more important detailed design work is put in hand, suppliers and contractors are approached and the first of many revisions to the budget or appropriation estimate is prepared. Now the estimate being discussed is supported by a degree of detail and the project engineer will find that everyone knows *something* about estimating. There are always one or more people prepared to oppose or criticise and who will seek to modify the figures that are being put forward. It is therefore very necessary that the project engineer has confidence in his data. If he himself does not believe the total he has prepared to be a reasonable estimate of the ultimate cost of the project, how can he convince anyone else? And it is indeed very important that those involved in the project have, and believe that they have realistic targets. Unrealistic targets are of no use for cost control. They only dishearten and mislead. So it is a first essential that the project engineer himself has every confidence in the approach to ultimate cost that is being made. He should firmly believe that whilst the details may vary—and they will—the validity of the estimate can be maintained at least in total. Any estimate can be disproved in detail and some figures can be shown to be high, others low. But in the end it is the grand total which is significant and it is by this that the project engineer should stand or fall.

Responsibility

Whilst the project engineer and his team have a very responsible job, they must not be overwhelmed by its implications. Engineers, in general, seem to find the monetary aspects of project management formidable. The project team will be spending other people's money. This can be great fun—or appear so—but it carries with it duties which must be fully appreciated, and it seems that it is the monetary aspects which have the greatest impact. This can be, of course, a consequence of the fact that any project of magnitude involves a total sum entirely outside the personal experience of those involved, and usually beyond their comprehension. Sums of the order of one million pounds or more cannot be visualised.

Another aspect of significance is that it is more than likely at this more detailed estimating stage that the project engineer and the design engineers learn the real cost of many of the items of plant and equipment to be incorporated in the project for the first time. It must never be forgotten, in this context, that the purchase price of an item is by no means the real cost of that item to the company or the project. In very general terms, the direct purchase cost of any item of equipment will be doubled by the time it is installed—sometimes trebled. The real cost includes the cost of design, delivery, erection, start-up and commissioning. Thus, when a design is being prepared, money is being spent by implication. When the material is being ordered, money is being spent, in fact, much more money than is represented by the face value of the order. If the design is extravagant, then money is being wasted.

Time Factor

Up to the day when the decision to build was taken, everybody took their time. Evaluations were made, feasibility studies were developed, the market analysed and the potential project assessed. These stages in project development usually go forward without undue haste and there is rarely any pressure on the individuals involved to reach the necessary decisions. But once the decision to build has been taken, time becomes all-important and presses relentlessly on the project team. The proposed completion date seems, all of a sudden, to be far too near for comfort. The completion of any project is always and inevitably a race against time. There are unpredictable hazards, such as abnormally bad weather, strikes or industrial unrest, and there is always looming ahead the final problem—will the plant come on stream satisfactorily when complete? The establishment of a proposed capital investment is a dynamic problem and there is never enough time.

The Heart of the Matter

Once the project is really under way the question continually asked is whether all is well. Will the project cost stay within the estimate? This question lies at the heart of cost control, and is only equalled in importance by one other question, the one asked when all is not going well. Then the question is—what are we going to do about it?

To answer the first question at any time in the life of the project requires a knowledge of the costs committed to date (oustanding commitments plus the value of materials received and work in progress), a knowledge of the costs still to come (estimated cost to complete), coupled with the assurance that there is no gap or overlap between these two sets of figures. Since the position is changing daily this knowledge is most difficult to attain. The techniques which have to be employed are entirely different to those used by the accountant, for instance, when he starts to prepare a balance sheet. Systems have to be employed which give an extremely quick reaction to the changing circumstances and careful planning to this end is required *before* the project gets into its stride. Records will be required that make the necessary cost data immediately available without research, and a reporting schedule has to be established and maintained. The procedures outlined later are designed to this end.

If procedures such as those that are outlined in later chapters are followed faithfully, then up-to-date costs should be readily ascertainable. But this is not the end. It is the *estimate to complete* that constitutes the greatest challenge to the project engineer. It must be realised that the problem becomes very real once the project reaches the field, and it will never be answered by sitting at a desk. It is essential to go out and survey the actual physical progress that is taking place.

In all this human fallability plays a very significant role. Costs are incurred by people, people who make mistakes and do not necessarily care to admit them. The project engineer, too, is yet another person, with the strengths and the weaknesses inherent in us all. Recognition of this fundamental fact will help towards a realisation that the reports—the columns of figures—the pluses and the minuses—are not everything. If the report is but figures and graphs, it is incomplete. The columns of figures should be clothed with words—words that are direct and to the point. Regular reporting, not only of the figures but also of the job status, is another fundamental to effective cost control and should be maintained throughout the life of the project, to the bitter end. It then becomes a most valuable history, as well as having been a project tool. The following points can be made in this connection:

1. The mere writing of a cost report is a valuable discipline, and induces control by demanding a logical assessment of the problems that are present.
2. Action should be taken as the report is being written, long before the report is finalised and issued to management.
3. Reporting the facts is not enough. These must be presented logically, in sequence, and interpreted.

A close and careful combination of the technical and psychological aspects of reporting can result in the effective control of costs and a successful conclusion to the project. It is, or should be, far more than a necessary chore undertaken to placate management.

4

Project Evaluation

Project evaluations are required for management decisions at various levels, usually culminating in proposals which require approval by the board of directors of a company. At all stages in the development of a project, there is the problem of choice and the decisions which have to be made. The choice which has been made, will have economic implications. This interrelationship between choice and cost is not always realised and it is more than likely that, even when the relationship *is* realised, the actual cost implications are not fully appreciated. That is, the cost implications of the choice are almost certainly underrated, and undervalued—the full financial implications and economic importance of the choice not being clearly evaluated.

The usual reason for the full implication not being realised is that all the relevant factors will not have been considered. The most usual factor to be ignored is time—the fact that everything takes time and that 'time is money'.

Basic Principles

Once the problem of making a choice is considered in the context of *time* the *length of time,* over which considerations are allowed to range, becomes very significant. When planning was first discussed (in Chapter 2) the concept of time in relation to the making of decisions was divided into three groups:

1 Short term—up to 18 months
2 Medium term—one to five years
3 Long term—three to twenty years

It is true so far as management is concerned, that to know what *is* is of extremely limited value. The main relevance is what *will be.* But what is not realised is the extreme fallibility of the statements made in respect of what *will be.* The problem of placing a true value on data in this context has been increased in recent years as the use of computers has grown. With the advent of the computer, increasing emphasis is laid upon the facility now available at the 'press of a button'. Real time information systems are the 'latest thing'.

The result of all this, when used, is a constant flow of information, but rarely does someone stop to ask—'is it information, or is it really misinformation?' Data is calculated and presented in a most authorative way without any indication as to its reliability or validity. It is usually supported by such a volume of figures in the form of computer print-out that the very volume of paper gives an impression of reality and actuality.

The time horizon

The real problem, the further projections are made into the future, is the range of choice available. As the time horizon extends five, ten, fifteen years into the future, the planner is freed from many of the constraining influences of the present. He is therefore able to consider an ever widening range of possible alternatives. But there is a price to be paid for this freedom, a price which is measured in terms of the difficulty which he has in specifying anything definitively, and the uncertainty with which he must live. In the last analysis, indeed, the number and kind of alternatives the long-range planner considers are limited only by his imagination. Potential markets, alternative products, alternative processes, the variety of mix—most things are possible and quite a few are even probable. The only real limitation is the base from which it all starts—the existing plant or plants.

It has to be recognised that long-term planning is therefore completely indeterminate. The best that any study can do is to indicate that *given certain assumptions,* which may or may not be valid, one alternative is to be preferred to another. Usually, major policy issues will be at stake and the data on which the study is based does not necessarily include the overriding policy decision. The political and social implications, for instance, may well be overriding in the event, but they are completely indeterminate and cannot therefore be assessed. For these reasons, long-term planning must be seen as a means of illuminating issues rather than resolving them.

Medium-term decision-making

Here, in the normal production concept, sales forecasts will be available which are possibly accurate for nine months ahead, but the data normally demands decisions relating to possible events up to two years ahead. This is the normal time that any plant takes from its first inception to being in full production. Studies are made, often a series of studies, the purpose of the studies being to achieve a decision. The obvious reaction is to look for the easy solution. If the easy solution is not apparent from the data available, then more studies are demanded, until the decision becomes obvious. The danger in this approach is that the variances become more important in the decision-making process than the result. The problem can be broken down into four major areas:

1 *Market potential* This relates to the product. A number of answers are required, including the potential selling price, the size of the unit sale, the cost of marketing (or selling) and the cost of distribution.
2 *Capital cost* This relates to the plant. What is the total investment? This must include not only the fixed investment in the plant itself, which may be described as the process capital, but also any investment in related facilities and in working capital.
3 *Operating cost* This is the cost of running the plant. Here consideration has to be given not only to direct costs but also to indirect costs.
4 *The budget* This is the capital resource from which the construction and operation of the proposed plant will be funded.

Before entering into any detailed consideration of the foregoing aspects, it is necessary to bring to mind once again the intent and purpose of this particular book. The subject is *the control of investment.* The immediate interest, then, is the capital cost, area 2 above, and it is proposed to consider the other areas only insofar as they contribute to the control of the investment. The prime concern of management, as has been said before, is to make a profit, and detailed consideration has to be given by management to the viability of the project, and also its relative viability. That is, where there is a choice of projects, a decision has to be made as to which, of the several projects under consideration, will best serve the interests of the company.

The choice is made on the background of calculations and financial statements relating to the proposed project, which are the result of detailed work in the first three areas mentioned above–marketing, capital cost and operating cost. These calculations are then related to the budget and a decision taken.

Relating Evaluations to Company Accounts

From the point of view of control, the important point is that the validity of the statements made once the project is accepted and approved, can be checked when the project is in production. Insofar as the fixed capital investment itself is concerned, estimates have been provided, and costs collected which can be compared in total with the original forecasts. But what of the statements made with regard to marketing and operating costs? Control can only be effective where there is a standard for comparison. It is here that failure so often occurs, since not only must there be a standard for comparison, but it must also be possible to make the comparison.

Once a plant is in production, its costs are integrated with the costs of all the other facilities and activities, and the accountant will be able to state whether the company is operating at a profit or at a loss. But if the profits are not as large as were anticipated, to what extent is this fault of the new plant, now in production? This is the question that it is often difficult to answer. Even more difficult is the determination as to which particular forecast (apart from capital cost) was wrong, *and to what extent.* Answers to these questions are vital to the proper control of the investment. In any particular case the answer is historic and nothing can be done about it, but if the questions can be answered then the process of control can be improved. The areas where poor data was provided will be known and action can be taken to improve the data in those particular areas. This may not always be possible. It could be that the answer given was, in fact, the best possible answer in all the circumstances. In this case, management at least has a better appreciation of the value of the statements being made to them and this can well influence the decisions they take.

Discussion of aspects other than that of the capital investment itself will be limited to the most important in this particular context. It will be seen that the most important aspect for control purposes is that of definition. The boundaries, between many of the costs that are being handled, are indeterminate, but precise boundaries should be drawn if control is to be maintained. Next in importance is that the manner of presentation of project evaluations should be such that they can be related to the company accounts. Only if this is so will a later assessment be possible, since the company accounts are the 'continuum' in which all else is set. The evaluation has to be related to the balance sheet and also to the operating results, or the profit and loss statement. These aspects are dealt with in detail later.

Appraisal of Risk

The nature of the project is the aspect most likely to influence the considerations of those involved in the profitability calculations. For instance, if the use to which a company puts its money is related to the risk it takes, a company normally expects a higher rate of return in relation to a higher risk. Projects can therefore be scheduled in a risk order and related to the investment of the money with a bank—the 'minimum risk' situation.

If a project is of a 'utility' character, such as a new boiler house, then it can be assumed that if the process units which caused the increased demand fail, then other process units will take their place. In other words, utilities have a long life and a longer payout (or lower rate of return) should be considered acceptable. This implies an appropriate 'pricing structure' for utilities as used in the process units. An attempt to make the same profit from utilities as for process units will inevitably distort the figures. Process units themselves can also be divided into those making base products, and those making 'exotic' or more complex products. Once again, a plant making a base product (say sulpuric acid or steel) will have the chance of a longer life, since the scope for its production is greater. But to compensate for this the acceptable return must be seen to be less than with the more complex products, which are often rapidly replaced by others, falling from popularity as quickly as they gained the attention of the market in the first place.

This is the first approach to the problem. The larger the company—the greater the problem, due to the steady increase in the number of possible alternatives. It will be found in seeking to make a selection from among a number of competing potential investments, there is rarely a lack of ideas. The difficulty lies in giving the ideas substance. A method of screening is required, and the most effective method of screening is financial. But there will always be projects which are implemented for other then purely financial reasons. A typical example, growing ever more important now that *environmental control* is to the fore, concerns plants for effluent disposal. These rarely show a profit. However, it is inevitable that these plants must be provided. Similarly, the time arrives when a utility has to be extended, and the nature of the extension will be such that an investment has to be made without immediate return. The hope lies in future growth. Once again, the project will look a poor one from a purely financial viewpoint.

It is not within the scope of this book to enter into this problem of economic analysis in any detail. It is important, however, to realise that all the intensive efforts that can be made, and should be made, to control the capital investment can be undermined by the *risk* taken in other areas. In general, indeed, in any project, the risk taken in relation to the actual capital investment (in the sense of the evaluation of the magnitude of the investment) is far less than the risk taken in relation to marketing prospects, or product price on the market.

The objective, of course, is to select the most desirable alternative. A project is relatively more desirable when it has greater usefulness, lower risk and lower cost. This is a generally recognised and accepted situation, and this interrelationship is commonly expressed in a formula of the following type:

$$\text{Desirability} = \frac{\text{project value} \times \text{feasibility}}{\text{project cost}}$$

Whilst it is true that each of the three basic factors entering into the equation are composed of a number of smaller units which may vary, often unexpectedly, the 'project cost', which is our immediate concern, is the only concept of the three which has a direct monetary value. The other two factors are concepts which have to have a monetary value attached to them in some way, but it must always be arbitrary. The one consolation is that the numerator in the equation actually varies far less than might as first be supposed. This occurs because as feasibility increases, feasibility must also be increasing for others interested in the same business—the competitors. But as a project becomes more feasible, or easier to accomplish, the potential profit will fall, due to increased competition. So the attractiveness of the project, or its value in the eyes of management also falls. Thus, as feasibility increases, project value falls, and the combination of the two, the numerator in the above equation, can be relatively constant.

It is the *feasibility* aspect which incorporates the largest element of risk in the overall appraisal. It should not be forgotten, moreover, that a very significant element in feasibility can be the availability of capital. If the capital resources are not available, or are limited, then feasibility is immediately reduced. It is an interesting thought that the more ingenious and the more inventive a company is, the more potential projects will come up for consideration. But, since capital is always limited, the less feasible will any particular project become. It tends to become a self-negating process, and this fact has resulted in a number of major companies becoming far less interested in research in recent years.

5

Profitability Calculations

The basic requirement in relation to establishing the profitability of any particular project is a *project evaluation.* In this context the basic yardstick used is 'payout', and any calculation of payout must be so organised that the presentation for each project is uniform. This ensures comparability. The other aspect, already mentioned, is that the payout data must be correlated with the operating results, since this is the basic medium for management control of the business of which the project is going to form a part.

The initial problem is one of definition. Considering, first of all, the investment capital, the scope of the capital cost estimate has to be defined. This is particularly important, of course, where the new project is being integrated with or built alongside an existing installation. The new plant, when built alongside existing facilities, will inevitably make use of those facilities. Indeed, initial planning may well have taken the possibility of expansion into account, and capital will already have been invested in supporting facilities to make expansion easier. Similarly, facilities may be provided with new plant which would serve, and have been planned to serve, other plants in prospect. This is the practical context in which the evaluation has to be made.

Various solutions to this problem have been found in practice, but the principle to be adopted should be that the capital investment stated should be that which it is proposed to make then and there. If, for instance, steam is used in the plant from an existing boiler installation, the capital element relating to steam raising should not be included. The capital cost should appear as part of the operating cost. That is, the cost of steam for the process, as included in the evaluation, should include the burden of the capital employed. This assumes that this is the accounting procedure, and it almost invariably is. The further consequence of this is that general facilities, which serve more than one plant, will have to be presented separately, and will require their own project evaluation and financial justification.

Payout Calculation

The purpose of all payout calculations, however made, is to establish the time taken to regain the money invested in the project. All the activities have to be scrutinised, therefore, from the point of view of the amount of cash which they will absorb or generate. Normally, a project begins by demanding money—the cash flows out. This outward flow steadily increases as time passes, reaching a maximum at about the time production starts, or shortly thereafter. The next phase is that money starts to flow in at a rate which should increase steadily until full commercial production is reached. The rate at which money flows in will vary from year to year, but it is usually assumed to stabilise itself at the point in time when it has been forecast that the plant will be in full production. This process is illustrated by Figure 5:1. The payout calculation is usually satisfied to follow this cash flow process only to the point in time when the accumulated cash income equals the accumulated outgoings. It is only after that point is reached that the project will show a profit, in the sense that more money is flowing back than has been spent.

It has to be remembered that the *profit* shown by the specific plant, as outlined above, is not the same thing as the conventional profit declared by the accountant. The accountant will determine the profits of the company on a year to year basis, in accordance with certain rules, and it may be that the plant will be returning a profit, in relation to company accounts, long before the end of the payout period has been reached. However, the company has a 'cash flow', just as much as every project has its own cash flow. This must be so, since the sum of the company business is normally the sum of the result of operating a series of plants, or projects. The cash flow situation in relation to the company as a whole is illustrated by Figure 5:2. It is with this cash cycle that the payout calculation has to be integrated. The cash cycle as presented in the diagram is a continuing process. It never stops and the basic concern is what an engineer might call 'transmission losses'. Typical of such losses are:

1 Unnecessary costs due to inefficient operation
2 Old and surplus stock
3 Bad debts

The cost of inflation and borrowing money are transmission losses of a different kind. The important thing is to recognise, yet once again, the influence of time on the situation. If the cycle moves slowly, then the volume in motion builds up. This increases the incidence of transmission losses to a marked degree.

In relation to this cash flow through a company, the profit and loss account deals with a period of time, whilst the balance sheet shows the position at a particular moment in time. Into this continuing accounting framework comes the new project, contributing to the cash flow and hence, influencing both the profit and loss account and the balance sheet.

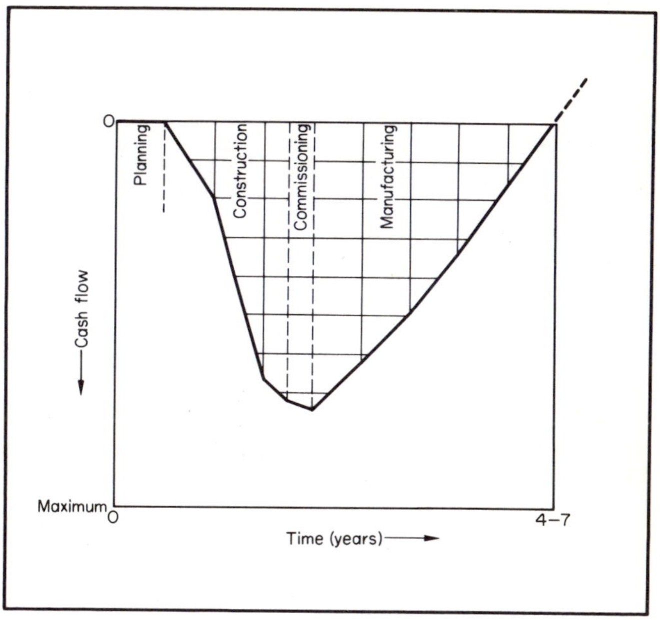

Figure 5:1 Project cash flow. A typical earnings profile. The relationship between time and money is critical. For major projects the time span can be as long as seven years and there are few projects where the time span is less than three years.

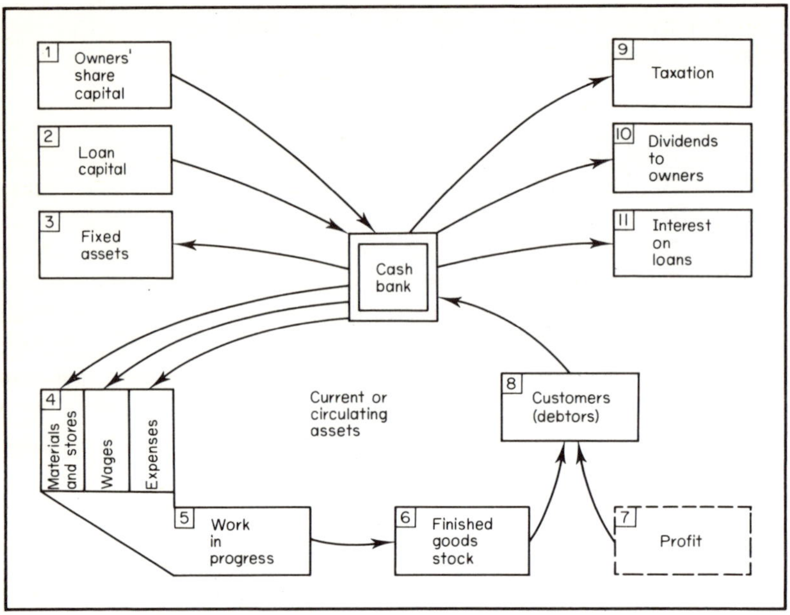

Figure 5:2 Company cash flow. The profit, after taxation, must be enough to cover:
(a) cost of inflation in relation to materials, wages and expenses;
(b) cost of money, such as the interest on loans and dividends to shareholders;
(c) cost of growth, in the provision of further fixed assets and additional working capital for stores, materials in progress and finished stocks. With respect to item (c) there can also be the injection of new capital for growth.

Payout Time

The payout time is an important element in assisting a company to make a choice from the various possibilities that are before it. It should be clearly seen that the payout time is only one of a number of factors, and not necessarily the most important one. Other factors, which can sometimes be of overriding importance, are:

1 The risk involved in the investment
2 The policy of the company
3 The nature of the project

The interrelationship of these several factors has already been discussed. It is important to remember that the various arguments cannot usually be translated into concrete financial terms. Those dealing with the profitability calculations will be fully aware of the arguments which should be mentioned in the supporting data, but the distinction should be maintained. All the while factors cannot be evaluated they should not be allowed to influence the calculation.

Whilst the whole object of the calculations is to establish whether or not the project is going to be profitable, it is nevertheless advisable in payout calculations to avoid the notion of profit completely and to think only in terms of 'cash flow'. This cash flow has been illustrated in Figure 5:1. The payout calculation is designed to follow, step by step, throughout the life of the project, the sums of money actually spent or received, and then to strike a balance between the two. This concept is different to that of the accountant, as can be illustrated by 'depreciation'. For the accountant, depreciation is a debit, but it does not involve the actual disbursement of money. It should not, therefore, be a part of payout calculation, although the relationship between the payout calculation and the company accounts has to be kept well in mind. This means that the payout calculation cannot ignore depreciation, even though it is not a part of the cash flow. The simplest form of expression of payout is:

$$\frac{\text{Total capital investment}}{\text{Annual cash generation}} = \text{Payout}$$

This relates the earning on the investment to the investment being made. However, the investment is not being made at a single point in time, but over a period, and the cash generation also occurs over time, and varies over time. For instance, the plant may not operate at maximum output from the moment it is put into service. A realisation of these facts introduces the first degree of sophistication into the *payout* concept. The point in time at which the investment was to be made was assumed to be midway through the construction period. This period is the period of maximum expenditure and whilst the cash flow varies over this period, it averages out and it is allowable to assume that this average spread is equivalent to making the total investment at one moment halfway through the period.

Relating investment to cash generation as indicated in the above formula gives a number, which is in effect the number of years it will take to recover the investment. This is referred to as the *payout time* and previously was the basic yardstick for judging the viability of a project. That was in the days when money was 'cheap'. A five-year payout represented an annual return on the investment of about 20 per cent. With the cost of money in those days at about 5 per cent, a return of the order of 15 per cent or more was considered appropriate in relation to the commercial risks involved. The higher the risk, or the shorter the potential life of the project, then the shorter the payout time would have to be in order for the project to be a commercial proposition.

Discounted Cash Flow Approach

As the cost of money became steadily more expensive, the assessment of the attractiveness of projects by means of payout time became dangerous, particularly when projects were being compared. Payout time ignores a factor of extreme importance when money is expensive. This factor is the rate at which the money is required, and when the money is required. The later in time that money is required, the less expensive it becomes. If all the projects considered had an identical cash flow curve (Figure 5:1) there would be no difference. But the profile does vary, and when money is expensive, the variance can be significant, enough to make one project more attractive financially than another, even though the payout time is longer.

To overcome this problem, the technique of *discounted cash flow* was developed. In essence, the value of the cash flow is related to the time at which it is required. It is not the purpose here to expound this particular method. It is however mentioned because time is an important factor in connection with cash flow, and the importance has to be recognised when considering the validity of cost control techniques. That is, it is not sufficient merely to control the cost of a project in terms of keeping the total investment to the minimum. The time at which the money is spent is also important and could be critical. The point must therefore be continually borne in mind that cost control is concerned not merely with the magnitude of the sums being spent—that is, in keeping within a budget—but also *when* they are being spent.

The discounted cash flow approach is, then, a particular way of measuring the attractiveness of a capital investment proposal, which takes account of the time at which the money is required. The method produces a percentage figure, usually described as the 'earning power' of the project, which is analogous to the average annual rate of interest that would be earned by the investment being made in the project. The DCF method differs in two major respects from the straightforward 'payout time' approach mentioned earlier. These are:

1. It takes into account the estimated earnings over the whole life of the project.

2 It puts a higher value on income received earlier, rather than income received later.

One definition of the earning power is: 'The "earning power" of a project as determined by the DCF method is that rate of discount which, when applied to the deferment of all future cash movements to present value, will make the future cash income expected from a project just equal to the present value of the project's cost.' Putting it in other words, the *earning power* is that rate of discount (it is expressed as a percentage) which will make the present value of the sum of all cash outflows and inflows equal to zero. The actual earning power of any project is found by trial and error and various methods are possible. It is not proposed to enter into these methods of calculation, but, for any approach, the fundamental data required is the same, and this is:

1 The amount of the initial investment, revenue expenditure and working capital as used in payout calculations, but specified year by year.
2 The annual amounts of cash income, calculated as in the usual manner for a payout calculation, but over the total lifetime of the project, and with each year specified separately.
3 The residual value, if any, of the assets at the end of their life.

This means that a life expectancy has always to be determined for the project. The value of the approach depends almost entirely on the quality of the cash income estimates, although the effects of inaccuracy in the estimates, when they relate to later years, is much reduced as a result of the compound discounts which then take place. There are various ways of getting out of this difficulty of forecasting cash flow over periods of time. One way is to assume that, for any given project, the investment will earn, for fifteen years, the same income as was calculated for the last year for which a reasonable estimate was possible. Another is to terminate the project at the last year for which reasonable estimates can be made, and the following year take in the residual value of all assets—say, the scrap value of specialised plants, or a transfer value if it is possible to use the plant for another process. Estimates of plant life are difficult, but since the future market estimates are even more difficult, these usually bring such a terminal point much closer than does plant life.

Payout and DCF Compared

The discounted cash flow approach to project evaluation is complicated and usually finishes up in the hands of the accountant. The average engineer has considerable difficulty in appreciating the finer points of the calculations being made and careful definition of the ultimate yardstick is required if it is to be understood by those not normally involved in 'discounting'. This gives rise to the question: 'Does the approach give a better answer?' The answer to that can well be that it gives a *different* answer—whether the answer is *better* depends very much on the validity of the particular assumptions that have produced the difference.

This point can be best illustrated by an example. Figure 5:3 presents two alternative projects, A and B. It will be noted that the basic difference between these two projects is the rate of sales build-up, and a different assessment of the allowances to be made for depreciation.

	PROJECT A £X 1000	PROJECT B £X 1000
Total capital investment	1,500	1,500
Total netback when in final production	1,000 p.a.	1,000 p.a.
Manufacturing cost, fixed	210 p.a.	210 p.a.
Manufacturing cost, variable	440 p.a.	440 p.a.
Pre-operational expenses	100	100
Tax on profits	50%	50%
Stocks (created in first year) as percentage of capacity	25%	25%
Depreciation allowance (per year)	10% for 10 years	30% for years 1 & 2, then 5% for 8 years
Debtors (as percentage of annual sales)	10%	10%
Raw material stocks	Assume financed by creditors	
SALES DEVELOPMENT		
Year 1	500	600
Year 2	750	900
Year 3	1,000	1,100
Year 4	1,000	900
Year 5	1,000	900

Figure 5:3 Two typical projects. The basic difference between these two projects is in the assessment of sales and the allowance made for depreciation.

The cash flow from these two projects would be as indicated in Figure 5:4, giving a difference of proceeds from year to year as tabled. If a payout calculation were now to be made in respect of both projects, the answer would be the same, since the figures which vary, namely the rate of growth of sales and the rate of application of depreciation, do not affect the payout time. As can be seen from Figure 5:4, the payout time for both projects is some eight years. If, however, a DCF calculation is made, the results of which are presented in Figure 5:5, a different picture emerges. The two projects are indeed evaluated differently when this approach is used. Taken over an eight-year period, project B looks the most attractive. However over a ten-year period, there is little to choose between them. Over a twenty-year period, project A becomes the more advantageous.

But think of the assumptions that have to be made and have been made. Assumptions have been made regarding sales; an assumption has to be made as to the potential life of the plant, and this involves the further assumption that sales will be possible at maximum production

	CASH FLOW		PROCEEDS	
YEAR	PROJECT A £X 1000	PROJECT B £X 1000	PROJECT A £X 1000	PROJECT B £X 1000
1	90	190	500	600
2	210	360	750	900
3	235	420	1,000	1,100
4	250	165	1,000	900
5	250	163	1,000	900
6	250	163	1,000	900
7	250	162	1,000	900
8	250	162	1,000	900
Sub-total:	1,785	1,785	7,250	7,100
9	175	125	1,000	900
10	175	125	1,000	900
Total:			9,250	8,900

Gross investment, Project A: £1,800,000
Gross investment, Project B: £1,790,000

Figure 5:4 Cash flow and proceeds for Projects A and B. The gross investment is the capital investment, plus stocks and debtors. This varies, since stocks and debtors are related to sales, which are different in the two cases given.

throughout that life. So, whilst there *is* a difference, that difference may be far less important that at first appears, and payout time may still have much to commend it. Decisions to build or not build, do not—or most certainly should not—rely upon such fine distinctions. Even if it is only a matter of simple choice—that is, the decision is made, but alternatives are available—it should be recognised that the value of the DCF approach as a selectivity tool hinges on the ability to define the life of the plant *and* its sales accurately over long periods of time. In practice, this is never possible and success then comes from good fortune rather than good management. The value of good management is that it can make the best use of good fortune and minimise the effects of unfortunate decisions.

	PRESENT VALUE	
YEAR	PROJECT A £X 1000	PROJECT B £X 1000
1	82	173
2	173	297
3	176	315
4	171	113
5	155	101
6	140	92
7	128	83
8	118	76
Subtotal, years 1–8	1,143	1,250
9	106	69
10	97	63
Total, years 1–10	1,346	1,382
Years 11–20	415	296
Working capital	45	43
Totals	1,806	1,721

Figure 5:5 The DCF calculation. The table shows the 'present day value' of the cash flow given in Figure 5:4. This value has been assessed using a 10% discount rate. If the project has a 20-year life, then the earning power of Project A would also be 10%, and that of Project B slightly less. A shorter life would result in a lower discount, since the earning power would be less.

Fixed and Variable Costs

In making the project appraisal outlined above, reference was made to fixed and variable manufacturing costs (Figure 5:3). These need a degree of definition, since confusion can easily arise. The terms are used in relation to the cost of production. The capital cost is, inherently, a 'fixed' cost, but it is treated separately, and is, in fact, represented in the day-to-day costs of operating a plant through the allowances which are made for depreciation. Depreciation was, originally, a means of valuing the asset, once created. It was presumed to fall in value over the years and would be 'written off' over a period which was, in effect, the 'lifetime' of the plant.

However, this simple concept has been complicated over the years by the ever-increasing rate of escalation, which meant that the real value of the plant could possibly grow over the years, rather than fall, assuming that it could be maintained in production. Further, the use of depreciation as a fiscal tool also affects the position, since the significant factor then becomes the depreciation which one is allowed to set against profits, rather than the physical realities.

All production costs must fall into one of two categories, variable or fixed. Variable costs are those costs which tend to vary with changes in the level of production in the plant unit under consideration. These include the cost of:

1 Raw materials of production
2 By-products from the plant (which appear as a credit)
3 The products, including packing materials
4 Auxiliary services to the plant, including the supply of utilities such as steam, water and electric power
5 Fuels
6 Charges on production, such as process royalties.

Fixed costs are those costs which tend to be unaffected by variations in the level of production. These costs include:

7 Operating
8 Maintenance
9 General overheads
10 Depreciation (which is a reflection over time of the original capital investment in the plant)

All these expenses (1) to (9) above—that is, excluding the last item—are elements of what is called *working capital,* in that, to run the plant, these activities have to be funded. This funding relates not merely to the obvious items, such as the stocks of raw materials and finished products, maintained for efficient operation, but also to costs of utilities, wages and salaries.

The important point in valuing the above items is to remember, particularly when considering a plant which is being integrated into an existing installation, that utilities should be charged for at costs which include the related capital investment. Where raw materials are provided by another plant or division, the price should include not only the full production cost of the material, but also a profit. Similarly, when by-products are passed into other parts of the plant, the value should also include the profit of the plant producing them.

The level at which these values are to be set can be productive of prolonged argument, but one equitable way to resolve such arguments is to appraise the *alternative use* value. What is the value on the open market? When by-products cannot be disposed of without incurring further expense, all such expenses should be taken into account in assessing both the capital and manufacturing costs. A typical example is the disposal of effluent through existing systems.

Scope of the Evaluation

The ramifications from a financial point of view, when a new capital project is integrated with an existing organisation, are innumerable. It becomes necessary, therefore, to establish certain boundaries to project evaluation and recognise that it is just not possible to take *everything* into account. Indeed, the cost of meticulous attention to detail outweighs the effect a limitation in scope on the study would have on the validity of the evaluation being made. Major exclusions can and should be mentioned. Typical of this is the exclusion of the cost of the purchase of land. Such an exclusion should be mentioned, even when the land was purchased at some earlier time. In addition, the incidental expenses associated with land purchase, such as legal charges and surveyor's fees, would also be ignored, and their omission could well go unmentioned.

Similarly, in considering the time over which the evaluation will range, early initial expenses can often be ignored, and perhaps retentions, if they are long delayed after the start-up of the plant.

On the other hand, there are a number of aspects in cost evaluation which can easily be overlooked, but which ought also to be studied and appraised. From experience, the following are mentioned as being particularly significant, in that they are often overlooked:

1 Division between home and export trade in relation to the product, and the estimated selling prices in each area. If a product can sell at a premium because of some specific situation (such as a protective tariff) this should be mentioned, since it is open to change without notice.
2 The amount of money absorbed, and hence required as working capital, by the particular credit terms being given to customers.
3 The costs of marketing should include blending and formulation, where applicable, storage, handling, packing and selling costs, *together with* the related administrative and overhead costs, including market development and advertising activities.
4 Where by-products from the processes are used in the process, such as for fuel, they should be properly valued (for instance at market prices) and credited as a by-product before being charged as a cost. Such actions should be highlighted, since alternative fuels may become available which are cheaper than the current market price of the by-product.
5 If the plant accepts, for instance, high pressure steam, and has a volume of low pressure steam as exhaust, credit should be taken for this steam as the cost of production elsewhere on the site, where such steam is required.
6 Assessment of the overheads on operating labour should include special transportation, if provided, and the cost of engaging and releasing labour.
7 Maintenance cost, or the cost of keeping the plant in good running order, is usually estimated on a statistical basis, as a percentage of the total fixed capital investment. In assessing maintenance cost, the effects of corrosion, and high operating temperatures and pressures, should not be overlooked.
8 The costs of general overheads, not provided specifically for the new plant, should always be included. Typical of these are laboratory services, fire protection and safety services, maintenance workshops, medical services, training facilities, canteens, watchmen, and general transport facilities.
9 Pre-operational expenses, such as special start-up teams. Consideration should also be given to the possible loss of product in the early stage, or the production of substantial quantities of materials which do not meet their specification.
10 Where the product is already being marketed and stocks of the

finished products exist, only the increase in working capital in this area attributable to the increased volume of product should be taken into account. Working capital should always include provisions for debtors, stocks of finished products in the plant (stocks held for marketing purposes should be part of the marketing cost), and stocks of raw materials, chemicals and catalysts maintained.

Report to the Board

When the estimate of capital cost is available and all the various assessments have been completed, and an evaluation made, then that evaluation will have to be presented to senior management, such as the board of directors, for approval. Most companies have fairly rigid procedures in this respect, which begin with a budget. It is usual to forecast the company accounts for three, or perhaps five years ahead, and the major factor in any such forecast, or budget, is the proposed future investment. Such investment is usually divided into two groups. The first is routine investment, largely for minor plant changes, incidental improvements and other necessities. The second will consist of major development projects. From year to year the immediate future will be established in some detail and budgets or financial targets established. These targets then serve as a standard of reference by which actual progress can be assessed.

In relation to such budgets, the report to the board may be either a contribution to the budget data or a request for an appropriation. It is the latter that is of prime interest, since it is only when capital has been appropriated, or approved for expenditure, that the project is initiated and 'control' is needed. In all such presentations the most important consideration is to ensure that all the capital required is declared. The evaluation will include not only the capital required for the plant development itself (the process unit) but all *directly related* facilities. It can be, of course, that utilities or other general facilities are also required, and it is possible that such extensions are more than is immediately required for the project in hand. This is due to the fact that such facilities can usually only be extended in discrete steps. This means that if the capital for such requirements were included with the immediate proposal that proposal would look much less attractive, because an investment was being made for the future, on which there would be no immediate return. This means that such items should always be presented separately; separate authorisation being sought with a separate justification. Nevertheless, the essential nature of the development in relation to the project under consideration should always be made very clear. The justification for such investment in the 'future' can be based on two major factors:

1. Its relationship to the existing production and forecast expansion as planned.
2. Its relationship to the plant under immediate consideration.

It is often found that expenditure, other than capital expenditure, will be incurred when proceeding with a project. This is particularly so when a new plant is being built adjacent to existing facilities. Such expenses should always be mentioned, although the approval procedure may ignore them. Such expenditure can materially affect the profits of the company. It is, for the same reason, important that such expenditure is estimated carefully in detail, and controlled.

Presentation of the Report

The basic objective, in presenting a report, can easily be lost sight of in the anxiety to 'make a case'. This often results in the highlighting of matters which are often largely irrelevant, whilst matters of considerable importance, to those who have to read and act upon the report, are forgotten. The basic objective of any report is to pass on information to others, and a good report writer will always keep that in mind and never assume that the 'others' have the same familiarity with all the facts as he has himself. There are four questions which should always be asked and answered before any report is written:

1. What is the subject of the report?
2. What is the purpose of the report?
3. Who will read the report?
4. What do its readers already know?

The answers to these questions will give a lead to the type of information which should be included in the report, the amount of detail required and the best method of presentation. Any report supporting a budget appropriation will be a formal document and the format for the financial data will probably have to conform to standard company practice. There is no merit, therefore, in enlarging further on this aspect.

6

Investment Ratio

The ultimate success of any company depends upon the ability of its managers to make the correct decisions in relation to the profitability of both the existing and proposed activities of the company. The overall objective of the company, regardless of what might be considered technically desirable, is to survive. In order to survive, its customers have to be induced to buy, its employees have to be induced to go and work for it, and its owners have to be induced to invest in it. It is this latter aspect that is now under consideration and it is the prime consideration because if the owners fail to invest, then the company will fail, however eager its employees are to work or its customers to buy.

The basic inducement in relation to investment is the earnings which the investor receives in relation to the investment, often expressed as a ratio, price/earnings. The higher the ratio, the more attractive is the investment. Existing company operations will establish this ratio at a certain level, and the attractiveness of any proposal for further investment will depend upon the effect that the investment will have on the price/earnings ratio, or the earnings per share (EPS). Will it enhance it? The appraisal of the earnings of a company comes from a study of its balance sheet, in relation to the profit/loss account, or income statement, as it is sometimes called. The balance sheet shows the financial status of the company at a particular date, whilst the profit/loss account records the events which affect the balance sheet over a period. The balance sheet sets assets against liabilities; the profit/loss account sets income against expenses. Where income exceeds expenses a profit is made, some of which can be held in reserve, and some of which can be distributed to the shareholders. Generally, however, 'earnings' are the total profit, whether distributed or not. This profit comes from the cash generated by the company and the new project is designed to contribute to the cash generation in the *process of time.*

Basic Relationship

Let us now consider project A (see Figure 5:3) in relation to both the balance sheet and the profits/loss account. To simplify the approach, consideration of the effects of the new project begins when the plant is completed and goes into the books of the company in its entirety. It is assumed that the complete plant is taken up as an asset in the books within one financial year. Figure 5:4 gives the cash flow and gross proceeds, or the income from sales.

If it is assumed that the company is financing the building of this plant from its own resources, then it will not incur interest charges in relation to loans for the project and the effect of the project on the balance sheet at the beginning of year one will be as shown in Figure 6:1. This is compared there with the situation at the end of year one. During year one, the plant will have started up and will produce 75 per cent of its rated total capacity. It has been assumed that of this production, two thirds will be sold, the balance going into stock. The effect of this on the profit/loss account for year one is shown in Figure 6:2.

If the viability of the project were to be assessed at this point and judged by its effect on the accounts of the company in terms of the usual yardstick, the earnings ratio, it would be condemned out of hand. What has to be appraised, therefore, is the cash flow in relation to the gross investment. Comparing Figures 6:1 and 6:2, this is seen to be 90/1780, or 5.1 per cent. The reciprocal of this, 1780/90, is the payout rate at this point, which is 19.6 years. It is interesting to note—as those involved in a project will know—the way in which the figures such as the cash flow and the payout time, are now 'buried' in the accounting statements and have to be derived from the figures presented. They are no longer directly available.

After One Year

The exercise can be repeated for year two, as illustrated in Figures 6:3

and 6:4. It will be noted that although the total funds employed in the business are growing, the investment is falling. The financial appraisal is now very different to what it was a year ago. If cash flow is related to gross investment once again, this is now 210/1805, or 11.6 per cent. An earnings ratio can now emerge, since a profit has been made. The real capital employed is now the book value of the plant (1200) plus the working capital of 305 (in effect, 230 + 75) and this gives a ratio of about 4 per cent.

After Two Years

It is perhaps of interest to follow the life of this plant in the company accounts for one further year. This is done in Figures 6:5 and 6:6. The cash generation is now 235/1800, or 13.1 per cent whilst the profit ratio is 85/135, or 6.3 per cent. The net investment in the project will continue to fall as cash is generated until the eighth year, when the investment will be cleared. The investment is cleared in the eighth year because the plant has a 'payout' of eight years. At that point in time the cash generation is still about 13 per cent, but the profit ratio has risen to some 17 per cent. In a running business, of course, the amounts put by for depreciation are re-invested, together with a proportion of the profit that is being generated, the balance being paid out to the shareholders in the form of dividends.

It will be appreciated that the foregoing presentation over the years ignores escalation. In the event, escalation should not alter the relationships, since as costs rise, selling prices can be expected to rise to compensate for this.

Capital Cost Versus Operating Cost

Previously, when considering the basic principles affecting evaluation (see Chapter 4), the appraisal of risk was discussed in relation to the comparison of projects. But once a project has been approved and the overall decision to take certain risks has been made, the project engineer involved in the design and construction of the facility is confronted with a series of choices, which are very much influenced by his own personal appraisal of the 'risks' involved. He is also aware that the end result of his efforts is set down in the company accounts, in the manner that has been discussed in some detail. It is, of course, patently obvious to the project engineer at this point that once the plant has

	Beginning of year 1 £X 1000	End of year 1 £X 1000
ASSETS		
Plant at cost	1,500	1,500
Stocks of product	–	230
Debtors	–	50
Total funds	1,500	1,780
LIABILITIES		
Share capital		
(*a*) In fixed investment	1,500	1,500
(*b*) In working capital	–	280
Total funds	1,500	1,780

Notes:
1. The net sum invested in the operation at the end of year 1 is £1,690,000 and not £1,780,000 as might be thought, since there has been a cash generation of £90,000 in the year, as shown in Figure 5:4, and demonstrated in note 3 of Figure 6:2.
2. The book value of the plant is now £1,200,00, or £1,500,000 less two years' depreciation at £150,000 per year.

Figure 6:1 Abstract from balance sheet of the data relevant to Project A. This is outlined in Figure 5:3, giving the position at the beginning and end of the first year of operation.

been built and is operating, the continuing factor entering into the accounts is the operating cost of the plant.

The risks which the project engineer has to take in relation to operating costs fall under two main headings—'insurance risks' and 'process risks'.

Insurance risks

As the design develops, there will be a continuing desire to incorporate features that will minimise operational problems, minimise labour requirements and minimise the use of raw materials. This will be an insurance against complaints about the high level of operating costs and

	£ × 1000
INCOME	
Sales	500
Stocks at cost	230
Total (or gross) income	730
DEDUCTIONS	
Pre-operational expenses	100
Cost of production	540
Provision for depreciation	150
Total deductions	790
Loss before tax	60

Notes:

1. Cost of production is the sum of the fixed cost (£210,000) and 75% of the variable cost (£440,000), or £330,000.
2. The value of stocks is calculated by taking the cost of production (£540,000), adding depreciation (£150,000) and then taking one-third of this total (£690,000), being the volume in stock at the end of the year.
3. Cash flow, as in Figure 5:4, is £90,000. This is seen in the above account as the depreciation allowance (£150,000) less the loss before tax (£60,000). The cash flow is also the total income (£730,000), less pre-operational expenses (£100,000) and the cost of production (£540,000).

Figure 6:2 Details from the profit/loss account, relevant to Project A. This is outlined in Figure 5:3, being data relevant to the operation of the plant in its first year.

it can, possibly, be achieved at a cost. The cost that has to be paid is the investment of capital.

A further cost that can be insured against by increasing the capital investment is unplanned shutdowns. So the project engineer, left alone, will tend to build a plant having the minimum of shutdowns, the minimum operating cost and the minimum maintenance cost. The only inhibiting factor, in the pursuit of this objective, is the amount of the capital appropriation allocated for these purposes.

To follow this particular path is also a personal insurance for the project engineer. The result is, in general, achieved by building over-capacity into the plant, and incorporating stand-by plant. This procedure takes care of errors of judgment in the original design and if

	Beginning of year 2 £ X 1000	End of year 2 £ X 1000
ASSETS		
Plant at cost	1,500	1,500
Stocks of product	230	230
Debtors	50	75
Total funds	1,780	1,805
LIABILITIES		
Share capital		
(*a*) In fixed investment	1,500	1,500
(*b*) In working capital	280	305
Total funds	1,780	1,805

Notes:
1. The net sum invested is £1,505,000, since the cash flow (Figure 5:4) is £210,000 this year, and £90,000 last year, a total deduction of £300,000.

Figure 6:3 Abstract from the balance sheet at the beginning and end of year two, for Project A in Figure 5:3.

the product is a success, the course can well gain the approval of management. Why? Because as the plant is 'de-bottlenecked' substantial increases in output can be secured for a minimal increase in the capital investment, and the policy takes on an appearance of foresightedness which is commendable. But is it?

The plant should incorporate a sufficient degree of 'insurance' in these areas to be safe in operation, and direct hazard to life and limb must be avoided at all costs. But efficient design is not necessarily the safest possible practice and the degree of risk should be balanced against the cost of the provisions that will increase safety in operation. Often the insurance company becomes involved, and it is at this point that it is found that premiums can be reduced if certain provisions can be made (fire walls are a good example). But such provisions do not contribute to the efficient operation of the plant. In fact, they sometimes mitigate against efficiency, and they do not *have* to be carried out. The risk must be appraised and set against the benefits.

	£ X 1000
INCOME	
Sales	750
DEDUCTIONS	
Cost of production	540
Provision for depreciation	150
Total deductions	690
Profit before tax	60

Notes:
1. No tax is payable as yet, since this year's profit just cancels out last year's loss.
2. Cash flow, as in Figure 5:4, is £210,000. This is seen in the above account as the depreciation allowance (£150,000), plus the profit (£60,000).

Figure 6:4 Details from the profit/loss account for year two, for Project A in Figure 5:3.

Sometimes the only benefit is a reduction in the insurance premium.

Process risks

Many processes, especially new ones which have only just passed the 'pilot plant' stage are not too well defined when equipment size is under consideration. Once again the project engineer will tend to take a conservative approach and incorporate margins in the sizing which will increase in proportion to the lack of definition in design, or lack of experience in operation. This conservatism has the same, familiar effect–it increases the capital cost.

The subject of the working life of a plant has been discussed in some detail in considering payout time, since the potential life of the plant will affect its value to the company. In practice, the life of a plant is rarely determined by its engineer. Its life is almost always fixed by the potential sales of product from the plant. In theory, the most efficient

	Beginning of Year 3 £X 1000	End of Year 3 £X 1000
ASSETS		
Plant at cost	1,500	1,500
Stocks of product 230	200	
Debtors	75	100
Total funds	1,805	1,800
LIABILITIES		
Share capital		
(*a*) In fixed investment	1,500	1,500
(*b*) In working capital	305	300
Total funds:	1,805	1,800

Notes:
1. The net sum invested is now £1,265,000, being the net sum invested at the end of year 2 (£1,505,000), less the change in working capital (£5,000) and the cash generated in the year (£235,000)

Figure 6:5 Abstract from the balance sheet at the beginning and end of year three, for Project A in Figure 5:3.

approach would be to design the plant so that, at the point in time when the product went off the market, the plant was worn out and could be scrapped. In practice, once again, plants are normally maintained at something approaching their original condition throughout their working life. So a costly asset is left behind when production ceases.

If a realistic approach were to be adopted in this context, and less money spent on maintenance, then operating costs would rise. The plant will tend to have more unplanned shutdowns, and the cost of the raw materials and utilities used in the plant will tend to increase. Once again, an attempt should be made to evaluate the risks involved. Then logical decisions can be taken, based on a realistic financial appraisal of the situation. It should not be automatically assumed that the best approach is to maintain the plant at maximum operating efficiency. If this approach is accepted in principle, then maintenance costs can be

	£X 1000
INCOME	
Sales	1,000
DEDUCTIONS	
Cost of production	650
Provision for depreciation	150
Revaluation of stock	30
Total deductions	810
Profit before tax	190
Profit after tax	85

Notes:
1. Tax will now be payable. At 50 per cent, this would be £85,000.
2. Stock is 25 per cent of annual production, and was valued at £230,000. It now costs £200,000 to produce, since the plant is at full production, and must therefore be revalued by £30,000.
3. Cash flow, as given in Figure 5:4, is £235,000. This is seen in the above account as the depreciation allowance (£150,000) plus the net profit of £85,000.

Figure 6:6 Details from the profit/loss account for year three, for Project A in Figure 5:3.

reduced and, at the earlier stage, the capital investment can be cut. But for such an approach to be successful, the *policy* has not only to be accepted by management but its *implications* clearly seen and accepted.

If the policy as outlined above is adopted, then management must accept the consequences. Savings in initial capital investment of this type will inevitably increase maintenance costs, whilst savings in maintenance costs will inevitably increase operating costs. These are all costs which have a relationship the one to the other, being inter-dependent. They cannot therefore be considered in isolation.

Replacements

Another area where the company accounts play an often misleading role is in connection with replacements. In discussing the relationship between payout and company accounts plant depreciation was mentioned. Accounting policy will be to write down the value in the books of the asset as it is depreciated, usually in accordance with certain rules, which may or may not correspond with the depreciation allowances allowed for tax purposes. On the other hand, it has to be recognised that costs escalate over the years, so that a 'replacement value' is also maintained in the books. The depreciated value of a plant, which is its value as recorded in the company accounts, is usually referred to as the *book value.*

It has to be accepted that the book value of a plant is not its *real* value. The real value, in fact, depends upon circumstances and is only of interest when the plant is destroyed by accident or is going to be taken out of production and replaced by new plant. If the plant is destroyed by accident and has to be replaced as it was before, then the *replacement value* is the significant value and this will obviously be much higher than the original purchase price. If the plant is to be replaced, however, by another different plant then the value will be that realisable when it is dismantled: its *salvage value.* The difference between book value and salvage value is often referred to as the *unamortised value.*

When replacements are under consideration it is the unamortised value which gives trouble, because it tends to be seen as a loss. Indeed, from a purely accounting point of view it *is* a loss. A loss has to be written off in the company accounts. But when a replacement is being considered, any evaluation should ignore this difference and deal with the realities of the situation. The book value should not be used in evaluating the cost of the replacement, nor should the unamortised value be added to the cost of the potential investment involved in the replacement. The difference will, of course, have to be dealt with by the accountant once the plant has been scrapped and the replacement is in operation. The usual procedure is, as has been said, to 'write it off' against operating costs in the year in which the plant is taken out of service. But it should be clearly seen that there is no flow of cash in this context. The company is not out of pocket.

The salvage value of a plant tends to be an imponderable. Often a plant can be shut down, rather than scrapped, when the replacement unit is brought into operation. There is then a tendency to offset the new capital investment with a potential 'user' value in relation to the old plant. This is a very dangerous procedure—particularly dangerous when the book value is at a high level, since the accounts will not disclose the falsity of the assumption that has been made until it is too late. The result of such a procedure is that the replacement project is thought to be more attractive than it really is. Appraisal of payout in relation to replacements must be based on the conditions prevailing *at the time* the replacement is being made. History, as reflected in the book value, and the future, as reflected in the prospective use of idle plant, must be ignored. If a plant is shut down, the book loss should be accepted and the new venture considered wholly on its own merits.

PART TWO

PROJECT ORGANISATION

7

The Estimating Function

The project engineer requires a series of estimates throughout the life of a project. These estimates are required, in the first instance, to enable decisions to be made in conjunction with management, on the viability of the project. Then, later, the estimates are required as a basis for project cost control. The estimate serves as a basis for comparison, whereby both financial and physical progress is measured in terms of cost. Because this is so, the objective once the estimate has been established, will be to use it as a target and seek to maintain costs within that target. If the costs are contained, then the impression is created that it was a good estimate, and also that the cost control procedures were effective. But this may well be an illusion.

The capital cost estimate is an estimate, and those who prepare it realise that life will be that much easier if they ensure that the final cost stays within the original appropriation. So, having estimated and allowed for all the technical provisions which safeguard the 'minimum' approach, they will provide an appropriate contingency to cover any lack of definition at the stage when the money is appropriated for the project. Now everyone involved has room for manoeuvre and the plant is built. Built within the appropriation. Why? Because all problems can be solved if enough money is available, and as the job proceeds to completion, Professor Parkinson's well-known law comes into operation, and 'expenditures rise to meet appropriations'. At the end managements have been known to say 'That was a good estimate'.

What is the role of the estimator in all this? Estimating, or the ability to predict costs, cannot by itself either control or reduce costs. The estimator, considered purely as an estimator, will evaluate the design in the light of his own experience, and so set a target. But, once again, the existence of a target is not, in itself, any guarantee that it will be met. Here, then is one pitfall to be avoided. Every effort must be made to ensure that the estimate is realistic—not optimistic, nor pessimistic.

Need for Experience

In discussing the role of the estimate (see Chapter 2) stress was laid upon the need for experience in estimating. The techniques which are dealt with here and in Part Three will never be a substitute for such experience. They can, however, help in that they offer a method of approach to the problem which will enable the available experience to be utilised in the best possible manner and to the best possible effect. The ideal, in this context, is to have an estimating engineer available, or an estimating group with the necessary experience and competence to prepare all the estimates. These resources are, of course, available within the major engineering contractor organisations, and some of the larger manufacturing companies also set up separate estimating groups for project work. The type of departmental organisation which is applicable to these is illustrated in Figure 7:1. The activities outlined in the figure can be further extended by having sections dealing with the economic evaluation of projects and a cost control team on the site itself.

This departmental organisation has been presented to illustrate the scope of the activities that are always involved, at least to a degree, but it is not expected that in practice such a resource would be established. The usual compromise is for the specialist engineers—plant, electrical, civil, instrumentation—to prepare estimates for their portion of the work. This leaves the co-ordination of the several estimates to someone else and it is here that the basic failure so often occurs. When each of the disciplines considers its own problems only, many minor requirements are easily overlooked, and the consolidated estimate is often in error and always low. A real breadth of vision is required at this point.

The need can be illustrated by considering the qualifications and duties that are appropriate for an estimating engineer, as set out in Figure 7:2. In the absence of estimating engineers with this experience, the responsibility will almost inevitably fall upon the project engineer. The point is made so that the nature of the problem that has to be faced can be seen—a problem appreciated is always a problem well on the way to a solution.

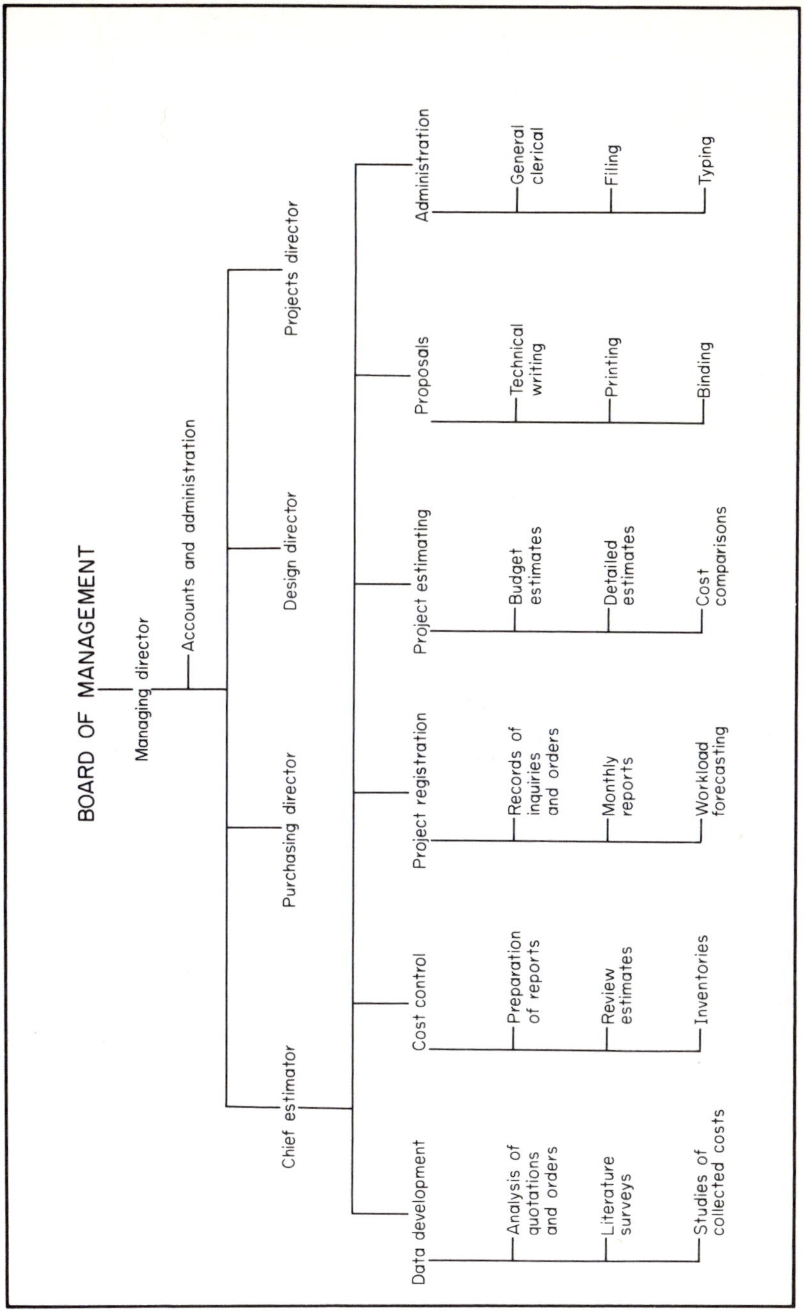

Figure 7:1 Typical organisation chart showing the range of activities in an estimating department which is part of a contracting organisation

QUALIFICATIONS	DUTIES
Professional experience in the fields of estimating and cost engineering.	Prepare budget estimates at the planning stage for management review and capital appropriation
Mature judgement, and the ability to work in harmony with professional engineers and architects	Prepare definitive estimates based on outline designs
Education biased to science, mathematics and engineering	Review costs and develop estimating data
Ability to comprehend specifications, read drawings and calculate	Consult with engineers and architects and establish relevent information
Office experience, design experience and some site experience on plant constructions	Confer with management on the implications of estimates and costs
Steady, reliable, confident, perceptive, able to work on own initiative, somewhat agressive, conscientious and interested	Keep abreast of economic trends and design developments affecting costs.

Figure 7:2 An indication of the requirements and responsibilities assumed in relation to the estimating function once a project has been initiated

To demonstrate the problem in a practical context, a simple process operation such as distillation can be considered. This illustration has been chosen because the operation of distillation occurs in a very wide variety of manufacturing industries and is thus well-known outside the chemical process field itself. At the estimating stage, the most that would be available would be an outline flow diagram of the distillation unit, and this might be as illustrated in Figure 7:3. Now compare this simple diagram with the finished section of the plant as illustrated by Figure 7:4. Sufficient acquaintance with both process and engineering matters is required to visualise the end result in terms of manholes, nozzles, platforms, access ladders, insulation, lights, and all the other accessories that will grace the tower when it is installed. This particular illustration is cited to force home a realisation of the problems

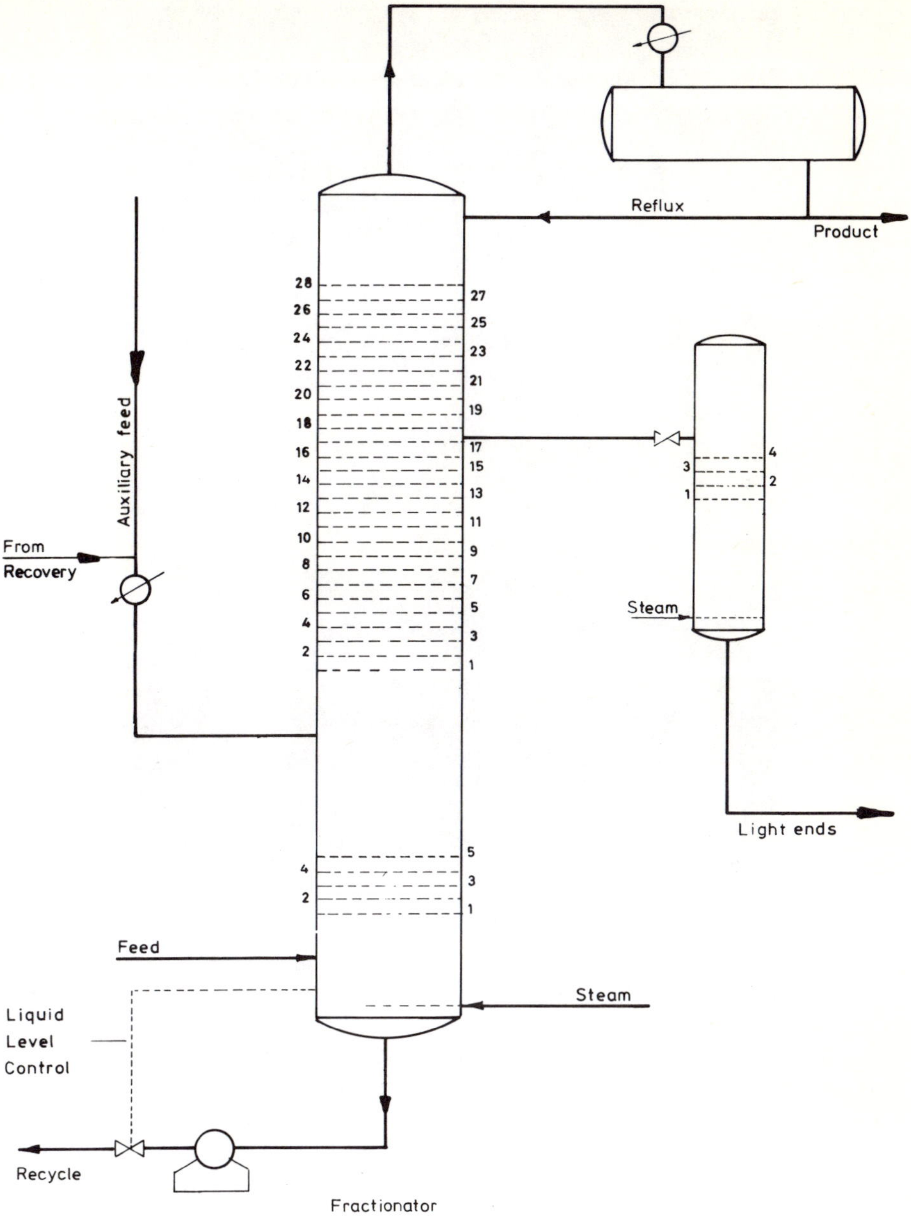

Figure 7:3 A distillation column (or tower). Detail abstracted from the process *flow sheet (Typical only)*

Figure 7:4 General view of distillation columns. This illustrates the complexity of the final design in terms of access, supports and insulation. It has no relation technically to Figure 7:3. (Photography by courtesy of Matthew Hall Engineering Limited, London)

involved. These can be solved, but a consistent, systematic method of approach will have to be employed if sound estimates are to be prepared.

Outline Design

The first stage in the development of the engineering design of the project is the preparation of a process flow diagram. The initial step, therefore, is the block flow diagram, a typical example of which is presented in Figure 7:5. Whilst it is possible, given the necessary cost data and the related experience, to estimate the capital cost of a plant from such a diagram, the margin of error will almost inevitably be large, and probably unacceptable. The next step, then, is the process

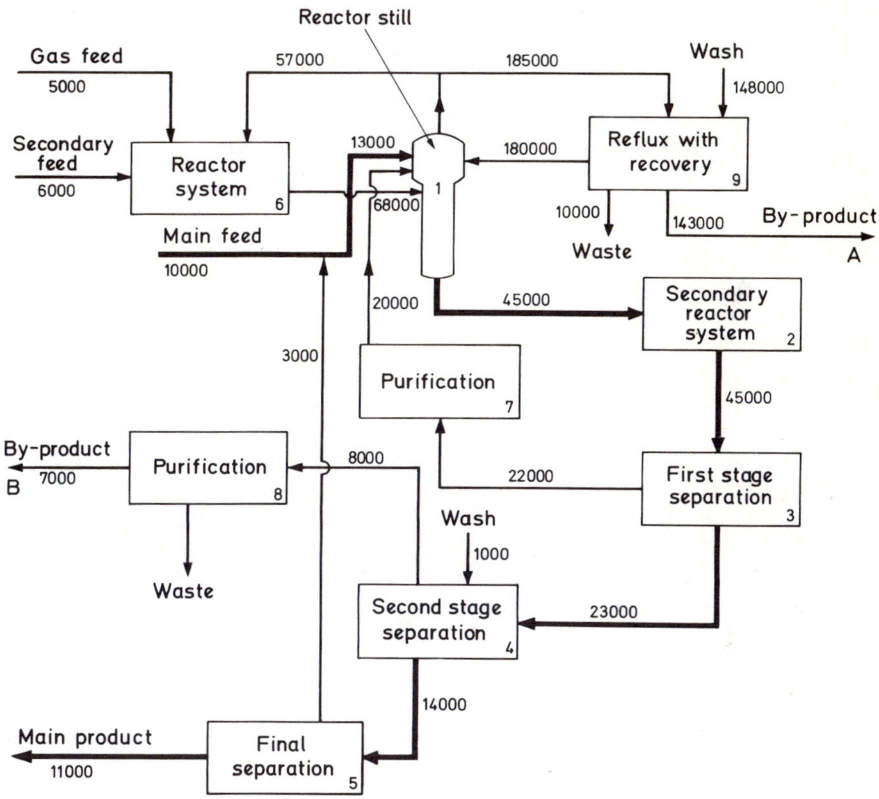

Figure 7:5 Typical process block flow diagram showing the main process flow and the related recirculation and side streams. A diagram of this type should be established for every production operation, whether gases, liquids or solids (loose or in containers) are being processed and handled. The principle remains the same whatever the process.

flowsheet. Figure 7:3 shows a small section from such a flowsheet. It is best if separate flowsheets are prepared for the process and the related services, or utilities, required. For estimating purposes, it is a vital preliminary, and an unavoidable step, that each piece of equipment shown on the flowsheet is 'sized'. The term 'sized' means that the capacity, or duty, of the equipment has been specified. Further, the operating conditions must be stated. To continue with the example of a distillation column, this means that the materials of construction of the column should be specified, it should be dimensioned physically (diameter, height, number of trays or depth and type of packing) and the temperature and pressure conditions under which the column will operate stated. Information in this degree of detail is necessary for each item of equipment and such information can normally be made available at a very early stage in the process development.

The Plot Plan

The 'plot plan', as prepared for estimating purposes, should give the proposed disposition of the items of plant and equipment, the appropriate building sizes, the run of pipe tracks, tentative suggestions

Figure 7:6 Low-cost model of new building project. This is a section only of a new food products factory. No building work is shown on the model: only the wall line. (Photograph by courtesy of Irish Biscuits Limited, Dublin)

for facilities such as railway sidings, roads and footpaths. Areas requiring concreting or special paving should also be indicated. If an elevation can be developed at this stage, so much the better, for it will be a further help in visualising the work involved and will also facilitate consideration of the problems that may arise in the course of construction.

The tentative character of such a layout at this point should not be a deterrent. Experience has shown that the most radical changes can be made in the interrelation of plant units and buildings without these having any material influence on the overall cost, provided always that the total plot area is not increased.

The Use of Models

An increasingly common approach to the problem of establishing plant and equipment layout by using models. Models have a number of advantages as compared with the preparation of layout drawings. They:

1 Facilitate plant layout and product movement planning
2 Increase co-operation between chemist, plant designer and the construction engineers
3 Improve the communication of ideas
4 Speed decisions
5 Reduce design costs
6 Have a continuing use in the guidance of construction and operating personnel

These advantages accrue even with the very simplest approach to model making in this field. The simple approach should not be despised and lack of previous experience need not be an inhibition. One company, known to the author, made the model shown in Figure 7:6 of a four million pound project. The model was prepared on a 'shoe-string' budget, under the guidance of the company's planning and manufacturing personnel. Substantial use was made of *Modulex* to the scale 1:50, together with some items in wood made by a joiner. The model was assembled by a girl with no technical experience. Apart from the advantages mentioned earlier, it was found that the model contributed to a better understanding, and eased negotiations with trade union and employee representatives when discussing manning levels for the plant, and general working conditions in the new factory.

Figure 7:7 Model of two parallel plant units. In this model, two parallel plant units are seen in the background with a pipe bridge. A single storey building is 'blocked' in the foreground. All pipelines are laid on such models, complete with valve indicators, using plastic tube or metal wire. The isometric drawings of the pipe-runs can then be developed directly from such models. (Photograph by permission of Humphreys & Glasgow Limited, London.)

The model illustrated by Figure 7:7 is a plant with a complex piping installation. This type of model is often used by engineering contractors. Since the materials used are available commercially, the method is of equal value when adopted by the manufacturer. Such a model, apart from its uses in relation to plant layout, is fully 'piped', and the contractor will usually develop piping isometric drawings for fabrication and erection purposes directly from such a model. The manufacturer, however, can adopt a similar approach. Having 'piped' his model he can call in a contractor and require him to make his own 'take off' and submit offers for the supply and installation of the pipework systems set out on the model. This is one of the most difficult areas of work to control, but a number of manufacturers have used such an approach to the installation of piping on new plants with a substantial degree of success. It is well worth delaying the request for tenders in such instances until the model is complete. Bulk orders for the piping can be placed to speed completion, but this step should not be taken unless it is felt to be absolutely necessary.

Off-site Facilities

There is a need to recognise, and separately assess, the process unit or units (that is, the plant concerned directly with the manufacture of the product) and the various supporting units, often referred to as 'off-site facilities'. The term 'off-site' derives from the petroleum industry, where there are invariably a series of refinery units, through which the petroleum is processed, and a series of service units, necessary for the proper operation of the process units. These latter are referred to as 'off-sites', although they are almost invariably immediately adjacent to the process units, within the same boundary fence. Most manufacturing installations will contain large or small elements of this character. In a completely new works, or *green site* development, as it is termed, the off-site facilities are usually substantial. A general indication of the potential scope of off-site facilities is given by Figure 7:8. Such facilities need careful survey, if adequate provision is to be made, not only for the new process units but also, for possible future extension. It is very easy to put an extension in hand and ignore certain aspects which, eventually, become very obtrusive. As production in the new plant builds up, it may become all too clear that the administrative offices need an extension to cope with the increased flow of materials, orders and larger pay roll. Or the canteen may become overcrowded. These facilities are required by the project, and should not be forgotten.

ACCESS

- Roads and paths
- Railway sidings
- Jetties and wharfage
- Fencing
- Weighbridge

ADMINISTRATION

- Office buildings
- Furniture and equipment
- First aid facilities
- Garage, gatehouse, etc.
- Telephones, hail systems
- Plant maintenance workshops
- Warehousing

BULK STORAGE

- Fuels
- Process chemicals
- Products

EFFLUENT DISPOSAL

- Oil separators
- Sludge beds
- Sewage treatment

ELECTRICITY

- Main feeders
- Substations
- Generating equipment
- Road lighting

FIRE PROTECTION

- Elevated water storage
- Sprinklers
- Carbon dioxide systems
- Fire station equipment
- Hand extinguishers
- Foam trucks and piping
- Safety equipment

FUELS, ETC.

- Gas storage
- Oil storage and pumping
- Inert gas supply and generation
- Plant air compressors
- Instrument air compressors and driers

STEAM

- Boiler house, building and plant
- Coal, coke storage
- Oil storage
- Ash disposal

WATER

- Raw water intake and supply
- Water storage
- Water treatment
- Cooling towers and pumping

YARD PIPING

- Steam, water, air and other services
- Interconnecting process pipework
- Pipe gantries

Figure 7:8 A brief outline of off-site facilities. The list is not intended to be exhaustive but to serve as a guide, illustrating the general scope of such facilities.

There is usually a tendency to discount and disregard off-site facilities as being of minor importance, but such facilities usually represent a much higher proportion of the total investment than is expected. The process unit is the focus of attention and it is all too easy to imagine that it commands the greater proportion of cost. It is not unknown, however, for off-site facilities, in certain circumstances, to cost more than the extension they are designed to serve. A small increase in steam load, for instance, can result in a major extension to a boiler house, since extensions of this type usually involve economic operating units of substantial size. All these matters, therefore, must be considered in detail and with care.

8

Management Structure

The various disciplines involved in the development, design and construction of new or additional production facilities, have already been discussed (Chapter 2). It has to be recognised that these requirements exist and will have to be met in the course of implementing the project. Who has to meet them and overcome them varies, but there are four major categories into which the situation will inevitable fall, namely.

1 Individual. A single individual, such as a Works Manager or a Works Engineer, is confronted with the task of setting up a new development.
2 Team. A 'project team' is set up, its members being taken from their routine tasks to develop and progress proposals for, say, a new factory.
3 Engineering Department. An established engineering department, engaged normally on maintenance work (with sometimes minor capital works), or perhaps a section specialising in new work, and then continuously involved in the type of work and the problems encountered in new construction.
4 Consultant/Contractor. A consultant, such as an architect or perhaps a series of consultants, or an engineering contractor, is employed to supervise the work and/or implement it.

The resources of these several categories are manifestly vastly different, but the scope of the organisational problem involved can perhaps best be demonstrated by considering the last, and most complex, with the employment of an engineering contractor and specialist consultants to implement the project. This is illustrated in Figure 8:1. In the 'individual' case, the same ground will in effect have to be covered, but the individual would have to do the work himself. This implies that the degree of detail and the volume of work must diminish. If the project is too large for the individual, or beyond his personal skills, then the efficiency of the operation will be much reduced, but the scope of the requirements remains the same.

The organisational development in this context is effectively unlimited: the controlling factor will be the size and number of new projects that have to be dealt with. In discussing the estimating function a typical estimating department is outlined (Figure 7:1): this department is but one block in Figure 1 of this chapter. The estimating function is a key function, the activities of which touch every part of the project, from its initial development through to its operation. This implies that, although the estimating function is a service function, any proposed organisation must be structured in relation to the needs of, and have the fullest capacity to co-operate with the estimating department.

The anticipated end result of all these combined activities, whether carried out by one man, or a complete department, is a profit. The talents involved are various, and demand the skills embodied in people such as process engineers, design engineers, sales engineers, estimating engineers, planning engineers, purchasing engineers, construction engineers, cost clerks, accountants, all combined with managerial skills of no mean order. Set out like that, this is an overwhelming requirement. Yet this requirement is placed, quite often, on a single individual, such as a works manager, or the production manager, at a factory unit. And it is placed on him, just as often, without absolving him from the day-to-day responsibility for running the plant in his charge.

The purpose of presenting the problem in this particular way is to allow the scope of the requirements, once a new development is contemplated of any substance, to be surveyed in detail. If the full scope of the task ahead can be clearly seen, then positive steps can be taken to forestall and deal with pending problems.

Help, if needed, can be organised before it is too late, or the available resources marshalled so as to be as effective as possible. The steps taken by management to implement new capital projects, particularly when they are extensions to existing factories, can be an example of 'fools rushing in where angels fear to tread'. There is a strong temptation to

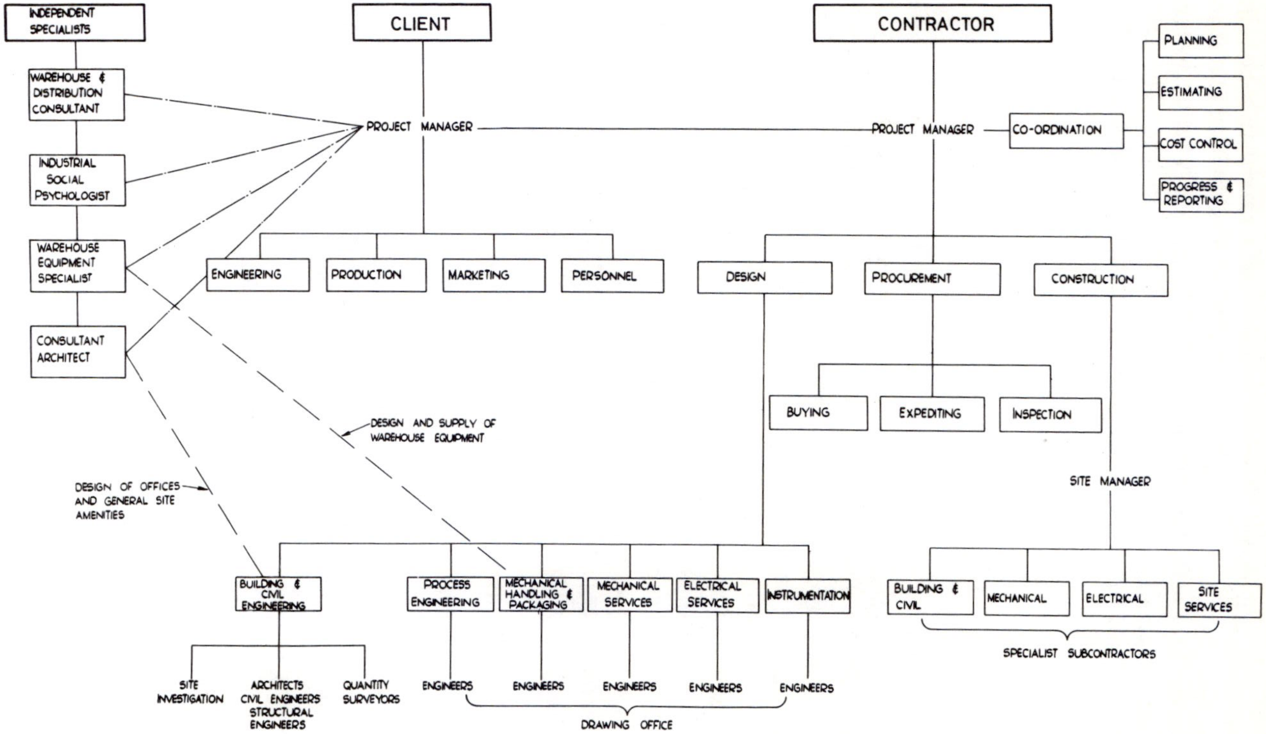

Figure 8:1 Typical project organisation, showing the framework of project management as established by an engineering contractor and the involvement of independent specialists.

assume, because it is merely an extension, that all the relevant data is available, and the task straightforward. But this is rarely the case in fact. To take another proverb, whilst 'ignorance is bliss', it is all too true that the bliss will not last. The problems are all there, very real, though dormant. They are, all too often, appreciated far too late. The end result of such lack of foresight is delay in completion and uncontrolled increases in costs.

Organisation

In discussing 'organisation', it is most important that the purpose and objectives of the organisation are always kept in view. One definition of organisation, found in *The Shorter Oxford English Dictionary*, is that it means a body formed 'into a whole with interdependent parts;' given 'a definite and orderly structure'. But this structure must have purpose: the purpose of organisation was well expressed by Dale (1960) in a study of the work of the great 'organisers' of industry, who wrote that organisation is a means to achieving ends that can only be gained when a number of people can work together. But can they work together? Once the project organisation develops beyond the single individual (the works manager or engineer) it is almost inevitable that there will be two conflicting objectives, two conflicting interests. This conflict exists and it may as well be recognised that it cannot be resolved. It must therefore be controlled and used.

The interrelationship of project functions

The first aspect of interest is the interrelationship between the administrative functions, directly responsible for implementing the project and the several service functions. These service functions are indicated on Figure 8:1 and are:

1 Accounts
2 Planning
3 Estimating
4 Cost control
5 Progress and reporting

Once again let it be said that whilst this subject is being discussed in a fairly substantial framework, the same concepts and principles apply in the smallest feasible framework through which a project can be

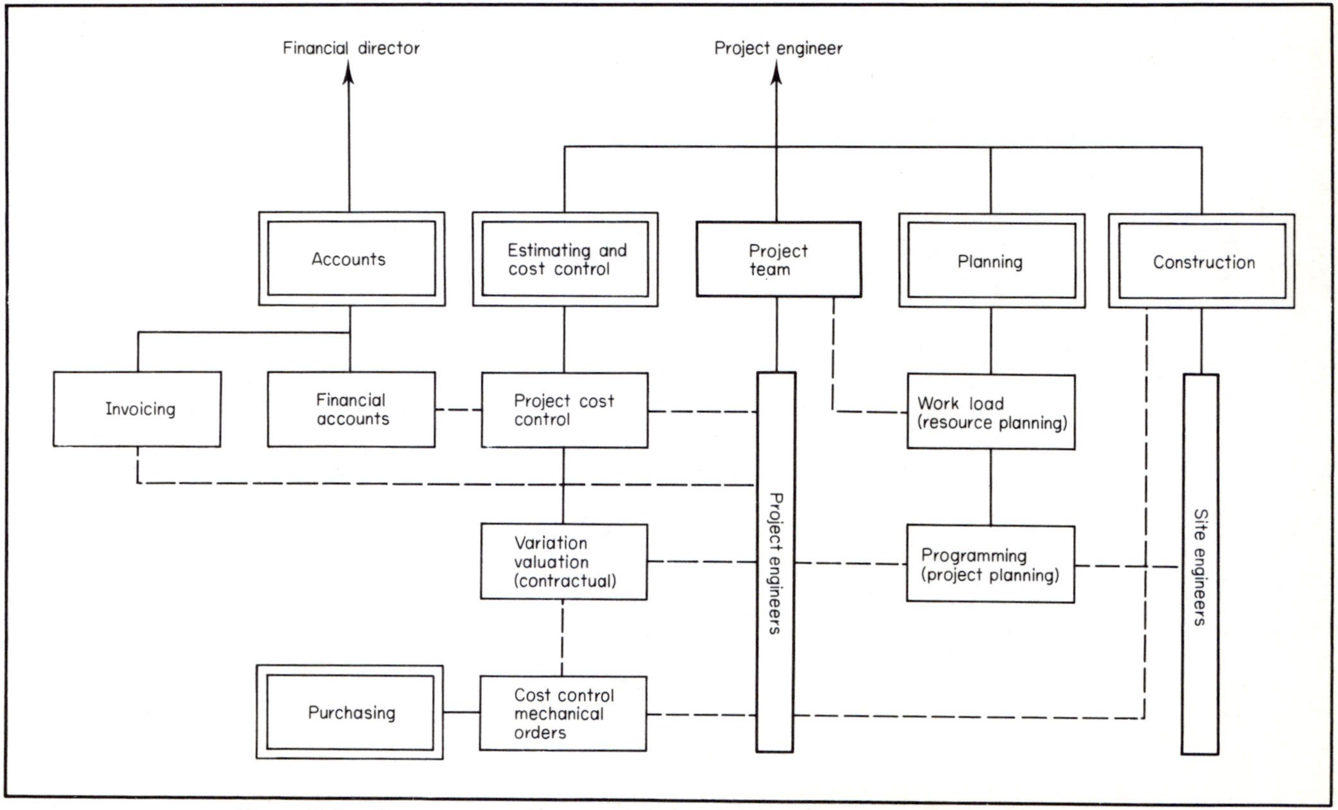

Figure 8:2 Organisation chart–project team. The interrelationship between the project team and the service functions is illustrated. Where the service functions could be separate departments, this is indicated by a double line around the description.

implemented. If it is the works engineer alone who becomes responsible for the job, and if he personally does the estimate, progresses the orders and plans the project, he will still be using the accounts department to process his invoices, and possibly the purchase department to place his orders. So organisation is still required and there will still be 'interdependent parts'. Considering then the interrelationship of the project function (one man or many) with the several service functions, the relationship should be as illustrated in Figure 8:2. In almost any company, the accounts department will be a separate department, indicated by the double line. With larger companies, estimating, planning and construction supervision will also be separate departments. The chart differentiates between administrative control and a functional relationship. As illustrated, there are only two administrative groups, financial and engineering, so that the respective responsibilities of the two groups can be clearly seen and easily defined. No reference has been made so far, however, to design.

In order that the project may be implemented, process design and engineering will be required. It is here that there may be an area of conflict. In setting up a design facility, or in utilising an existing design facility, the scope of the design functions will probably need definition. Care must be taken to see that the design engineers do not usurp the responsibilities of the purchasing department on the one hand, or the field construction team, on the other. That done, it will also be necessary to define the responsibilities of each of the several design disciplines that are to be employed, since once again conflict can arise, or aspects of the work be left undone. The 'code of accounts' can be a useful tool in this respect. Specific sub-groups can be said to be the responsibility of certain departments, and an outline definition of the scope of their responsibilities is then immediately available.

To summarise, the situation that develops once a project is implemented, is that there is both *direct* and *indirect* involvement. The functions directly involved are:

1 Project management
2 Design
3 Procurement
4 Construction

Other departments provide a service and thus, are only indirectly involved. These include:

5 Planning
6 Estimating and cost control

7 Financial and accounts
8 Personnel

The effective deployment of these resources, both direct and indirect, is the responsibility of the project engineer. His basic tool for this purpose is *management information,* which should lead to executive action. Success will only be achieved by team effort, the team being *all* the departments involved, and not only those directly responsible.

Conflict of Interests

For the smaller projects, and in the smaller companies, this deployment of resources may well be the function of the project engineer, developing the project in consultation with the chemist, the works engineer, and other technical and operating personnel in the organisation. Even so, with a small group, there can still be conflict, since although each function of the several contributing parties is largely advisory, they have a strong vested interest in the outcome, and are always anxious to see their own ends fully satisfied. With the larger projects, the problem intensifies, since it is then necessary to have a separate design organisation. Two groups are formed and the conflict becomes polarised. Nevertheless, this division into two groups is inevitable.

In Figure 8:1 the design function is shown as an element of the project organisation, but once design requirements grow and a variety of disciplines become involved, separate co-ordination of the design effort becomes essential for proper management administration. The interrelationship between the several aspects of design, such as building design, plant design, electrical design and instrumentation design is very close. These facilities are strongly interdependent and so need to be seen and managed as a separate organisation. This is illustrated in Figure 8:3. Here, the project manager is responsible for a group of projects and has a team of project engineers to support him in servicing those projects and bringing them to completion. Each project engineer (five are shown) will be responsible for one or more projects, depending upon size, and each engineer will require design services. The scope of the design service required will vary according to project and not all the project engineers will require the same services. This variation has been indicated in the chart. For instance, a warehouse project will not require instrumentation, another project will involve plant changes only. Ideally, the resources of the design department would be such

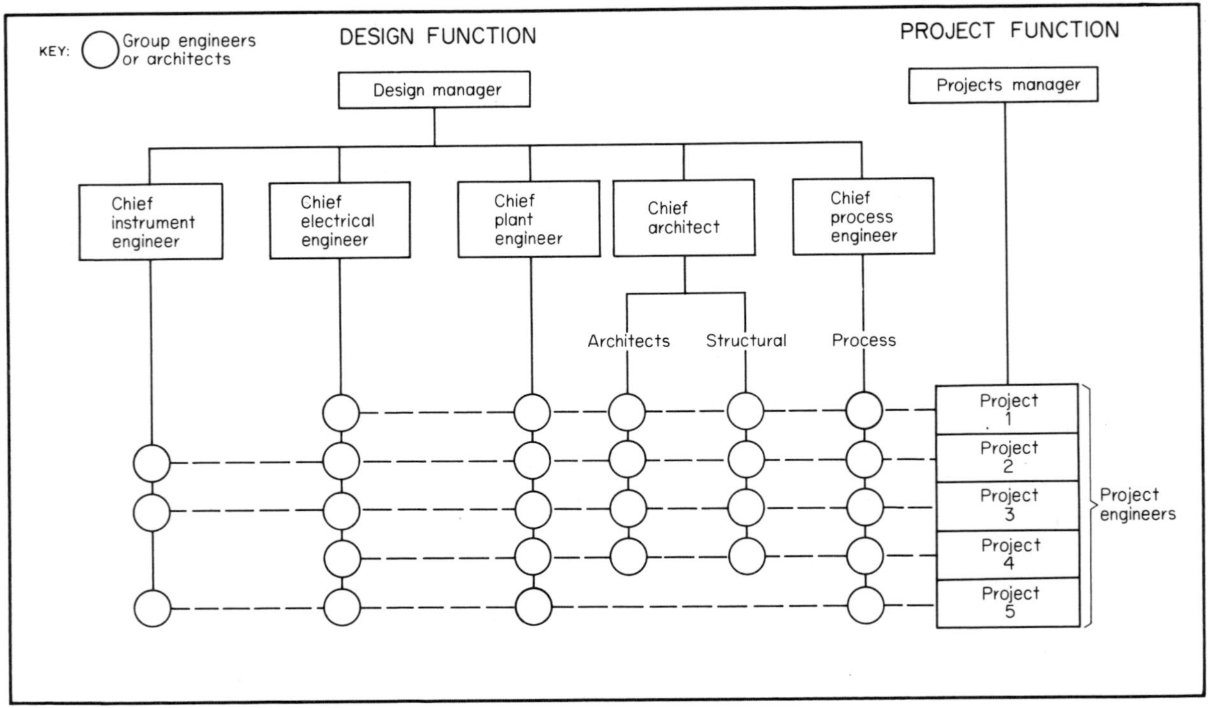

Figure 8:3 Organisation chart–design group. This chart demonstrates the manner in which the design department should be grouped under section leaders in order to integrate with the project management function. Whilst the design department is necessarily internally streamed and managed in accordance with the several disciplines involved, the external integration is on a project basis.

that they match the requirements of the projects group, but in practice this will never occur. The design resources will necessarily be limited and hence there will be competition between project engineers for its services, each wishing to progress his own project and maintain his own programme. This is the first point of conflict, requiring resolution by consultation between the departmental heads.

Another area of conflict arises in that the design manager will be seeking to ensure that the designs for which he is responsible are sound and safe, whereas the project engineer is seeking to minimise cost and speed up the design process. Such areas of conflict exist and need to be recognised. It is no contribution to project management to ignore them.

Resolving the Conflict

These various internal differences are resolved in part by a mutual recognition of the common objective: an installation for the minimum cost, within the minimum possible time, consistent with certain minimum acceptable levels of process operability and safety. But it is still necessary to determine where the dominant role lies. In the experience of the author there are two basic ways in which a project/design/construction team can be built up—the team can be design orientated, or it can be project orientated. The simplest approach is to have design orientation. This minimises conflict, but it does not necessarily result in minimum costs. The better approach, though more difficult from a managerial point of view, is to have the team project orientated. This is the approach adopted in Figure 8:3, the project engineer and design group working as a cohesive whole.

The project manager and his engineers will then relate each project to management or board directives. To implement those directives, they will lay down a design philosophy, seeking to ensure that the project is completed to programme, and controlling the costs by monitoring the performance of the design department and the construction department. This necessitates control of personnel, the review of orders as they are placed, review of progress and costs, together with involvement in the payment of invoices from suppliers and variations made to the project.

The prime responsibility of the design department will be to develop a sound design within the parameters established by the project engineers.

Principle of Accountability

If these concepts are to be expressed in management terms, then the project manager is 'accountable' to senior management for the project. An obligation is thereby placed, in the first instance, upon the project group. The usual problem is, that whilst the project manager is held accountable, he is often not given the authority to discharge his obligation to management properly. Once made accountable, he should have both the right and also the obligation to take those actions and decisions judged necessary to discharge his responsibility properly.

All too often there is a certain reluctance in this respect, from two sides. Senior management is reluctant to leave 'major' decisions to the project group, and design is thought to be a 'specialist' function with which the project engineer should not interfere. It is true that limits of authority have to be established and should be established in relation to certain decisions. These decisions involve factors outside the scope of the project engineer, so that a measure of control must be maintained by senior management. A common instance in this context is in relation to money. Limits may be placed on the power of the project engineer to spend discrete sums of money, despite the fact that blanket financial approval has been given for the project as a whole. Orders over a certain value, for instance, may be referred to senior management for final approval.

Care should be taken to see that these limits on the authority of the project engineer do not inhibit him from discharging his responsibilities. The textbooks seek to resolve such problems by providing the occupier of each position of responsibility with a *mandate.* It is suggested that a written description of each position can be prepared, which should be a brief but positive statement of the basic objectives of the position (in this case, that of project engineer or project group). This description can be further extended by a written description of the specific activities which it is considered are implicit in the mandate. In practice, however, such descriptions are most difficult to write in this particular context, and are probably best left unwritten. It is for this reason that no 'specimen' descriptions are provided in this book. It is better to strive after the basic objective, namely, that of having all the personnel involved working as a team, with individual members assuming responsibilities in co-operation with the other members of the team. The total responsibility of the team as a whole, however, will be clear enough.

Management by Exception

The system of project management and cost control now being presented in detail, is built around the principle of 'management by exception'. This is another long established principle, which implies that policies are established and plans laid, deviations from these approved policies and plans being reported upon. If management by exception is to be successful, there are four basic requirements which will have to be fulfilled:

1. There must be a plan
2. There must be the ability to delegate
3. There must be confidence in the ability and judgement of the subordinates
4. There must be a proper system of *management information*

The plan is the standard of reference against which the actuality is measured, so that exceptions, or departures from the plan, can be reported. The plan has to cover two basic areas–cost and time. The final result of the planning is a programme and an estimate. The programme and the estimate therefore become an integral part of the management information system. The term 'management information' is intended to embrace the reports, which should cover both the physical and financial aspects of the project, and which will provide the information needed at successive levels of management to enable them to make the appropriate decisions. Typical reports, and the appropriate formats, are discussed in detail in Part 4. It will be seen that in all the forms there is one basic feature. There is continuous comparison with the initial plan in relation to time and money.

Management needs to know the deviations from plan, since it is these that require consideration. Deviations or departures from plan thus become the subject of the reports and the level that they reach in management will depend upon their magnitude and significance in relation to the project as a whole. Good management information will provide the essential information only. This means that it has to be condensed, accurate, complete and up-to-date. Above all, reports at one level should not include data which is properly the concern of subordinates at a lower level. Whilst the senior executives are, of course, entitled to ask for and get any specific information they feel they want, excessive demands of this nature tend to undermine the concept of delegation. Thus, the basic principle around which project management is built, that of 'management by exception' is destroyed.

9

Purchasing and Material Control

The purchasing and material control functions are vital elements in cost control and the two go together to comprise materials management. The purchasing function is concerned, in the first instance, with the purchase price. The overall concern is not price, but cost, and this distinction should be recognised. If purchases are made on price considerations alone, they are more than likely to increase the total cost of a project. So far as the purchasing function is concerned, there are a number of separate elements to be considered in making a purchase, namely:

1 Time
2 Quality
3 Source
4 Availabity
5 Place of usage
6 Price

All these must receive consideration when selecting the source and it will be noted that price is only one element in six.

Selecting the Source

The source decision is probably the most important of those

SUPPLIERS INDEX OF PERFORMANCE
AS AT 30 NOV 1971
****

SUPPLIERS REF. NUMBER	SUPPLIERS NAME	PERFORMANCE INDEX
1238	A	220.00
2688	A	300.00
10304	A	162.50
13168		133.33
14848	A	100.00
15872	A	308.33
18688	Al	109.52
23072	Al	146.83
24320	Al	121.43
25600	Al	100.00
26496	Al	116.67
27840	Ar	83.33
30016	Ar	1000.00
33408	Gt	50.00
48152		200.00
48512	AS	106.50
57216	W	60.00
62464	BA	133.33
66686	BA	100.00
67200	BA	92.00
67264	BA	110.00
77440	JA1	224.11
82688	Bt1	188.89
87040	Bt1	167.20
95360	Fr	216.67
98048	BIt	144.44
98176	SAt	112.50
105472	Jt	92.30
114016	BUr	121.21
117888	BUn	157.14
125504	JD	225.00
130816	BRI	100.00
131328	BRI	110.00
145024	BRI	225.00
149760	BRC	100.00
151040	BRU1	300.00

151168	BRU1	159.56
153344	DAV	116.67
153600	DUN	175.00
154560	RU	226.46
159360	BUDE	90.28
176384	CAHE	137.50
188800	JCHR	151.23
232640	JDC	100.00
235392	CORR	171.43
238624	CORR	125.00
238720	COOR	140.00

Figure 9:1 Supplier's performance index. Each supplier is identified by a specific number (used also for accounting and payment by computer) and the index is the ratio between the promised delivery and the actual delivery, 100 representing the 'norm' where the promised delivery is met. Thus 200 means that the time taken is twice that promised.

enumerated above. A good selection of the source of supply will almost inevitably result in much saving of time and effort once the order has been placed. The project team can easily find that far too much time is being taken in 'chasing' suppliers and subcontractors. This is directly related to the source selected and leads to a consideration of the way in which such a selection should be made. The essential qualities required of a supplier can be summarised as:

1 Technical skill
2 Productive capacity
3 Appropriate financial resources
4 Managerial competence
5 Administrative ability

A weakness in any of the foregoing will affect the project programme and hence the final cost of the project. There are various techniques available for evaluating the performance of suppliers, but they are all largely dependent upon experience. One key measurement that can be made is the ability to keep a promise. Delivery can be promised for a certain date, but the actuality can often be very different. Excuses are always to hand, but nothing can compensate for failure to deliver on time.

If there is a flow of orders over time, with any one supplier, the actual delivery can be measured against the promised delivery, and a register of the performance of the suppliers developed, as is illustrated in Figure 9:1. This is a sophisticated computerised development of a principle that should be applied in the purchasing department as part of the contribution to the control of costs. Where projects are being handled only infrequently on any major scale, experience in relation to specialist contractors may be limited or even non-existent, but the experience of others can be asked for.

The result of such purchasing experience will be that certain suppliers are considered unreliable, and hence, unacceptable. Enquiries should not, therefore, be sent to such suppliers. It should be a matter of purchasing principle, indeed, that enquiries should only be sent to suppliers or contractors with whom one is fully prepared to place an order. Reservations in this context, when the offers are in, makes nonsense of the purchasing procedure.

The several offers, as received, need assessment both from a purchasing and a user angle. The user here, is in fact, the project engineer, but he may in turn, wish to seek advice from specific members of his team. Where a separate design department exists, the original requisition for purchase may have originated there and therefore, the initial review will be made by the originator of the requisition. Final approval however, should only be authorised by the project engineer.

Bid analysis

The review of offers to supply is often referred to as 'bid analysis' and a typical bid analysis form is given in Figure 9:2. The form provides for the situation where an outside contractor is used to place orders on behalf of the ultimate user of the facility, but exactly the same procedure should be followed in all cases. The use of external engineering contractors will be discussed later in Chapter 10.

Bid analysis introduces another problem which is often under discussion in purchasing departments. What is the optimum number of suppliers to be approached to obtain the appropriate competition in order to purchase at the most advantageous price? In assessing this problem, in relation to project and construction contracts, the implications of time should never be overlooked. It can often be advantageous to negotiate a contract with a single supplier in order to have the work started on site at a much earlier date. As a matter of general principle, however, it must be recognised that it is poor purchasing to approach a multiplicity of companies. Widespread enquiries give little long-term gain to the purchaser, because this

BID ANALYSIS

Item ______ Tag number ______

Amount allowed in control estimate ______ Clients code of accounts ______

Delivery required by schedule ______ Prepared by ______

Date ______

	Suppliers			
Name				
Conformity with specification				
Quotation details				
Price				
Duty payable (if any)				
Carriage				
Terms				
Delivery				
Other relevant information				
Estimated total price				

	For client's use
Purchasing recommendation	Client
Reasons	Approved for purchasing from
	Reason if different from engineering
Engineering recommendation	
Reasons	
Project engineer ______ Date ______	Project manager ______ Date ______

Figure 9:2 Bid analysis form. This form is designed to highlight those aspects of the quotations which are specially significant in relation to cost control, namely estimated price as well as actual; delivery; specific item identification (tag number) and code of accounts reference.

usually leads to the practice of negotiation with the potential suppliers, after the submission of the offers, playing off one supplier against the other. Such practices rapidly become common knowledge and are then anticipated by the supplier who adjusts the price accordingly. To negotiate a reduction in price may give the purchaser some satisfaction, but no real benefit has been gained. This is not cost control.

The best approach for cost control purposes is to measure the processed price, not against those of other suppliers, but against a realistic estimate. Then the number of quotations secured can be very limited and it only becomes necessary to go outside the original choice of suppliers if there are drastic differences between the estimated cost and the tenders received. The standard procedure in this context is also illustrated by the bid analysis form, (Figure 9:2). This form is designed to highlight those aspects which are significant for cost control purposes, the most basic of these being the relationship between the offer proposed for acceptance and the amount included in the appropriation, or control, estimate.

Purchasing Policy

Much of what has already been said may be thought to be an integral part of purchasing policy, but the point being made is that there are certain areas where the policy adopted should be governed by project experience, rather than by established purchasing techniques. It is a purchasing technique, for instance, to divide a total requirement up into sections, and purchase each section separately, on the assumption—which is sound—that the individual elements will be purchased more advantageously, both from the point of view of price and delivery. A common example is to purchase the materials required for a plant, such as piping, in bulk, and make this material available as a 'free issue' to erection contractors. This can have serious disadvantages when the ability to control costs in such situations is considered. As a matter of project policy, it is always advantageous to minimise the work done on site. The advantages of this are many, and include:

1 The benefits of continuous manufacture without interruption caused by adverse weather conditions.
2 A greater facility in controlling labour and ensuring fabricating efficiency.
3 Less opportunity for waste and pilferage
4 Simplification of the material control procedures

5 A better product, made to closer tolerances
6 Greater flexibility in production capacity

Purchasing policy should, therefore, be modified to give due weight to these considerations.

Another aspect of purchasing policy relates to the nature of the contract being established. The purchasing department, if use is being made of an existing organisation, may not be familiar with the buying of services. When materials are purchased, it is usually easy to specify the volume and price of those materials and so establish a firm fixed order price, but with services the problem is different. There are, essentially, three different ways in which services can be purchased:

1 As a lump sum
2 Via a schedule of rates
3 On a daywork basis

Lump sum

This is generally familiar, being the agreed price for a specified volume of materials and/or work. The possibility of price change is usually limited to 'escalation' and minor additions such as delivery and packing costs, apart from specific variations called for by the purchaser.

Schedule of rates

The rate is an agreed price for a unit of material or work, and the schedule details the agreed rates. The work as done is measured and paid for in accordance with the agreed rates.

Daywork basis

This is, in effect, a cost-plus reimbursement. Hourly rates are agreed for services (labour, and so on), possibly by trades, with percentage additions to materials as supplied. The rates and percentages allow the supplier to recover overheads and provide margins for profit.

Orders placed may have elements of all these three basic schemes for remuneration, but any order will fall into one of the three groups. If it is felt that there are going to be variations or changes made to a lump sum order, then it is expedient to specify the way in which these changes are going to be valued—and daywork rates might well be used for this purpose. However, all orders which are not lump sums should be considered to be 'open' orders in the sense that the scope of the order is not defined in precise detail, and hence, is open to adjustment.

Of course, if an engineering contractor is appointed who is going to undertake the purchasing either within a lump sum price or on a reimbursable basis, these matters of purchasing policy will become his problem and will be resolved in accordance with his own practice and experience. The use of such contractors is described later, in Chapter 10.

The fixed price

The reference just made to the possibility of a contract with a contractor incorporating a 'reimbursable' element, and the discussion of 'fixed' and 'open' orders, raises a further question of purchasing policy. There has been, in recent years, an overemphasis on the desirability of the fixed price, particularly in relation to contracts incorporating site erection of items of plant. This is often termed the 'package deal'. This anxiety to 'fix' prices may well be an over-reaction from the war and post-war years, when 'cost-plus' was a very common method of purchasing indeed. As a result of this method of purchasing—or so it was felt—companies found that their budgets were being grossly over-run when, at long last, the final price of the orders became known.

The development of the package deal is an attempt by the user companies to avoid this sort of situation and impose a discipline. The view was taken that the lack of discipline with 'cost-plus' lay with the contractor: in fact, of course, the prime failure lay with the user company. If a proper discipline of instruction and supervision of work is established, as a part of the cost control procedure—a discipline which applies equally to contractor or supplier on the one hand, and the user on the other—then the weakness inherent in the 'cost plus' approach can be overcome. If the discipline is transferred *in toto* to the contractor, he in turn seeks to protect himself and the net result will be that contingency provisions are included, the total cost increases, and the user may finish up paying more than would have been paid under a properly supervised and controlled 'cost plus' arrangement.

These considerations do not of course affect the desirability of establishing fixed prices wherever possible—but the fixed price approach should be limited to situations where the risks are clearly seen can be assessed and defined and so measured both qualitatively and quantitatively. Even with the fixed price, of course, certain elements which are considered to be an abnormal risk can be left out for separate adjustment, when thought appropriate. A typical example is, of course, escalation, which is often handled by means of some mutually acceptable formula related to published cost indices, rather than incorporated in the fixed price.

Standard Clauses

With an established purchasing department, the standard routines should ensure that all the significant aspects relating to the placement of an order will be covered. However, the smaller organisation, lacking the appropriate breadth of experience, may find the outline of significant aspects given in Figure 9:5 of value. Where an available standard form is used, this form will invariably carry certain standard purchasing conditions, often found in small print, almost unreadable, on the reverse of the order form. However suitable these may be considered to be in the context of the manufacturing operation, they should be carefully reviewed if the same form is to be used for purchase on a capital project.

For instance, compliance can be called for in respect of certain standards, such as safety standards, in very general terms. Such clauses should be deleted and the specific requirements of the project set out in the specification. All too often such standard conditions are very wide in scope, presumably because at some time, and under some circumstances, the purchasing department might find the provisions valuable. Since they are incorporated in the order, they have to be taken seriously. In practice, however, when such clauses are queried, the answer is given that they are 'not applicable in this instance'. Once again, the purchasing officer should take the trouble to peruse these conditions and delete the irrelevant. It is interesting to note, in this context, that government departments generally have very comprehensive conditions of purchase, but they do *indicate* which clauses apply to the particular enquiry and order.

Order Form Versus Contract

Every order placed and accepted is a contract, but it is usual for the order form to be used for the purchase of materials, plant and equipment, and the 'contractor' approach to be used for major orders involving services. For smaller orders involving services, the contract approach can still be adopted, with standard conditions of contract such as are described later. The standard conditions then govern the way in which the contractor will be employed, and the manner in which payment will be made.

With the smaller order, for services, care must be taken to ensure that the conditions are not too comprehensive. For instance, it is common in such conditions of contract to find that delivery time is a contractual requirement. This means that a failure to deliver is a breach of contract. A breach of contract can lead to a suit for damages, and the implication is that the contractor becomes liable for consequential losses, such as loss of profit due to the delay in delivery. It should be apparent that minor items, except perhaps in very special circumstances, cannot, in themselves, bring such drastic consequences. Such statements are, therefore, far better deleted. In any event, they can never be enforced in practice and will only lead to friction between purchaser and contractor.

The scope of *force majeure* is another source of such friction. It is always better to define *force majeure* and the writer would recommend that *force majeure* is deemed to include delays outside the control of the supplier or contractor, such as strikes, lockouts and failures in delivery by others. If the *force majeure* clause is equitable, then it is feasible and fair to have a bonus/penalty clause, although care must be taken to ensure that such a clause is not punishing. The magnitude of the bonus and the penalty should always be related to the value of the order, not to the potential benefit or damage which may result to the purchaser in relation to the performance of the contract.

Progressing

It is important to recognise that procurement does not end once the order has been placed. Procurement must continue until the goods, or services as ordered, have been delivered to the user. This means that the format of the order has to conform to this principle and take it into account.

It is inevitable that every company will have its own purchase order format and procedures and it is assumed that each and every order gets a unique identification. Where orders are placed in relation to capital projects, however, it is usually desirable to incorporate additional information in the order, either as a part of the format, as indicated in Figure 9:3, or as an appendix to the order. These items are all essential to cost control, in that they facilitate the progressing of the order once it has been placed, and ensure that all documentation follows the

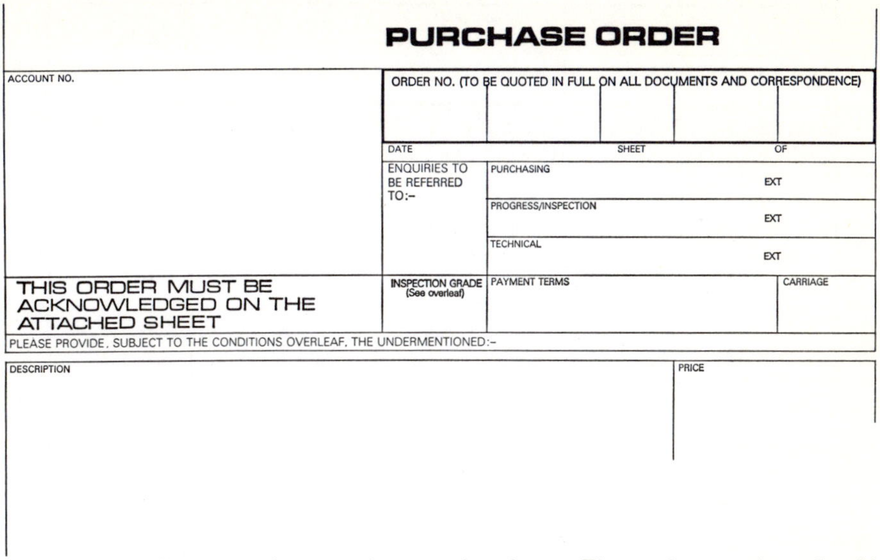

PURCHASE ORDER

ACCOUNT NO.

ORDER NO. (TO BE QUOTED IN FULL ON ALL DOCUMENTS AND CORRESPONDENCE)

DATE SHEET OF

ENQUIRIES TO BE REFERRED TO:-

PURCHASING EXT

PROGRESS/INSPECTION EXT

TECHNICAL EXT

THIS ORDER MUST BE ACKNOWLEDGED ON THE ATTACHED SHEET

INSPECTION GRADE (See overleaf)

PAYMENT TERMS

CARRIAGE

PLEASE PROVIDE, SUBJECT TO THE CONDITIONS OVERLEAF, THE UNDERMENTIONED:-

DESCRIPTION

PRICE

Figure 9:3 Section of a purchase order form. The order number should incorporate an allocation reference derived from the code of accounts, so that the five sections of the order number can be, for instance, order type; serial number; location reference; project number and sub-group number. Order type is a facility to separate, for example, materials from services.

approved pattern. The details are largely self-explanatory, but it is essential that the order number incorporates the code of accounts allocation as well as the purchase order reference.

Once the order has been issued, it is necessary to be aware of its progress up to the time when the material is delivered to site, or when work on site has been completed, where relevant. This is normally the function of the purchasing department and the control should be exercised order by order. This requires that individual order histories are maintained in the purchasing department. A typical form for this purpose is illustrated by Figure 9:4.

Inspection

The reference to inspection in both Figures 9:3 and 9:4 will have been noted. Inspection is another area where company policy can play a significant role, but it is recommended that, as a matter of policy, inspection at the supplier's works is reduced to a minimum—the absolute minimum. All standard items, such as pumps, valves, pipe, instruments—the list is unending—should comply with approved standard specifications, as supplied by the manufacturer, and the best

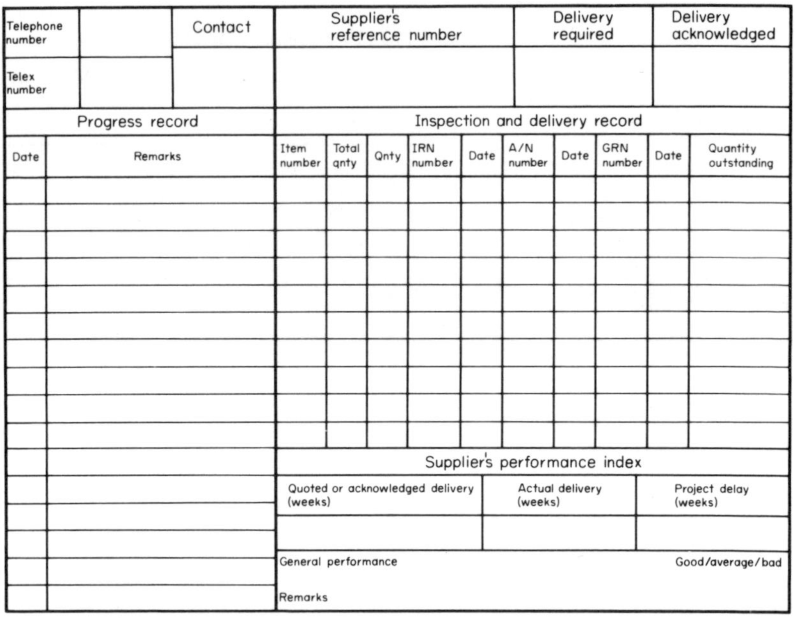

Figure 9:4 Order Process History. One such form should be maintained per order, until the delivery or the work is completed. Note the link (bottom right-hand corner) with Figure 9:1.

place to establish that the component meets the job requirement is on the site. With pumps, for instance, the manufacturer can provide an approved test certificate, and subsequent operation on site is the next stage of 'proof'. Referring to Figure 9:3, the more often *NONE* appears in the space under the 'inspection grade' heading the better. But in certain circumstances, such as in relation to insurance requirements, or the requirements of the factory inspectorate, inspection is obligatory. This means inspection at the manufacturer's works, and here, the best solution is to use the insurance company's surveyors.

Site material control

The reception, storage and use of materials received on site is very closely related to the purchasing function, and it is good practice to make the storeman and other staff in charge of materials on site responsible to the purchasing function. The purchasing department can then be responsible for certifying invoices in relation to the receipt of goods, resolving problems relating to shortages and rejected materials, without the intervention of third parties.

1 . PRICE

The price should always be analysed, where applicable, into:

1:1 ex-works price for equipment or materials.
1:2 freight and transport charges.
1:3 erection, testing and commissioning charges.

Every attempt should be made to fix each of these three elements.

2. SPECIFICATION

2:1 All optional extras should be defined and agreed.
2:2 All salient technical and performance requirements should be clearly indicated
2:3 The supplier should be responsible for conforming to UK statutory requirements and in particular the requirements of the Factory Inspectorate.
2:4 Any site labour requirements to be provided by the purchaser should be specified by number, grade and period.

3. DELIVERY AND SHIPMENT

3:1 Establish time-scale, mode of transport and guaranteed delivery date.
3:2 Identify overall dimensions and weights and consider the off-loading requirements.
3:3 Where an item is imported, take action in relation to the supplier's UK agent and/or shipping agents and define the responsibilities of the various parties in relation to marine insurance, documentation and customs clearance.
3:4 Determine passage of the title to the property.
3:5 Consider claims procedure for damage, shortage, etc.

4. PERFORMANCE AND MECHANICAL GUARANTEE

4:1 Ensure that workmanship and materials are guaranteed, preferably for twelve months from the date of handover.
4:2 Consider the desirability of a performance warranty.
4:3 Consider the value of a liquidated damages clause in relation to delivery or completion of work.

Figure 9:5 Procurement procedure. A schedule of the salient aspects to be considered for any major order. *(Continued overleaf)*

5. PAYMENT

5:1 Avoid letters of credit or the intervention of bankers (this is particularly relevant on overseas orders).
5:2 Arrange direct invoicing and payment to the supplier's account.
5:3 Establish settlement periods.
5:4 Seek stage payments allowing maximum retentions at all times.
5:5 With imported equipment, consider forward purchase arrangements for non-sterling currency.
5:6 With imported equipment, consider tariff and other import legislation with financial implications.

6. CONDITIONS OF CONTRACT

6:1 Modify supplier's conditions if considered appropriate.
6:2 Alternatively, seek to impose own proposals, preferably of a neutral character, such as one of the 'model forms' available.
6:3 Ensure that basis of contract is English (not Scottish) law and that place of settlement of disputes is the UK.
6:4 Provide for arbitration.

7. INSURANCE

7:1 Establish requirements in relation to:
(*a*) All-risks insurance on the contract works.
(*b*) Marine/transit insurance.
(*c*) Employer's liability
(*d*) Third party and public liability.
7:2 Scrutinise the policies or other certificates effected by the supplier (take nothing for granted).
7:3 Ensure that any policies taken out by the supplier are valid for the duration of the contract being agreed.
7:4 Check the 'limitations' in policies taken out by the supplier, to ensure that they do not preclude the application of the policy to the contract being agreed.

Figure 9:5 continued

The degree to which staff is established on site for material control will depend very much on the size of the project, but however small or large the volume of material flow, the principles remain the same, and material control must not be limited, as it so often is, to checking receipt. A site storeman should be competent to deal with general administration and documentation matters, quality control of materials delivery, and the co-ordination of 'open order' materials. This will ensure a continuing flow of basic materials, (for example cement) so that deliveries meet the programmed requirements. Materials should not be left to lie about on the site to become lost after issue from the stores. The storeman should recognise a responsibility for materials *after* leaving the stores, as well as whilst in the stores.

10

Consultant and Contractor

These days the line of demarcation between a 'consultant' and a 'contractor' is becoming more and more blurred. The basic difference between the consultant and the contractor is that the consultant is not financially implicated in the cost of the works for which his services are being made available. In addition, the consultant is, almost invariably, a member of a recognised institution or professional association, whereby remuneration is fixed, or related to a standard scale of fees and other charges.

The most well-known in this field are the architect and the quantity surveyor. There is also an association of consulting engineers, but the activities of its members are less well known, at least to the general public. This arises in part, because their numbers in the United Kingdom are relatively few—perhaps six hundred. And, of course, they are not allowed to advertise.

The contractor, on the other hand, can and does intrude into the 'consultant' field when a 'fixed fee plus reimbursable cost' type of contract is established, as discussed in detail later. Similarly, this complete divorcement of the consultant from the financial consequences of his work is none too acceptable to the user, so that consultants are tending to accept approaches which implicate them in the cost of the works in a more direct fashion than has been in the past. A common device in this context is, of course, to fix the fee paid, rather than have it expressed as a percentage of the cost of the works.

It is important to recognise, when considering the use of consultants, that the true consultant offers no challenge to the authority of the project engineer. The project engineer remains fully in control of the project. The consultant provides advice and an 'independent opinion' and there is no doubt that where there is scope for the services of a consultant his cost can be saved, sometimes many times over. This is achieved by the consultant's skill in design and fair administration of the conditions of contract.

Choice of Consultant

The selection of a consulting engineer is not a difficult matter. Where there is no prior experience or knowledge, application should be made to the appropriate institution and the chairman will put forward a few names from which a selection can be made. Insofar as fees are concerned, the several associations have laid down scales of fees which will be quoted on request. It should be noted that the rules provide for variations from the set scales to allow for difficult or special classes of work, or for the savings in time that result from repetitive work.

The role of the consultant

On accepting a commission from a client, the consultant's first task should be to ascertain the client's exact requirements. It is usual for these to be set out in a report, which is associated with an estimate of cost. Alternatives should be valued and discussed, with the objective of securing the most economical design. The consultant also prepares tenders, complete with specifications and conditions of contract, seeking to ensure that tenders, when received by the contractors, are on a comparable basis. The specification defines the work the contractor has to do, the conditions of contract lay down how it has to be done and how payment is to be made. Three parties are involved, the client, the consultant and the contractor, and the conditions of contract should recognise the existence of all three, setting out as precisely as possible their respective duties and responsibilities, and their relationship to each other.

Where, as is often found in practice, the construction work is subject to the supervision of the consultant, his representative will be on site to check the works in relation to alignment, measurements, quantities and quality. The consultant will authorise payments to the contractor based on the state and progress of the works. During all such contracts variations arise, which will be the subject of claims from the contractor.

It is the further duty of the consultant to hear these claims and suggest appropriate awards if he considers that these are fair and reasonable.

The 'packaged deal'

So far, the term 'contractor' has been applied to firms who are executing work to designs provided by the client or consultant. However, during the past decade the concept of the 'packaged deal' has been developed. A packaged deal is a contract placed with consultant or contractor that is all embracing. For instance, with a new factory, a single firm may take responsibility for carrying out the initial market appraisal of the product to be made, finding a suitable site, designing the buildings and plant required, negotiating with third parties, preparing drawings and tenders, dealing with the planning authorities, advising on tender selection and other negotiations, and finally handing over the plant as a running concern. The firm might even find and train the necessary staff.

The 'turn-key' contract

Another term applied to this type of contract is 'turn-key'. The implication is that the consultant or contractor will initiate the project and complete it, presenting to the client a plant in which all that has to be done is to 'turn the key' and commence production.

The advantage of such an approach is that the client is relieved of many problems. Indeed, most of the problems discussed in this book, but by no means all. The modern trend is for companies to confine their activities to those areas in which they have specialised experience, and a manufacturing organisation does not, therefore, have specialised experience of construction. Furthermore, the load in this respect is fluctuating—widely fluctuating in most cases—and this is another reason for seeking such comprehensive help from others. There are also the advantages to be gained from the employment of a team of specialists, working in harmony and competent to co-ordinate and integrate the many detailed facets of a project of substance.

Overall saving of time is another benefit claimed for the packaged deal. Tenders can be streamlined, material ordered ahead of final design, deliveries can be planned, subcontractors efficiently organised. It would often be quite impracticable for a company to achieve similar results by itself, even at the cost of an enormous increase in overheads. Savings in overall costs can also be expected. For instance, lifting problems can be pre-planned, a heavy item placed on site at an early stage, and the construction planned around it. The whole job is likely to run more smoothly because it is under the direct supervision of one overriding source of authority.

This is, of course, the concept presented in Figure 8:1 with one single point of contact between the client and the contractor. Those offering packaged deals as either consultants or commercial contractors vary in their internal organisation and method of working, so that this illustration must not be taken to be typical. It is, rather, a method of working. In particular, of course, the scope of the duties undertaken by the contractor will vary, according to the resources available. Generally speaking, however, the basic offer is of consulting and/or design facilities, together with the overall supervision of the project. Some companies go further and are able to undertake certain elements of the work, such as the civil works or the manufacture of some of the equipment, or perhaps the pipework. Advantages are naturally claimed for this further facility, and advantages do exist, but care must be taken to ensure that the prices paid for such work are competitive.

As stated previously, not only can this service be utilised from initial survey to final commissioning, but an additional service for the recruiting and training of personnel may also be available which would be put to good use. Throughout, however, it has to be recognised that there are certain principles fundamental to the success of such arrangements from a cost control point of view. These are:

1 Close co-ordination between client, consultant and contractor
2 Continuing effort throughout all the stages of the project
3 Complete confidence in the skill and experience offered
4 Proper use of the resources made available
5 Co-operation in both the technical and financial aspects of the project

If the approach to the packaged deal is to be summarised, and the question asked why use it? There are three basic reasons:

1 The client may not have a sufficiently large staff or resources for all or part of the work
2 The client is willing to pay a premium for the advantage of having assigned overall responsibility to another
3 The client is convinced that a particular process plant can be designed by a contractor with staff expert in the specific area

The last of these three reasons is often decisive.

Negotiation Versus Competition

It has to be recognised that a fundamental concept in the 'packaged deal' approach is that the contractor must be involved from the very beginning. Where the process is being bought from the contractor, it may still be possible to consider getting a lump sum offer, but where the process is essentially that of the client, then direct price competition is impossible. The contractor cannot possibly know enough to enable him to make such an offer. He has, in fact, to start work in order to learn what the basis of that offer could be. In such circumstances, it is usual to survey the technical competence of possible contractors in relation to the scope of the particular project, and perhaps make some general enquiry as to design cost rates and the percentage on cost required for purchasing. On data such as this a choice has to be made of a specific contractor. But the contractual procedure should be such that there is opportunity to withdraw at certain defined stages in the progress of the work should it be felt that the contractor is taking advantage of the specialised relationship that has been established, or should he prove incompetent.

The usual course is for the contractor to be progressively involved in the successive stages of project development, as follows:

Stage 1

Preparation of outline schemes and preliminary estimates. This is undertaken for a fee which is usually less than two per cent of the value of the project.

Stage 2

Submission of a fixed fee and reimbursable cost proposal on completion of, and based upon, the agreed outline scheme. The fee is fixed in relation to the agreed scheme, thus limiting the liability of the client to the contractor.

Stage 3

At the appropriate stage in the detailed development of the project, negotiation of a fixed lump sum in place of the reimbursable cost. This step, if accomplished, finally places the whole of the financial risk for successful completion of the project on the contractor.

Stage three may not necessarily be pursued. Successful negotiation of a lump sum depends very much on the existing financial climate. If conditions are stable a mutually acceptable sum is much more likely to materialise.

The alternative to the foregoing is, of course, the 'simple' competitive bid. But, if several offers are going to be sought for a project, or major plant units in a project, then two, three, or perhaps even six, months may elapse before the offers can be received and evaluated. This delay must be foreseen and the necessary time allowed for this procedure.

The attitude of the contractor in this connection cannot be ignored. He is asked to spend a considerable sum of money to prepare a tender—perhaps one per cent of the total value of his offer—and may be reluctant to spend such a relatively large sum if there is little prospect of success. The contractor, therefore, may have to be assured that there is a firm intention to build the plant and that the number of competitive tenders being requested is reasonable (usually less than four) before he will undertake the necessary work. This attitude is understandable. There ought to be a reasonable possibility of obtaining a profitable contract if he is expected to spend money on any scale.

Establishing a Contract

Consideration has to be given to the situation where the project engineer is able to decide that the interests of the company are best served by 'going it alone'. In this situation a series of contracts will have to be placed. Should the decision be taken to buy a process, then in that context a contract will also have to be placed. It is helpful, therefore, if the problems that are likely to be encountered are foreseen. It should also be recognised that the formulation of a contract is not the prerogative of the finance or the purchasing departments, nor is it the exclusive domain of solicitors and lawyers, even when their guidance is sought.

A sample from the broad spectrum of the engineers engaged in a project should be involved in the establishment of a contract, and involved throughout, from the preliminary discussions, held when the specifications are first prepared as a basis for enquiry, to the time when all the details are finally hammered out and a contract is signed. An understanding of the essential elements in a contract, and the factors which are significant in successful contract negotiation, is of considerable help to the engineers who will later be involved in the day-to-day administration of the contract, While the negotiations tend to be conducted at a fairly high level in the company organisation, the key decisions are invariably made by the engineers who have to prepare the specifications around which the contract is, in fact, built.

Negotiating procedures

On the assumption that the proposed plant is of a complicated technical nature (if this is not so a simple order will suffice) the first stage is to review the basic requirements with prospective contractors. This serves two purposes: the project team becomes aware of the possibilities and the contractor becomes aware of the seriousness of the enquiry. Against this background, carried out with say, two or three different contractors, an enquiry can be prepared complete with outline specification. These initial discussions should cover the following:

1 Plant size and possible cost
2 Programme
3 Process innovations
4 Standard specifications
5 The seriousness of the enquiry

As the negotiations proceed, and particularly once the offers are in, and detailed discussions are being held with the preferred contractor, care must be taken to see that unfair procedures are not adopted. These may not necessarily mitigate against the success of the particular contract being negotiated, but they may well affect the success of any future contract with that company, or even with others in the same field. A practice to be deplored in this respect is that of passing prices as tendered from one contractor to the other. It is also possible to set up unfair conditions of contract. If the contractor is under pressure by virtue of the market situation, and anxious to secure the order, these conditions may well be accepted by him. But at a later stage the inequalities in the contract may affect the progress and the quality of the work. Unfair conditions of contract are sometimes quite difficult to discern and the protests of the contractor may not be understood. An attentive ear should always be given to protests of such a nature. They should never be overridden by statements such as—'these are our standard conditions of contract', or 'no one else has ever objected.' The inequality may, of course, come from either side.

Where his own processes are involved, the contractor is anxious to maintain secrecy and overall control and he can then put forward conditions that are unfair to the purchaser. For instance a common clause in this context is:

'Purchaser guarantees to the contractor that he will not use *nor permit any other company to use* the process or the related designs in any other plant belonging to the purchaser or otherwise'

On the face of it, such a clause seems fair, since after all, the process has been developed by the contractor and naturally, he wishes to have the opportunity of securing orders for further plants of this type, both from this particular purchaser and, from others. But, in fact, the clause is too broad. It places an obligation on the purchaser which he is hardly in a position to fulfil. It is incumbent on the contractor to protect his own patents and processes. The responsibility of the purchaser should be limited and the words underlined modified. The limit of the requirement placed on the purchaser should be that he does not *knowingly and intentionally* disclose such secrets to others.

Round the table

All contract negotiations finish up with a group of people sitting round a table. The conduct of the various people at this time is very important—a lack of discipline can be very expensive. Looking at such a meeting from the point of view of the purchaser, the project team must do its 'homework' before going to the meeting, and parties to the meeting (such as the purchasing officer or the legal representative) must be properly briefed before the meeting begins. The following points should always be discussed before such meetings:

1 Terms that are essential to the project
2 Terms that are desirable but may be waived if necessary
3 Terms that the contractor may put forward that cannot be accepted
4 Terms that the contractor may put forward that would be accepted if necessary, but are not really desirable

Such a discussion leads, in effect, to a decision as to what the content of the contract should be: that is, the terms essential to both parties to the contract. It is always important before any such meeting to agree who is going to be 'leader' or 'spokesman', and care should be taken to ensure that the technical representation is of the proper status. It must always be possible to reach decision *at the meeting.* Reference back is a sign of weakness and can well lead to a poor contract.

How will the contractor react? The techniques of negotiation are limitless, but a very common approach is to have a *nice* and a *nasty* personality in the team. This permits a complete reversal of approach, if necessary, without it appearing that such a change has in fact taken place. Terms can be toughened, or relaxed, as negotiations proceed, by one or the other taking the dominant role. There are, of course, a number of basic rules which should always be observed. Once again, the list is extensive, but the following should never be forgotten:

1 Do not make sudden decisions. Reserve a decision when a point is not fully understood, or has not previously been discussed by the team.
2 Be prepared to listen. If the contractor spells out his terms, they may well be more favourable than was expected. Let the contractor tell you his reasons—this may tell you how important the point is to him.
3 Watch for reactions. This may reveal far more than the spoken word. Loss of patience may be a warning to stop, although some points may be important enough to be pursued—whatever the reaction. Whispers and furtive notes are to be abhorred—this creates an air of suspicion.
4 Maintain a sense of proportion. Once the important points are settled, get the meeting closed as quickly as possible. While you are discussing a triviality in detail, the contractor may well be reviewing the merits of earlier decisions.
5 Do not press too hard. The purchaser is always in the dominant position, as the buyer. Advantage should not be taken of this to secure complete capitulation. The negotiating team from the 'other side' should always be allowed to take home some 'successes' to their own management.
6 Do not display your feelings. When an unexpected victory has been won, do not labour it. Leave it. When a point has been conceded by the contractor, do not go on 'excusing' yourself for its necessity. Of course, expressions of satisfaction at a successful conclusion are in order.

Terms and conditions of contract

Most of the negotiation will centre around the specification, but the terms and conditions of contract are also extremely important and must never be taken for granted. The best approach, and one which is usually acceptable to the potential contractor, is to use as a basis the standard terms and conditions as published by one of the professional associations, or public bodies. These 'model forms' of contract are generally accepted as being equitable, although they may require adaptation to suit them to the specific needs of a particular contract. Redundant clauses, in particular, are a nuisance and can be extremely confusing.

The Institutions of Mechanical and Electrical Engineers publish forms of contract appropriate to engineering plant, the Royal Institute of British Architects has a form for building works, the Institution of Civil Engineers has a form for civil works, and the Institution of Chemical Engineers has published a form of contract which is very appropriate where a 'process' is being purchased. One or other of these several forms of contract can be used for contracts within the United Kingdom. Where contracts are being negotiated with overseas suppliers and contractors the position becomes much more complex, but the United Nations Organisation for Economic Affairs has published standard forms which have the intrinsic merit of neutrality. Where possible, therefore, such a form of contract should be adopted. Extreme caution is needed if the supplier's conditions are accepted in such circumstances, because of the complications that can ensue owing to the problems of language and the differences in contract law, that exist from one country to another. These differences are often fundamental in this context and expert advice should always be sought in such cases. Blind acceptance in 'good faith' can have the most disastrous consequences without there being any evil intent on the part of the overseas supplier.

11

Site Administration

Reference has already been made to the control of materials of site (Chapter 9), since this is seen as a part of the responsibility of the purchasing department. Where a main contractor is not being employed to take overall responsibility for work on the site, it will fall to the lot of the project engineer to co-ordinate and control the several contractors who are employed there. He will have to ensure that they make proper use of such plant, equipment and materials, as are supplied to them. This can be a real problem and is one reason why it is desirable to make site contractors responsible for their own materials, insofar as that is possible. The time advantage secured by the pre-ordering of materials and the cost advantage secured by the bulk ordering of materials has to be weighed against the losses than can occur once those materials are handed over to others. It is best, therefore, if pre-ordering is limited to clearly recognisable and definable items, such as equipment, switchgear and instruments, and to allow the contractor to supply the miscellaneous materials such as jointing, cables, brackets, insulation, paint and so forth.

Construction Team

The cost of construction on the site always represents a significant proportion of the total installed cost of a project and, as a matter of experience, the most difficult to control. In general, there will be three major parties involved in site operations, the owner, the contractor and the labour force. The labour force may not necessarily be restricted to the employees of the various contractors, but can also include labour normally engaged on maintenance or miscellaneous capital projects by the owner. This is often the case where the extension is adjacent to an existing production unit.

The various site activities require administration and control, which has to be exercised by the owner himself, through a section of his project team, or by a main contractor. The type of organisation necessary on a project of substance is illustrated in Figure 11:1. This chart gives an outline of the potential site activities and hence can serve as a check list in relation to the establishment of an organisation in a specific context. The degree of elaboration of the actual site organisation will depend upon the size of the project but as a rough guide usually two men are required per £100000 of total project cost (at 1971 price levels), for site supervision above foreman grade. Not all these people are necessarily in the employ of the owner and on the smaller project there is a tendency towards duplication of effort, in that the owner will maintain an interest in site activities which are already being quite adequately supervised and controlled by the contractor.

The level of activity on the site will, of course, vary as the project progresses, reaching a peak normally after two thirds of the total duration of time over which the site activity is spread, as is illustrated in Figure 11:2. As a 'rule-of-thumb', the total labour force at peak will be roughly twice the average labour force throughout the duration of the project. This is a useful guide to the maximum level of site activity, since an approximate estimate of erection cost and duration allows one to derive the average level of activity.

Live Site Working

The nature of the work on site falls, from the point of view of the owner, into two distinct groups. The first is construction work on a separate and distinct plant, which can be pursued without interfering with the existing production facilities except, perhaps, to quite a minor degree for tie-ins. The second is where a major integration with existing facilities is involved, necessitating the shutdown of plant for a period. The usual objective, for obvious reasons, will be to minimise the shutdown period, but this can only be achieved at a cost. The cost of shutdown has therefore to be weighed against increased construction cost.

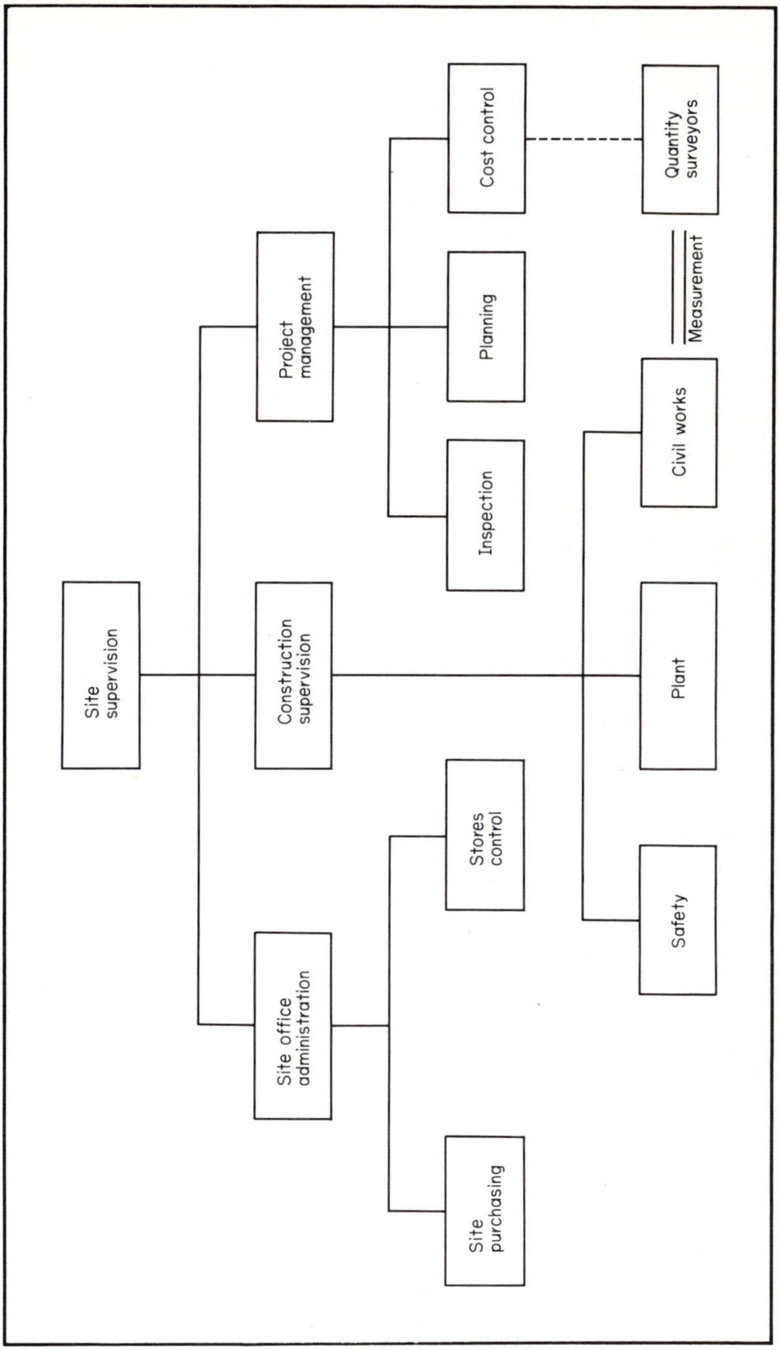

Figure 11:1 Typical Site Organisation. The degree to which individual activities are combined in one or more personnel will depend upon the size of the project and the nature of the contracts awarded.

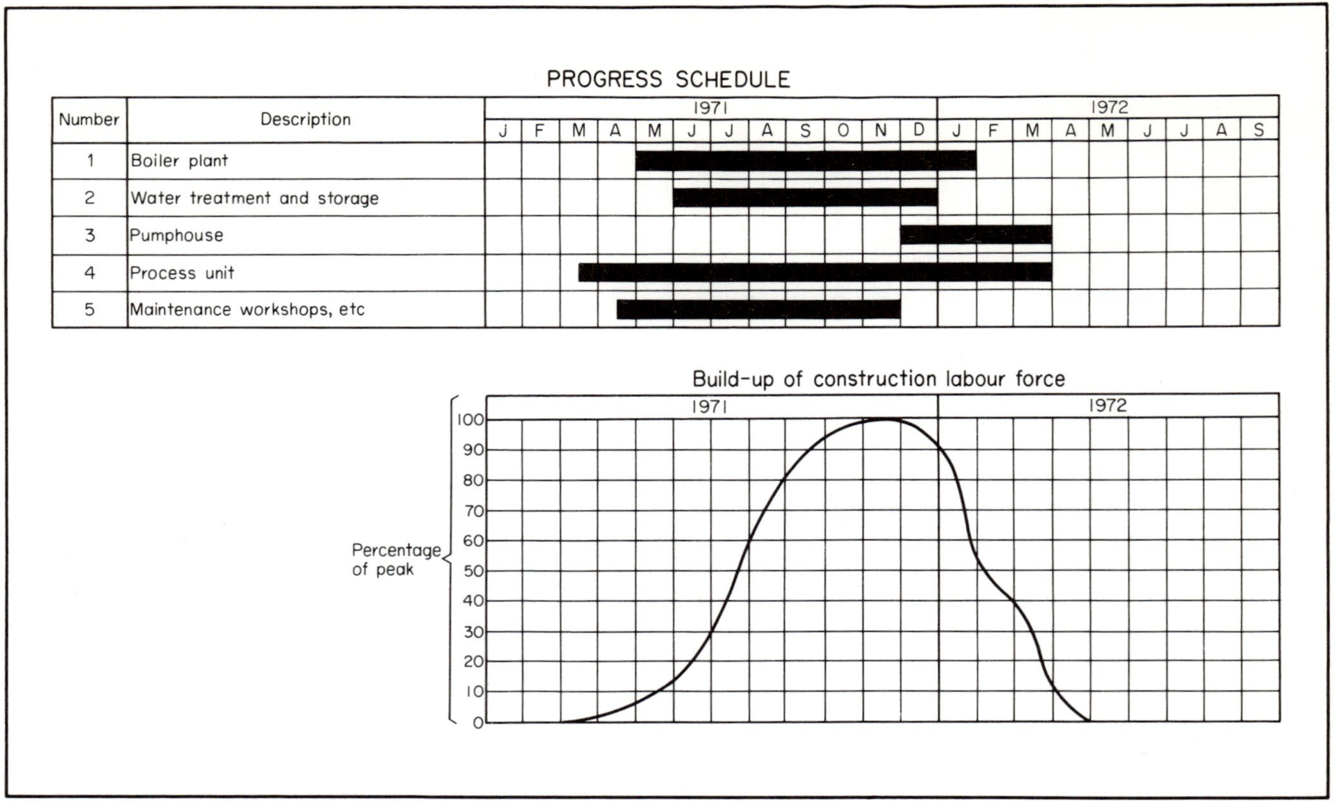

Figure 11:2 Erection programme. The Gantt chart is developed into a labour loading curve. More sophisticated techniques, based on critical path planning, are of course available.

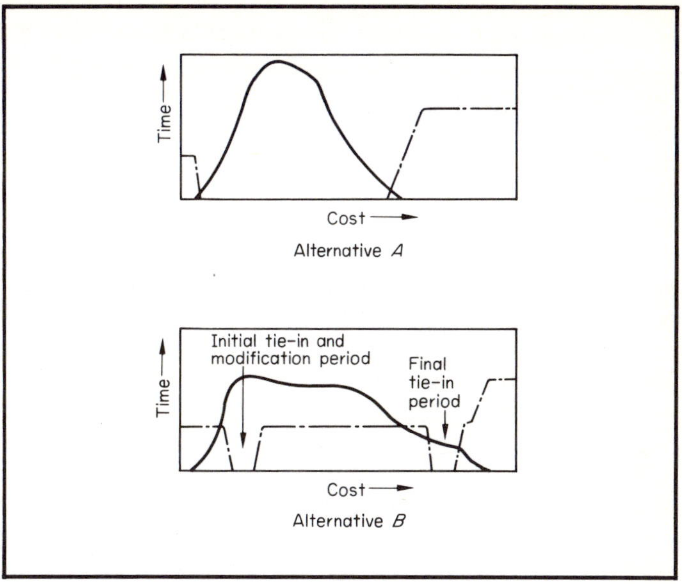

Figure 11:3 'Live site' working and suspension of production. Alternative A represents the situation when production is suspended during the construction period. Alternative B demonstrates what is known as 'live site' working, where production continues during the construction period.

Taking the same graphical approach as presented in Figure 11:2, two alternatives are generally available, as is illustrated in Figure 11:3. The second alternative, employing what is known as 'live site working' requires a high degree of sophistication in the planning of the site work if it is to be successful, but it will then result in an overall saving despite the increased cost of the project itself. The direct monetary benefit can usually be demonstrated by calculation, but this is not all. There are usually less tangible benefits as well, largely in the marketing field. For instance, the product remains available for sale, even if the total falls, stockpiling of raw materials and finished products is largely eliminated, and staff problems are reduced to a minimum.

Labour Problems

Pressure on the project team reaches a peak when the project enters the construction phase and this leads to an approach where completion at the earliest possible date becomes *the* target—often to the detriment of logical, planned progress. If the project is being carried forward on an existing site, where two types of labour are present, the maintenance labour for the existing plant and the contractor's labour on the new plant, these problems are often compounded by claims relating to site working conditions and wages that are not met with on a 'green field' site. A series of guidelines can be established in relation to site administrative which should serve to minimise these problems with site labour. These are:

1 Plan the site start date carefully. Too early a start, before materials or design details are available in adequate volume will set a poor standard in relation to labour productivity.
2 Minimise the peak labour force. Almost invariably peak conditions have to be met by the importation of labour from outside the normal area of labour availability. This is not only very expensive but it also mitigates against efficiency.
3 Minimise overtime. As overtime becomes systematic, the rate of absenteeism rises and productivity falls. Not only does absenteeism give an unbalanced and hence less efficient labour force, but the related overtime is worked at a higher yet less productive hourly rate. There is, therefore, a two-fold loss of efficiency.
4 Maximise co-operation. There should be the fullest exchange of information in relation to labour availability, local rates, factory rates and conditions between the owner and the several contractors employed on the site. Neither party should act unilaterally, without prior consultation, even though he has every right to do so.
5 Use the minimum number of contractors. The division of site work into a series of small contracts often appears to be financially attractive, since it increases the possibility of competitive tendering. But smaller contracts attract higher overheads, when expressed as a percentage of basic cost.

A multiplicity of contractors on a site will also reduce the efficiency of operation, usually by extending the total time taken to completion. This means that the owner's costs for the overall management of the site will then be higher.

Extra Works

It is as construction proceeds at site that all the mistakes made, from the first design fault onwards, together with all the earlier failures to take appropriate action, are finally seen as inescapable problems that *have* to be solved. Equipment arrives late and sometimes damaged, drawings have errors, so that items do not fit or clash, and things are forgotten. Everyone is fallible, including the site construction team, who can also fail to supervise the work on site properly, or plan it well.

Over and above all this, which we may refer to as the 'acts of men', we have conditions which are referred to as 'acts of God'. They come under the general description of *force majeure* and exercise a powerful influence on progress at the site. There are such things as bad weather, fires, strikes—everything hinders and nothing helps. The writer has known good weather (a prolonged, hot summer) to have an adverse effect, let alone rain and fog, the incidental accompaniments to the normal English winter.

The best defence here, as always, is knowledge—knowledge of what can happen and why it happens. Knowledge of what gives rise to extra works and variations on site, and why. The major types of extra works and their causes, can be tabulated as follows:

Type of extra	
1 Rectification of design errors	Careless design or poor design co-ordination
2 Alterations to avoid plant or buildings	Poor construction supervision or ill-defined drawings
3 Dismantling and re-erection of plant or buildings to allow other plant in	Poor construction planning, or poor site supervision
4 Rectification of damage caused by other contractors	Poor construction supervision
5 Rectification of general damage	Weather, fire, poor site or stores control
6 Assistance to other contractors	Lack of co-ordination and pre-planning. This can be justified, but should be foreseen
7 Extra works	Design omissions, or can be deliberately left for the site to order, or is due to late changes

8 Extra overtime	Late design and ordering, or late delivery, or poor construction planning, or poor construction supervision, or to meet a new and urgent situation

If this list is perused it will be seen that most of the causes are generated at site, and this is very true. This means that a good, strong and comprehensive site organisation with sound administrative techniques, whilst appearing expensive in the first instance, and perhaps a luxury, can in fact, more than pay for itself by minimising total project cost to an appreciable extent.

PART THREE

ESTIMATING TECHNIQUES

12

The Estimate

Having considered in broad outline the type of detail on which a capital cost estimate will have to be based, it is now possible to examine the way in which the estimate itself can be tackled. To do this it is desirable to have an appreciation of the underlying principles involved. As a project develops the details available for the preparation of such an estimate also grow, and even if it is the intention to prepare a detailed estimate at a later stage, it is always advantageous to prepare preliminary estimates at the earlier stage. If there is no more cogent reason than that it is always desirable in estimating to approach a cost problem from two or more different angles, such an estimate will have served its purpose. Usually there is such pressure, from a wide variety of interested parties, for a figure at the earliest possible moment—a 'quickie' or a 'guesstimate' as it is often called—that the estimator is driven to produce an 'order of magnitude' indication (another common term) whilst still in the throes of gathering together the necessary information that will enable a figure to be prepared which can be substantiated in detail.

The major difficulty involved in putting forward such estimates at an early stage, is that the figure first quoted in this way tends to have more weight attached to it than is normally warranted. Such figures, once published, are often taken to be substantial and accurate. An unfortunate situation can develop if the final estimate, produced after more detailed consideration and calculation, is higher. Every effort has to be made, in such circumstances, to ensure that the figure quoted covers all possible contingencies. On the other hand, management, presented with such figures, must be prepared to recognise that these figures are *estimates*, subject to a margin of error, and not the ceiling figures that they are usually taken to be. A ceiling figure will not serve the purpose for which the estimate is being prepared, since it will inevitably overstate the case.

However, despite the largely psychological problems involved in the handling of such figures, the rapid solution can still serve a purpose. If the detailed estimate agrees reasonably well with the earlier figures then there is every reason for confidence. Any gross discrepancy can be investigated and its cause established. It is often that in this way omissions in the detailed estimate are brought to light.

Using the Correct Criterion

The basis of the approach to estimating now being considered is the application of what is called the 'scientific method', whereby the results of experience gained in one field can be conveyed to another with the minimum of mental exertion. This concept is fundamental to engineering, and estimates of capital cost present but another facet of an abiding problem. It is necessary to appreciate and assess the value of the principles underlying any particular aspect of estimating, if the experience already gained in comparable fields is to be of use.

Sometimes, even technically trained people are deceived into jumping to conclusions and fail to convey their experience from one field to another, even in a proper arithmetical manner. This can be a failing with engineers when they estimate costs. For instance, a series of experiments could be conducted on a small scale, and in one part of the process adequate cooling would be achieved in a vessel by surface loss. The next step is to consider a plant having ten times the output. The engineer would realise at once that it would be a fatal error to multiply by ten all the linear dimensions of the vessel, or even to increase its capacity ten times. He recognises immediately that as the vessel increases in size, the surface exposed for cooling bears a varying relation to its bulk, so that the time required for cooling would be affected. Yet how often is the error made of assuming a linear relation between capacity and cost in the bulk storage of liquids? The major cost factor, with storage tanks, is the area of plate in the tank, and this follows the same rule as the one we have just cited in relation to cooling. The cost, therefore, will not increase in proportion to the increase in storage capacity.

How do costs vary? Cost is one expression of the results of engineering design, so presumably known engineering design principles can be related to cost. In engineering work it is recognised that the use of models is only of value when some criterion which enables the performance of the production unit, operating on a larger scale, or under different conditions, is to be estimated from the results of experience with the model. The principle relating to this matter, in the purely mathematical field, has been stated as the principle of similitude. By way of example, the limiting piston speed in different sizes of engine is the same, and assuming the same steam pressure, two engines could be built by the same drawing to different scales, and both would be satisfactory. On the other hand, if the stability of towers or chimneys is being studied, a very different situation exists.

Taking this problem of the stability of chimneys as an example, consider two geometrically similar chimneys, as illustrated in Figure 12:1, and consider each chimney in turn when it is being acted upon by the wind. A simple, straightforward example. If n is the relationship between the linear dimensions of chimney A and chimney B, then the resultant wind pressure P_2 as compared with the wind pressure P_1 will be $P_1 n^2$, and the respective turning moments will be:

Chimney A: $P_1 \times X_1 Y_1$

Chimney B: $P_1 n^2 \times X_2 Y_2 = Pn^3 \times X_1 Y_1$

That is, the turning moments are proportional to the cube of the linear dimensions. The resisting moments, however, are:

Chimney A: $W \times X_1 Y_1$

Chimney B: $Wn^3 \times X_2 Y_2 = Wn^4 \times X_1 Y_1$

where W is the weight of chimney A. So we see that whereas the turning moment is proportional to the cube, the resisting moment is proportional to the fourth power of the linear dimensions. In consequence it would be both stupid and dangerous to design a small chimney simply copying a larger one to a smaller scale, safe as that proposition seems at first sight. Danger usually comes by copying small things to a larger scale. Here the reverse is the case, and the smaller chimney, if so designed, would not be equal in stability to the larger structure. This is a simple example, but it does illustrate that knowledge and experience have to be soundly applied, if it is to be

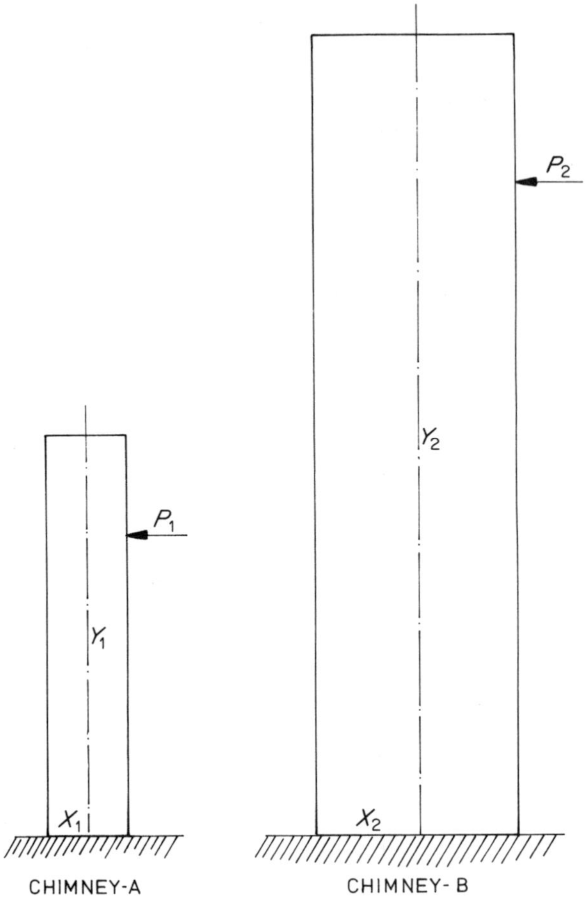

Figure 12:1 Basic factors in the design of chimneys. The mathematical relationship is discussed in the text.

really profitable. It also emphasises the danger of so-called judgement and common sense.

So then, it is extremely important to realise 'how things vary' and also to select the correct variable, the *applicable* variable.

The 'Six-Tenths' Rule

The other principle which is fundamental to estimating capital cost is that things do not, as a general rule, proceed be leaps and bounds. The various functions involved in both process and plant design are continuous and, when plotted, will give smooth curves. Plotting such relationships on logarithmic paper usually approximates to a straight line, and substantial accuracy can be secured, at least between certain limits, by setting down the results as though they gave a straight line on logarithmic paper. Such straight lines on logarithmic paper can be expressed in the form of an equation of the type:

$$X = Cy^r$$

This formula is well-known in the engineering profession. It has the merit of being generally applicable, and lends itself to quick calculation on a slide rule or incorporation in a computer program, where such a resource is available.

Since cost is, ultimately, but a reflection of engineering design, it is only to be expected that costs will follow a generally similar pattern. It should, therefore, be possible to rationalise and correlate costs in a similar fashion. There is every reason to expect that 'monomial' formulae of this type, if developed from costs, would be a useful summary of an extended range of estimating data, even though the rule would be purely empirical.

The most widely known rule of this type, commonly used in cost estimating and based on the principle just discussed, is almost universally referred to as the 'six-tenths' rule. The rule is given in Figures 12:2 and 12:3. The exponent in the equation is cited as 0.6 since this is the reason why the expression is referred to as the 'six-tenths' rule. The actual exponent can vary quite widely, being influenced by the field of application of the formula, but there are a large majority of instances and circumstances where the exponent is within the range of 0.5 to 0.7. When complete plants are being considered, the original area of application for the relationship, the exponent is almost invariably very close to 0.6. It was in this context that the relationship was first discovered, hence the description.

The formula was first given wide publicity in engineering circles in 1947,[1] but it was well known as a 'rule of thumb' method for many years before that.

As already demonstrated, such a relationship should be applicable over a wide range and, it is in fact, applied with confidence, not only to the comparision of costs for complete plants, where these are similar in process, but also to the individual items of plant and equipment. Its usefulness, where extensions to existing installations are under consideration, is immediately apparent, and the rule can find continual application in such circumstances. Caution is, however, continually necessary, and the manner in which the cost of existing plant installations is analysed can often be of great importance.

IF:

a = Size of unit of which cost is known, expressed in the appropriate terms such as capacity, throughput, etc.

b = Size of unit for which cost is required, expressed in the same terms as *a* above.

c = Actual cost of *a* above.

d = Cost being sought—that is, estimated cost of unit size *b*.

e = Correction factor (see note below)

THEN:

$$d = \left(\frac{b}{a}\right)^{0.6} \times ce$$

(The index can vary from 0.5 to 0.7)

Note:
The correction factor *e* has been introduced to ensure that the necessity for adjusting the price *c* to take account of the variation in costs, arising with the passage of time, is appreciated, since in almost all cases the price *c* will be years old.

Figure 12:2 The 'six-tenths' rule. This formula can be applied not only to complete projects, but also to individual items of plant and equipment provided that the limitations discussed in the text are respected.

The relationship is, with the exponent at 0.6, a 'rule of thumb' method in every sense and little tricks have been developed over the years to get approximate answers even whilst such figures were being discussed. For instance, if the exponent is assumed to be 0.666 recurring, then, with the appropriate scales available on the slide rule, it is possible to establish the ratio between, say, two similar plants in terms of output, square the figure, take the cube root, and have the cost ratio forthwith. Estimators in continual contact with such figures know that to double the size of a plant adds only 50 per cent to the cost, whilst to reduce a plant to one third of its capacity will only halve the investment cost.

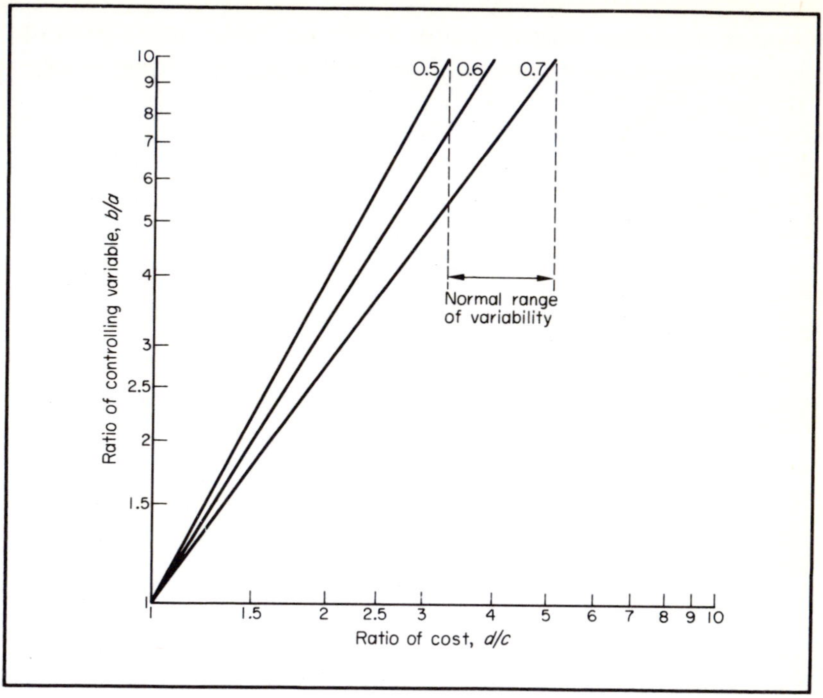

Figure 12:3 A plot of the six-tenths rule. This chart can be used for a quick assesment of the cost ratio, once the size ratio is known.

Choosing the Applicable Variable

The importance of taking the correct criterion when applying the principle of similitude has already been discussed and this is an aspect which must never be ignored. With a complete plant, output (or sometimes input), expressed in terms of tons per year, is usually a fairly reliable 'yardstick', but careful consideration must always be given to this point. If a process has a recirculation cycle, then the magnitude of that cycle can be such as to overshadow the influence of either input or output capacity on the size (and hence cost) of the other parts of the plant. The volume of recirculation may not necessarily be related to either input or output but affected by something entirely different, such as the quality of the product required, which varies from one product to another. In such circumstances the rule would be invalidated.

The use of this technique is perhaps best illustrated by considering a specific item of plant, rather than complete plants. One very common item of plant is the heat exchanger, and this can serve as an example. A heat exchanger is, in the mechanical sense, a relatively simple piece of equipment. For those unfamiliar with heat exchangers, a typical section is shown by Figure 12:4. The design variables are many and, the possibilities from an engineering point of view, diverse. The potential variables include the inlet and outlet temperatures of the two opposing streams, their viscosities, and the consequent heat transfer coefficients. The final cost of such an item of equipment P can be expressed in the form:

$$P = K.x^a y^b z^c \dots$$

where x, y, z, ... are the various design factors involved and a, b, c, ... are indices whose value would be an expression of the influence of that particular design factor on cost. However, with heat exchangers, a great many variables are resolved when the area of required heating surface has been established. There still remains a series of engineering design variables related to the particular duty of the exchanger.

A choice can be made between fixed or floating heads in a 'shell' exchanger as illustrated. Other types are also possible, such as the condenser, the kettle or the U-tube. The materials of construction of both tubes and shell can vary, the operating temperatures and pressures will differ from one type to the next, and so on. All these additional factors will influence cost to some extent, but to a lesser extent than the area of heating surface. In other words, the area of heating surface is the basic criterion when cost is being considered. In practice, it is found that most of the other variables can be disregarded within the limits of accuracy normally required. In the heat exchanger example, the estimating formula is reduced to the following expression:

$$H = a.c^v.p.t.m$$

where:

a = heating surface area (bare tube surface) as calculated
c = cost per unit of area
v = exponent relating area and cost (established empirically)
p = factor for shell design pressure
t = factor for type of exchanger
m = factor for the materials of construction

The end result will produce curves as shown in Figure 12:5.

The merits of the 'exponential' approach have been discussed, and the fact that a straight line produced on 'log-log' paper has already been mentioned. It may be wondered why, after all that, the data on heat

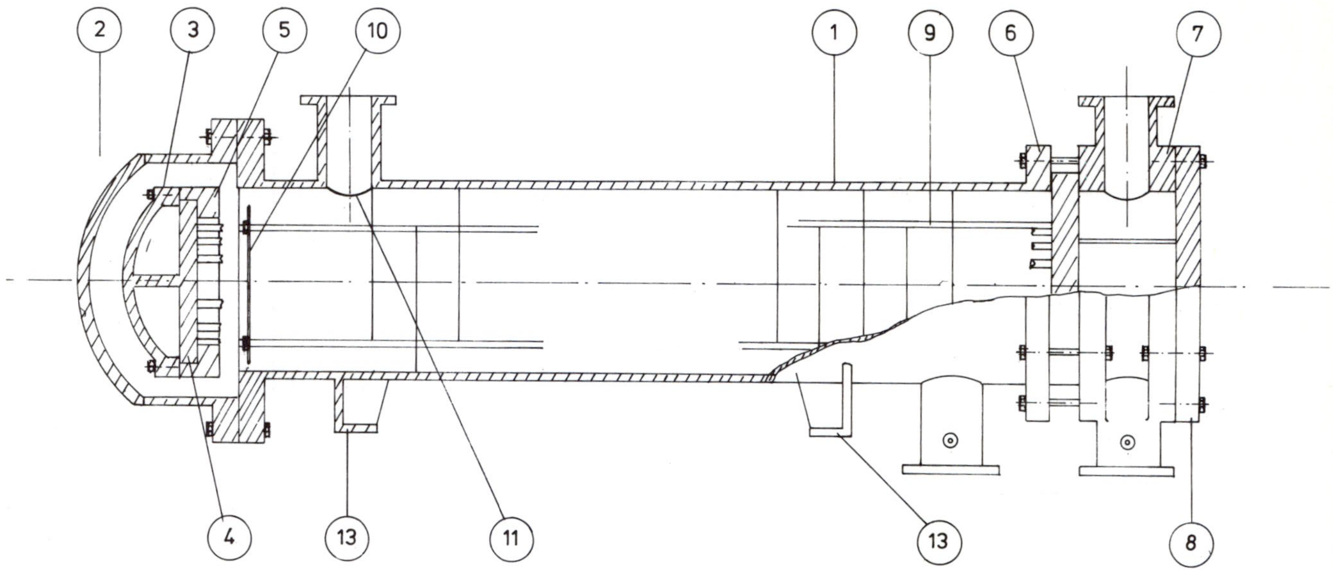

1 SHELL
2 SHELL COVER
3 FLOATING HEAD COVER
4 FLOATING TUBE SHEET
5 CLAMP RING OR HOOK BOLTS
6 STATIONARY TUBE SHEET
7 CHANNEL
8 CHANNEL COVER
9 TIE RODS AND SPACERS
10 TRANVERSE BAFFLES OR TUBE SUPPORT PLATES
11 IMPINGEMENT BAFFLE
12 LONGITUDINAL BAFFLE
13 SADDLES

Figure 12:4 Section through a typical heat exchanger. The heat exchange takes place between the medium circulating through the tubes and that circulating around the tubes, in the shell. A steam consdenser is a typical heat exchanger, the steam in the tubes condensing when cooled by water circulating in the shell.

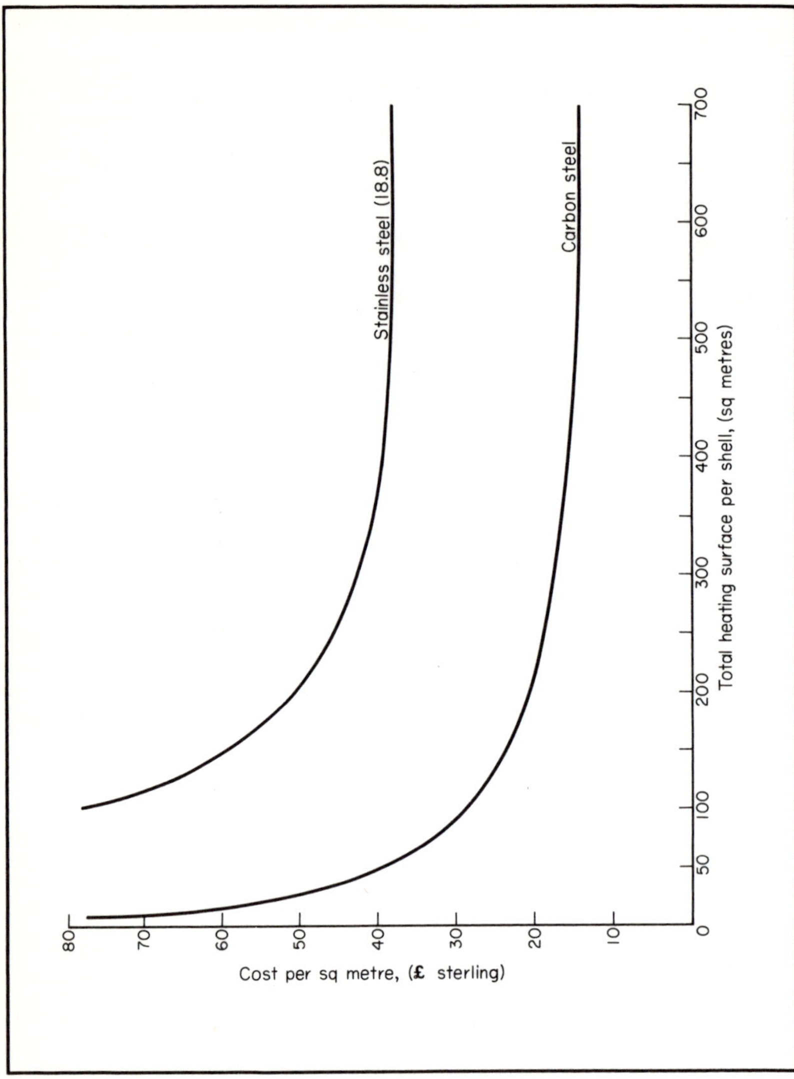

Figure 12:5 Heat exchanger cost curves. Approximate costs of shell and tube types for various materials of construction are given in the medium pressure range. They are plotted for tube and tube sheet material, disregarding the shell materials, which would normally be mild steel.

exchangers, as presented in Figure 12:5, is presented in the form of curves on ordinary squared paper. The reason is two-fold. Not only would a straight line be a dangerous approximation over the smaller sizes in the range, but also, the curve illustrates a fact which a straight line does not, that the cost per square foot rises very sharply as the total area of heating surface in the unit falls.

Distinctions without a difference

Having laid so much emphasis on the all-pervading influence of the principles underlying the 'six-tenths' rule, it is important to realise that this principle is not of universal application. Whilst there may appear to be no good reason why a method of rating could not be applied to any, and every type of process equipment, by synthesising the many prime variables into a few characteristic variables which apply in the normal, economic operating range of the equipment in question, this is not necessarily the simplest or the quickest approach. A typical example in this context, is the pump. Any given size of pump has, usually, quite a wide range of operating conditions and the pump capacity is dependent, to a degree, upon the pressure head demanded. This is illustrated by the characteristic curves for pumps under operating conditions, when capacity is plotted against head (see Figure 12:6).

The performance of any given pump is related to an 'area' of duty, rather than to a specific duty. It is often possible to fit various sizes of impeller into a given pump casing, thus extending the range of duty of the pump quite considerably, although the influence on cost is marginal. Yet again, dependent on the nature of the fluid being pumped, the materials of construction can be varied, not only in total, but also in relation to parts of the pump, as further illustrated by Figure 12:6. All this leads to the conclusion that any attempt to draw a 'graph' relating price to capacity, for instance, could be extremely misleading.

As a consequence of these various possibilities, which really follow no rule, the best approach, when pricing pumps, is to have a list of catalogue prices and evaluate the pumps required from such pricing data. Price lists of this type are normally readily available from the pump manufacturers, who are also prepared to provide prices against specific pump duties at very short notice.

Another example, of a rather different nature, is to be found in the field of linings. Equipment, particularly vessels, is often lined—with refractories, acid reisting brick, glass, rubber and so on. Here the normal approach is to price on an area basis (price per square foot) irrespective of the total area involved. Whilst it is true that the

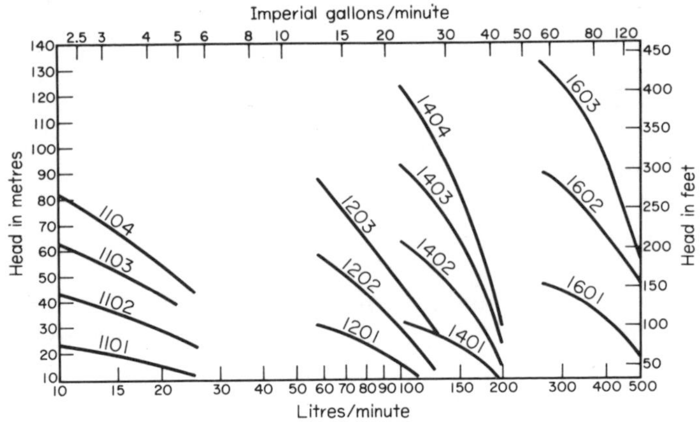

Materials of construction

Pump series	1100–1200–1400–1600				
Pump parts	Materials 01	02	32	42	51
Suction and delivery cover Intermediate casing	C.I.		Zinc-free bronze	18/8/3 s.s.	High grade s.s. 20 Ni 25 Cr 4 Mo
Impeller	g.m.	Ct St			
Sleeve bearing	Special carbon				
Shaft	Chrome steel		Cr Ni St	18/8/3 s.s.	High grade s.s.
Shaft sleeve	Packing rings or mechanical seals				

Figure 12:6 Typical capacity table and materials of construction for a range of pumps. Note the way in which the range of a particular size of casing (identified by the first two digits in the code) is extended by minor modification. There are also five different combinations of the materials of construction.

'six-tenths' rule is still in the background, and that the cost per unit of area will vary according to the total area involved, the variance over the normal range of use is usually so small that it can be disregarded. It is well within the normal estimating error which is, in any event, associated with the figures being used. In other words, the exponent is very close to unity and it can be applied as unity for all practical purposes. The estimated cost of lining becomes, in these circumstances, a *unit cost.* Unit costs are discussed in detail later.

Factorial Method

A second basic principle employed in estimating is well illustrated by what has now become widely known as the 'Lang factor'.[2] The Lang factor, in a nutshell, is:

	A for solid process plants		Total
Delivered equipment cost x	*B* for solid-fluid plants	=	estimated
	C for fluid process plants		plant cost

The factors *A, B* and *C,* as published by Lang, ranged from 3.10 to 4.74, but this was for the United States and the figures are, in any event, outdated. It is the principle which is of interest—the fact that there is an empirical relationship to be established from a study of the available cost data. This means, with access to the collected costs of the appropriate plants, that comparable data can be accumulated and applied in a variety of fields with a degree of confidence. Further, the principle is of the widest application.

The principle which has been established is that certain costs are dependent upon and have a constant relationship with other costs. In its widest application, the approach is often referred to as the *factorial method* of cost estimating. Its application to an estimate is demonstrated in Figure 12:7, which presents a typical estimate summary sheet. The *Lang factor* in this particular case is the relationship between the total cost of plant and equipment (a) and the total erected cost of the installation. The other relationships to which attention is drawn in the notes under this particular illustration are, however, further demonstrations of the same principle and can serve as the basis for the development of estimating data.

This simple, direct approach to the problem of estimating a variety of cost elements, such as pipework, erection and design is the best approach to be made in the absence of any further data. It is better to know that the total erected cost will be three to four times the cost of the basic equipment, than to know nothing at all. Such knowledge will enable a project engineer to be extremely suspicious of an estimate where the factor is only two. There may be reasons for this, but these reasons need to be investigated and validated. However, it should also be realised that, as presented, this concept of Lang is an oversimplification.

Taking erection costs as an example, the figure seen for the particular 'mixture' of plant and equipment set out in the estimate given in Figure 12:7 is 70 per cent of the total material cost. But the actual relationship, over the range of materials embodied in this particular example will vary between 5 per cent and one and a half times the total, dependent upon the material. Plant and equipment

ESTIMATED CAPITAL COST

EQUIPMENT SUBGROUP	DESCRIPTION	ESTIMATED COST £	
20	6—Columns	83,700	
21	30—Heat exchangers	46,800	
22	20—Vessels	9,500	
25	2—Reactors	8,000	
25	1—Furnace	29,700	
25	1—Steel stack	3,000	
25	6—Sets of vacuum equipment	4,000	
26	35—Pumps and drives	13,900	
26	1—Compressor and drive	4,000	
27	2—Stirrers	400	
	Plant and equipment	203,000	(a)
	Instruments	30,000	
		233,000	
	Piping and other materials	157,000	(b)
	Total materials	390,000	(c)
	Freight, purchasing, etc.	48,000	
	Erection	270,000	(d)
	Design and project supervision	67,000	(e)
	Sub-total	775,000	(f)
	Contingency	75,000	
	Total erected cost	£850,000	(g)

Notes:
1. Total erected cost (g) is 4.2 times the estimated value of plant and equipment.
2. Total materials (c) is approximately 2 times the value of the plant and equipment.
3. Erection (d) is approximately 70 per cent of the total value of the materials (c).
4. Design (e) is some 17 per cent of the total value of materials (c).

Figure 12:7 A typical project estimate. The factorial method is illustrated by the notes.

erection costs may vary between the limits 5 to 15 per cent, electrical materials may be about one third, pipework erection can range between 80 per cent and 120 per cent and so on. Once these variations are seen to exist, it is also evident that here is an area open for still more detailed anaylsis. Furthermore, the fact that a range has now been cited, rather than specific figures, in some of the examples, indicates that the relationships are not constants, as was at first implied, but variables.

The major factors influencing the magnitude of these relationships are:

1 Plant size
2 Type of plant (for example, fluid, gas, solids handling)
3 The process (this has particular reference to the materials of construction)

The extent of the detail developed in relation to such factors will depend both, on the data available and, the degree of accuracy required in the estimate. However, the principle can be demonstrated by a consideration of the overall Lang factor (see Note 1, Figure 12:7).

The effect of items 1 and 2 above will be seen, ultimately, in the schedule of plant and equipment, which forms the basis for the estimate and comprises the total (a). If, therefore, factors can be developed for each equipment sub-group in turn, a further refinement of the estimating process has been achieved and estimating accuracy improved. Yet the time taken to prepare the estimate, once the data is available, is very little longer.

This further refinement in approach is illustrated by Figures 12:8 and 12:9. Figure 12:8 relates to air coolers, where the changes in the materials of construction, that normally occur, have very little effect on the cost of the equipment and can be ignored. The cost of the liquid cooled heat exchanger, however, (Figure 12:9) is radically influenced by the materials of construction employed. If the cost of manufacture in the actual materials of construction employed are related to a base, say, the cost of construction in commercial quality carbon steel, then a ratio results. This is R in the graph.

Cost of Design

Further insight into 'the way things vary' can be gained by considering the cost of design. The scope of the project engineering service has

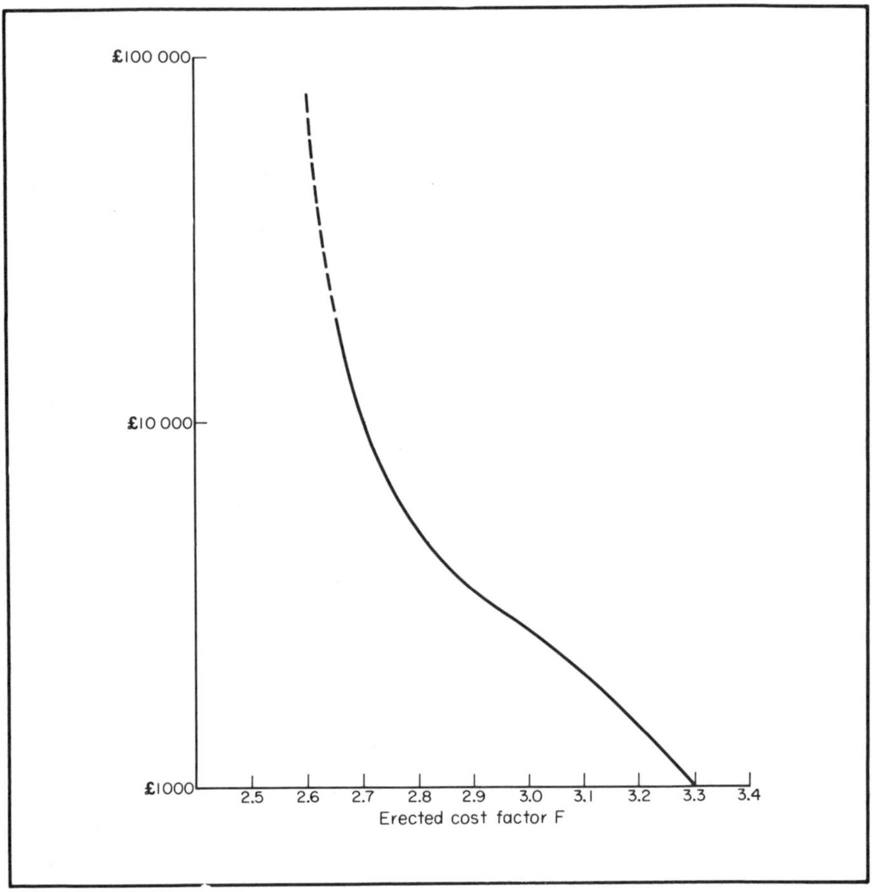

Figure 12:8 Air coolers–erected cost factor. The cost used to establish the curve is the average cost of the air coolers in the unit being estimated.

already been discussed in Part Two. The estimate presented as an example in Figure 12:7 assumes that design is carried out within the manufacturing organisation, with minimal project supervision. The other administrative expenses, such as purchasing and the supervision of erection, are included elsewhere in the estimate. When the cost of design is considered in detail and related to the cost of the equipment, or the materials being purchased as a result of that design, it is seen, for instance, that plant and pipework requires much more intensive design than buildings or instrumentation. Furthermore, the cost of design, when so related to the cost of the equipment or materials being designed, is influenced by the size of the project. All these several

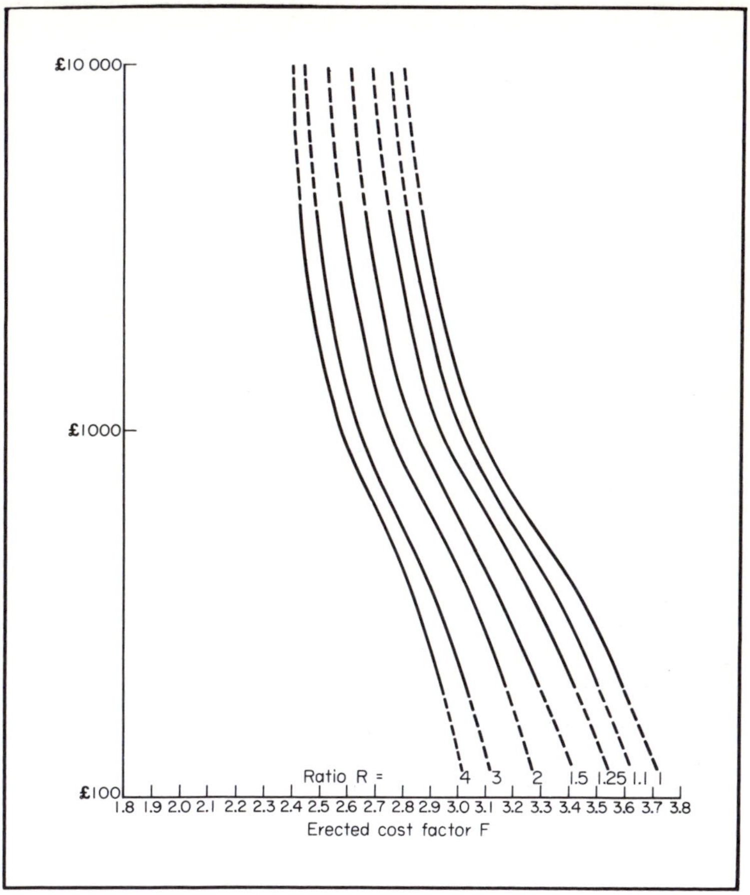

Figure 12:9 Heat exchangers—erected cost factors. The cost used to establish the factor is the average cost of the heat exchangers in the unit being estimated. R is the relationship between the cost in the materials of construction being used and the cost if this was made in mild steel.

interrelationships are illustrated in Figure 12:10. The estimate (Figure 12:7) includes approximately 17 per cent for design in total but, of this, about three per cent will be required for project supervision, leaving 14 per cent as the direct design cost in terms of the chart presented in Figure 12:10.

The comparable reading on the chart at £390000 (total materials) is 12 per cent, which means that the average plant indicated by curve A has a somewhat lower 'plant and pipework' content than the specific plant illustrated by Figure 12:7.

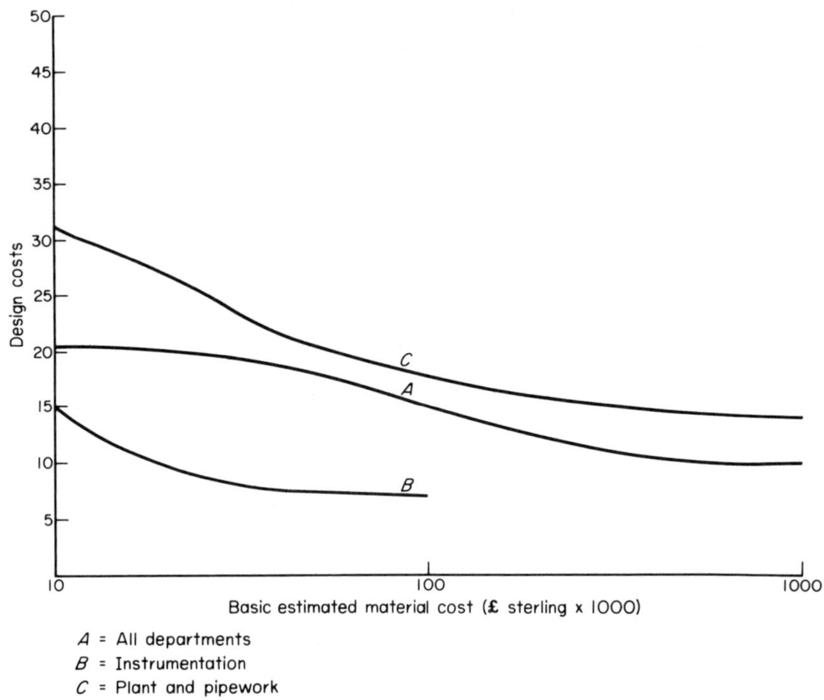

Figure 12:10 The relationship between design costs and the basic cost of materials (or equipment) dealt with by the design discipline. The curve for 'all departments' illustrates an average interrelationship, where plant is 85% and buildings and civil works 15% of the total cost.

Analysing the Interrelationships

Once it is recognised that these *factors* are not constants, it is recognised, once again, that the primary principle, the six-tenths rule, also plays a part. The various functions involved in plant design are, in general, continuous, and the empirical relationships between design and cost are there to be ascertained, if sufficient data is available. This means that it is possible to reduce the estimating procedure to a series of formulae, and this approach is strongly recommended. It is recommended because it compels a logical analysis of costs, and develops an awareness of the way things vary. To illustrate the approach, the process of estimating the cost of a simple vessel (or

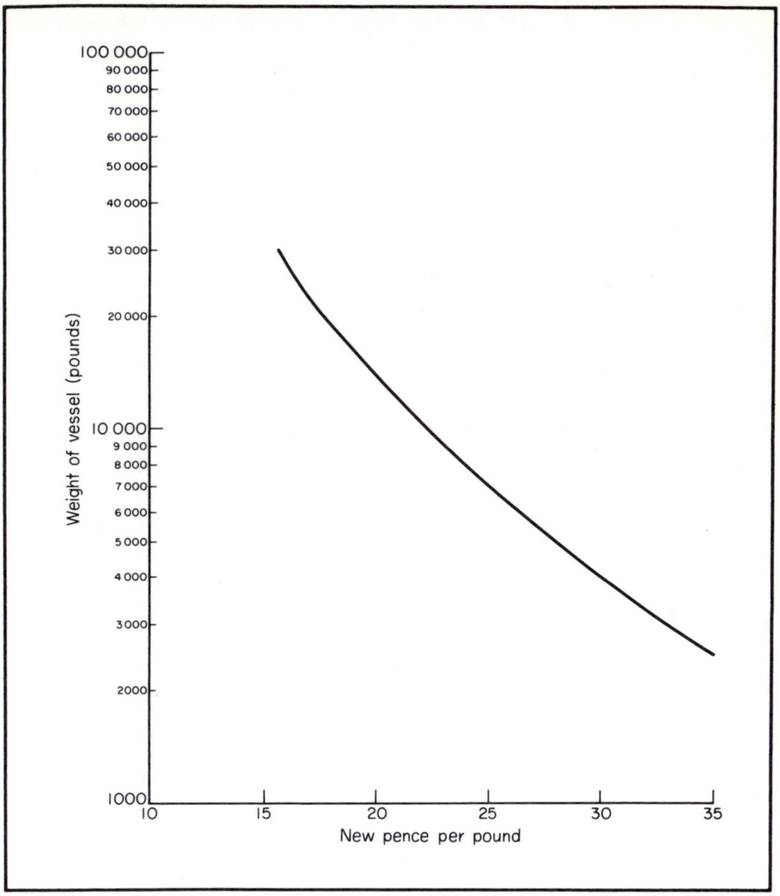

Figure 12:11 Mild steel pressure vessels: cost curve.

drum) can be analysed in detail. Figure 12:11 expresses an empirical relationship between cost and total weight, ascertained by the analysis of quotations and orders. The estimated cost of the vessel (E) can be established, using this relationship, as follows:

$$(E) = (0.67\ tDL)\ fcm$$

where:

t = wall thickness expressed in sixteenths of an inch, plus corrosion allowance

D = inside diameter of the vessel, in inches.

L = length of vessel between tangent lines, in feet

f = factor to provide for the weight of nozzles, heads, skirt or support, manholes, etc

c = cost factor, taken from Figure 12:11

m= factor for the specific materials of construction employed, as compared with commercial quality carbon steel

Graphs similar to that shown in Figure 12:11 can also be developed for the factors f and m, whilst t is a function of the design pressure, related to the overall dimensions of the vessel. Hence, it becomes a direct mathematical calculation, based on the basic design data, to establish the estimated cost using these several factors as related by the formulae. A similar approach can be adopted for quite a wide variety of plant and equipment. The analysis made, and the formulae developed, should always indentify and relate the significant cost factors. This demands critical appraisal of the many variables and the selection of those which have a significant influence on cost for inclusion in any formula.

Unit Costs

A brief reference should be made to unit costs, since these are still *factors*, but now expressed in great detail. A typical example would be a schedule of rates such as used in assessing the cost of building works. Each element of work is priced and the size of the element is so chosen that the factor is a constant within the limits of accuracy demanded. The principles under discussion are still there, although, those

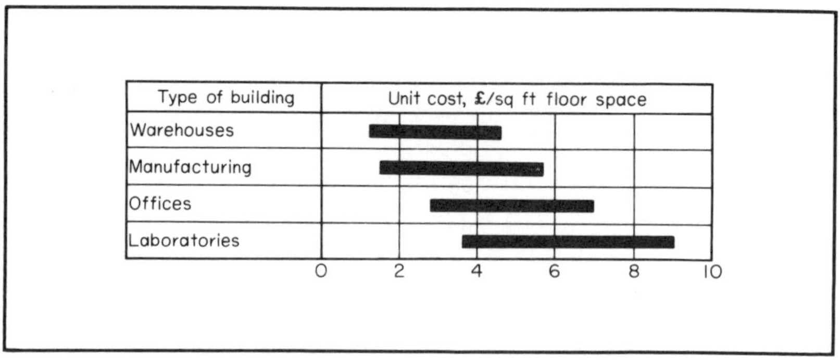

Figure 12:12 Unit costs for various types of buildings (excluding equipment) met with in industry. Notice the relationship between complexity and cost.

developing and using unit costs may not necessarily recognise this. For instance, a typical schedule of rates expresses the cost of supplying and fixing reinforcing rod in terms of weight. The unit cost is given per hundredweight. But this is not a constant. Size enters in. Since this is so, the schedule will quote a series of rates, one for each size of rod by diameter. The table of figures presented in the schedule of rates in this instance could, in fact, be plotted. A size/cost graph could be drawn, but this is not appropriate for inclusion in a schedule. What *is* important is to recognise that the two basic principles which have been discussed, the six tenths rule and the factorial method, are still playing a part.

This *unit cost* approach is employed not only in a detailed schedule of rates, but also in relation to estimates for complete buildings. The cost is then expressed as £/sq.ft. of floor space, or £/cu.ft. of building volume. It is, of course, important to recognise the differences in design between buildings when using such an approach and if the range of unit costs is tabulated, as in Figure 12:12, a curve can once again be seen.

This particular approach can be very useful when estimating the cost of heavy mechanical equipment for which there may be very little cost estimating data available to the estimating engineer. Once again a curve can be formulated: one parameter is cost per ton, the other parameter is mechanical complexity. If mild steel (as opposed to alloy steel) constructions are considered, ordinary mild steel plate, whose price involves no fabrication, will appear at the bottom of the scale. Going up the scale, the first degree of complication is to be found in fabricated steelwork and simple tankage. The cost has now doubled. Introduce a degree of complexity in design, as in a pressure vessel, and the price per unit (ton) trebles. Roto-dynamic machines (pumps and compressors) are still more complex, so that the unit cost continues to rise. The basic raw material cost has now to be multiplied by a factor ranging between ten and fifteen. But weight is still the major cost parameter, and a very effective estimating tool, despite its apparent crudeness. It is often a far more reliable parameter, and hence more valuable than a performance parameter (horsepower, for example).

Another example of the principles involved is found with mechanical presses. Presses incorporate movement, but movement of a much more limited character than is to be found in roto-dynamic machinery. However, the principle can still be applied. The problem may well seem insoluble at first sight, when confronted with a press in all its complexity, as illustrated by Figure 12:13. But the basic parameter is still weight and it is usually possible to estimate the weight of such equipment fairly easily—certainly much more easily than estimating

Figure 12:13 22 Daylight Siempelkamp press. The 22 daylight Siempelkamp press seen here is centred in the new Warerite factory at Aycliffe. (Photograph by courtesy of British Xylonite Limited, Birmingham)

the price.

If the process is novel, as illustrated, and the size of sheet to be produced in the press is materially larger than that in current production, then the size of sheet will be known. This determines the overall dimensions of the press and hence its weight. This data can be related to the known weight/cost/dimensional relationship, the weight of the press estimated and a potential cost established, long before the press has been designed by the manufacturer and a formal offer made. Indeed, at the point in time when the estimate is being made, it might be a question of whether the larger size of sheet was feasible. Nevertheless, an estimating approach based on weight will give an estimate within the limits of accuracy normally expected at this stage.

Thus far, this discussion has centred on mild steel constructions, but the materials of construction do represent another parameter. Once again there is a consistent relationship. A change in the materials of construction will affect the end cost of the equipment, but the relationship is fairly reliable over quite a wide range. The type of price relationship that can be expected is illustrated by the following table.

Material of construction	*Cost relationship*
Iron and steel	100
Ductile iron	125
Carbon steel	150
Austenitic iron	200
Bronze	250
Stainless steel	300
Monel	400

The foregoing examples covering diverse fields, are introduced to demonstrate, as forcibly as possible, that the 'unit rate' approach—essentially a simplification of the six-tenths rule—and the factorial relationships already discussed, is a valuable tool if the right parameters are chosen. It can be adopted as a basic principle in estimating techniques and enables all cost relationships to be analysed in a way which results in useful estimating data by the proper identification of the significant variables.

Notes

1 See *Chemical Engineering*, June 1947, page 162. The article was by Roger Williams, Jr., and entitled 'Six-tenths factor aids in approximating costs'.

2 See *Chemical Engineering,* September 1947, which contains the first article by Hans L. Lang on this subject entitled 'Simplified approach to preliminary cost estimates'.

13

The Cost of Accuracy

The study of the manner in which estimates are prepared should make it very plain that estimating is, inevitably, an inexact science. So true is this that some are inclined to describe it as an *art,* rather than a *science.* Any estimate will have a margin of error associated with it, the magnitude of which, will depend upon a variety of factors. The most significant of these factors are:

1 The quality and reliability of the process and engineering data on which the estimate has been based
2 The validity of the estimating data used in the preparation of the estimate
3 The accuracy and scope of the knowledge that is available relating to the actual location proposed for construction.

Influence of Design Data

The quality and reliability of the design data made available for estimating purposes, is largely dependent upon the time spent on them. Estimates of capital cost are required at a very early stage, long before a detailed design can be developed, and are usually based, in the beginning, on an outline process flow diagram. Such block diagrams are hardly sufficient at this stage unless, one is dealing with a well known process and the content of each process stage is already known in some detail. The next step in design development is the process flow sheet,

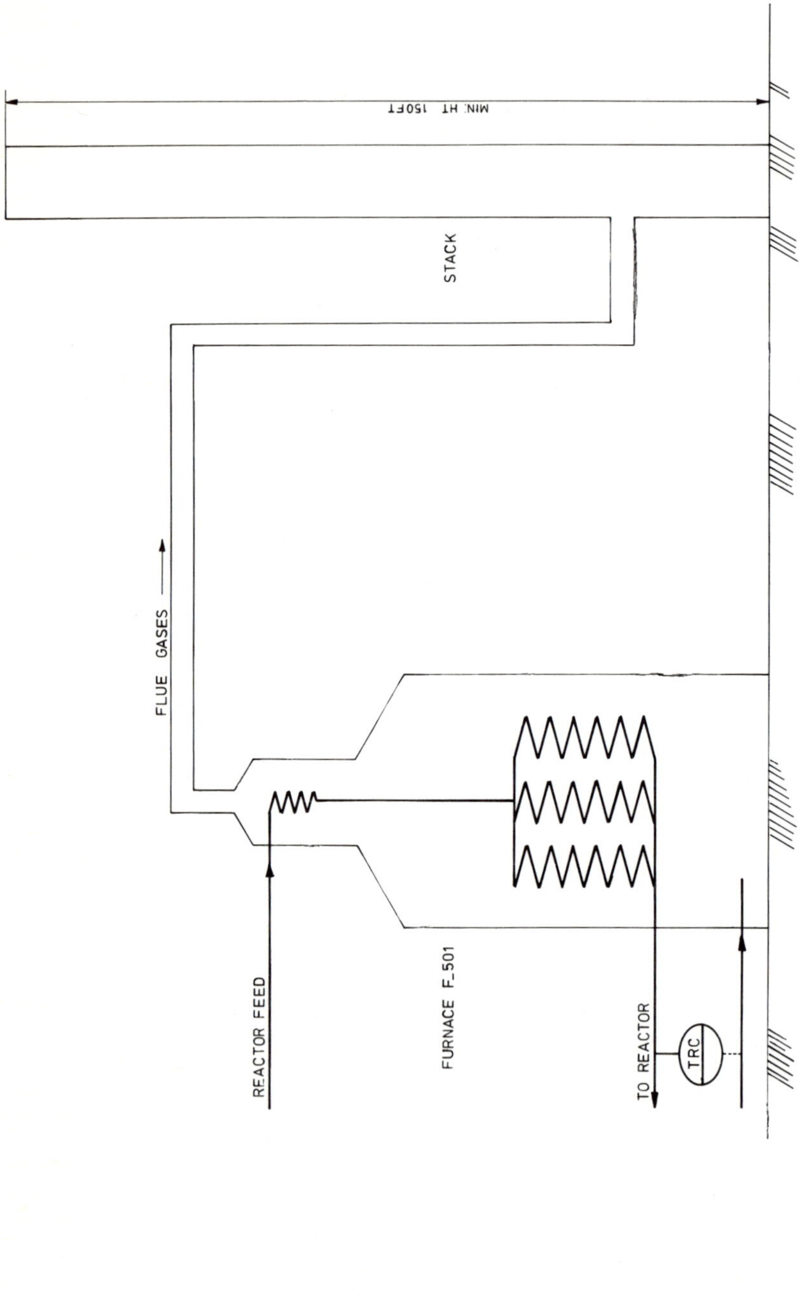

Figure 13:1 Furnace F101—abstract from a preliminary flowsheet.

such as discussed in detail in Chapter 7—The Outline Design. The section given of one such flowsheet in Figure 7:3 is typical of the detail usually available at this time on the flowsheet. This flow diagram has, therefore, to be coupled with an outline specification. Another abstract from such a flowsheet, showing a furnace (or heater), is given here in Figure 13:1. The normal data given at the estimating stage to enable the cost of such a furnace to be estimated would be:

	Expressed as
Absorbed duty:	MM Kcal/hr.
Fired duty:	MM Kcal/hr.
Number of tubes:	Qty
Tube i.d.:	inches
Wall thickness of tube	inches
Materials of construction:	code reference
Convection section	
Area:	square metres
Materials of construction	code reference

These are the most significant criteria in relation to cost. Eventually the furnace will be designed in detail in all its complexity by a specialist manufacturer. The ultimate complexity of this design is illustrated in Figure 13:2, whilst Figure 13:3 shows such a furnace, complete and erected. As engineering proceeds, the details grow and the data available becomes fuller and more complex. But the development of increased detail costs both time and money. Firstly, the design itself costs time and money, but secondly, the estimating takes longer, and will also cost more.

This relationship is shown graphically in Figure 13:4. Whilst it is true that all the design work will eventually have to be done, so that time spent in this way is not necessarily wasted, it is not usually desirable to wait until the designs are completed before estimating commences. The viability of the project may well depend on the magnitude of the estimated cost of the project. Should it be decided later that the project is not, in fact, viable, then the investment made in design, up to the point in time when that decision is taken, is lost.

The other aspect which needs to be appreciated, and which is demonstrated by the graph in Figure 13:4, is that this increasing detail does not necessarily improve the accuracy of the estimate to any material extent. In fact, speaking from experience, and provided that the initial *global* estimates have been based on relevant data, then such global estimates are often more reliable than subsequent estimates

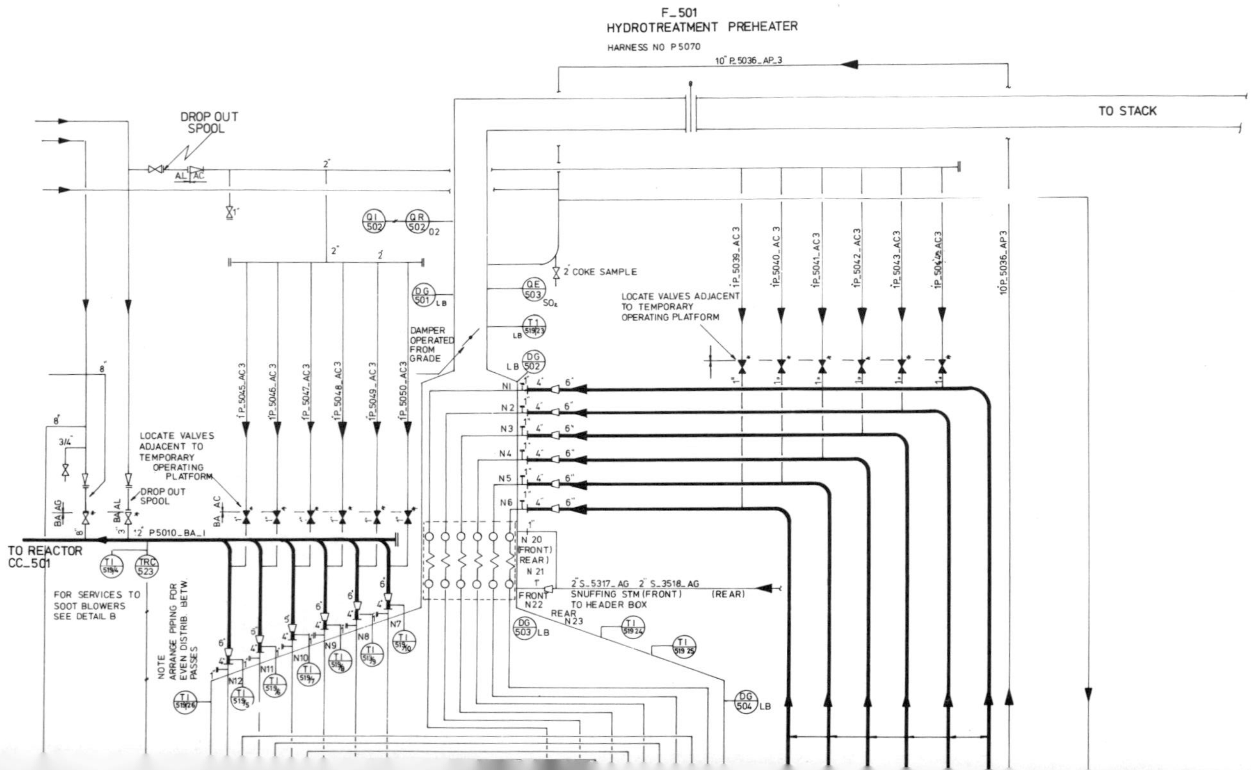
F_501
HYDROTREATMENT PREHEATER
HARNESS NO P 5070
10" P 5036_AP_3
TO STACK
DROP OUT SPOOL
LOCATE VALVES ADJACENT TO TEMPORARY OPERATING PLATFORM
2" COKE SAMPLE
DAMPER OPERATED FROM GRADE
DROP OUT SPOOL
P5010_BA_1
TO REACTOR CC_501
FOR SERVICES TO SOOT BLOWERS SEE DETAIL B
NOTE ARRANGE PIPING FOR EVEN DISTRIB BETW PASSES
2" S_5317_AG 2" S_3518_AG
SNUFFING STM (FRONT) (REAR)
TO HEADER BOX
10" P 5036_AP3

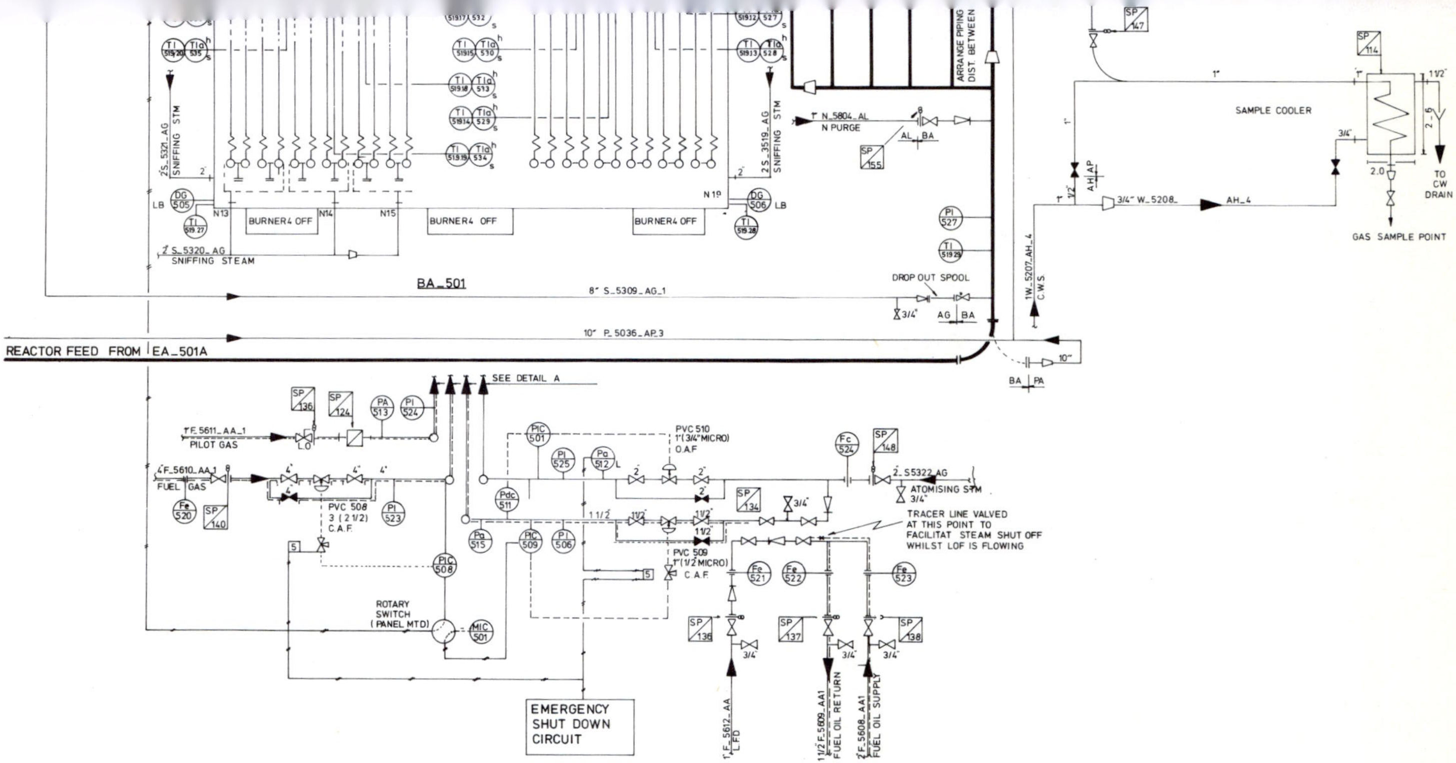

Figure 13:2 Furnace F101—abstract from the final detailed engineering flow diagram.

Figure 13:3 30,000 BPSD (barrels per stream day) *distillate hydrotreater and fractionator unit for BP.*. A furnace is seen in the foreground left, with the stack immediately behind. (Photograph by courtesy of Matthew Hall Engineering Limited, London, who were the main contractors for the process and engineering design, procurement and construction of the unit.)

based on much more detailed data. It is usual for the estimated final cost to fall in the early stages of the project, but then as time passes and work intensifies in the field, for the estimate to rise until it at last reaches and overruns the original figure. This occurs because when detail becomes available it is assumed to be complete—but never is.

Escalation and Learning

Another interesting experience is to watch the design change as time passes, due to the project being studied in ever-increasing detail. Time gives the opportunity for reflection, for new ideas to be brought forward, for the validity of earlier design concepts to be checked. Such changes can, in general, be expected to have a beneficial effect on cost. So lapse of time, in this context, can produce a reduction in the final capital invested. But also, as is well known, price inflation is a continuing fact of life. The result of *this,* as time passes, is that costs

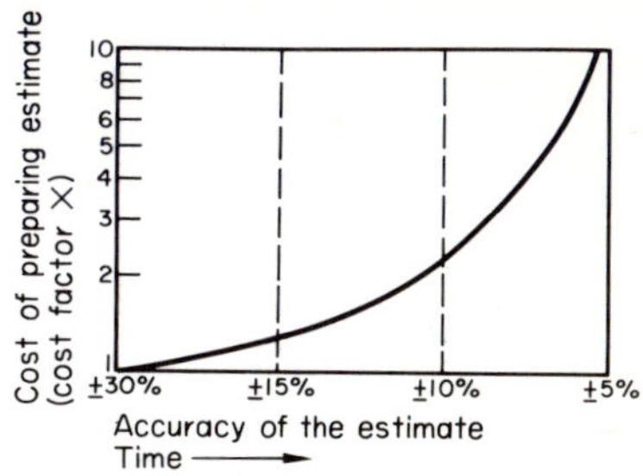

	AVAILABILITY OF DATA								
BASIC PROCESS DATA									
Plant type and size	X	X	X	X	X	X	X	X	X
Outline flowsheet		X	X	X	X	X	X	X	X
Heat and energy balance			X	X	X	X	X	X	X
Equipment and instrument list				X	X	X	X	X	X
Equipment data sheets				X	X	X	X	X	X
Details of plant location							X	X	X
Details on utilities							X	X	X
ENGINEERING DESIGN DATA									
Equipment sketches				X	X	X	X	X	X
Plant layout with elevation				X	X	X	X	X	X
Layout of off-sites					X	X	X	X	X
Schedule of piping							X	X	X
Piping layout							X	X	X
Electrical oneline diagram							X	X	X
Piping isometrics								X	X
Instrument loop sheets								X	X
Electrical control drawings									X
Foundations, detail drawings									X
Buildings, outline drawings									X
Suppliers quotations, equipment									X

Figure 13:4 The cost of accuracy. The cost of an estimate depends on the data involved and used.

increase. The longer a project takes to complete, or the longer it is delayed before it is initiated, the more it will cost in the end.

The approach to cost inflation for estimating purposes is discussed in some detail later in this chapter. For the moment, the point to be seen, recognised, and remembered, is that time is a significant parameter in the cost relationship, but not always in an upward direction. The point can be illustrated by a simple example, typical of many, in the 'mass production' field. Figure 13:5 shows how the price of bearings has been held steady over the years, despite the escalation in the cost of raw materials and production labour. This demonstrates the need to distinguish between *inflation* and *price escalation* (or *actual escalation*). Much study has been devoted to the relationship between these two

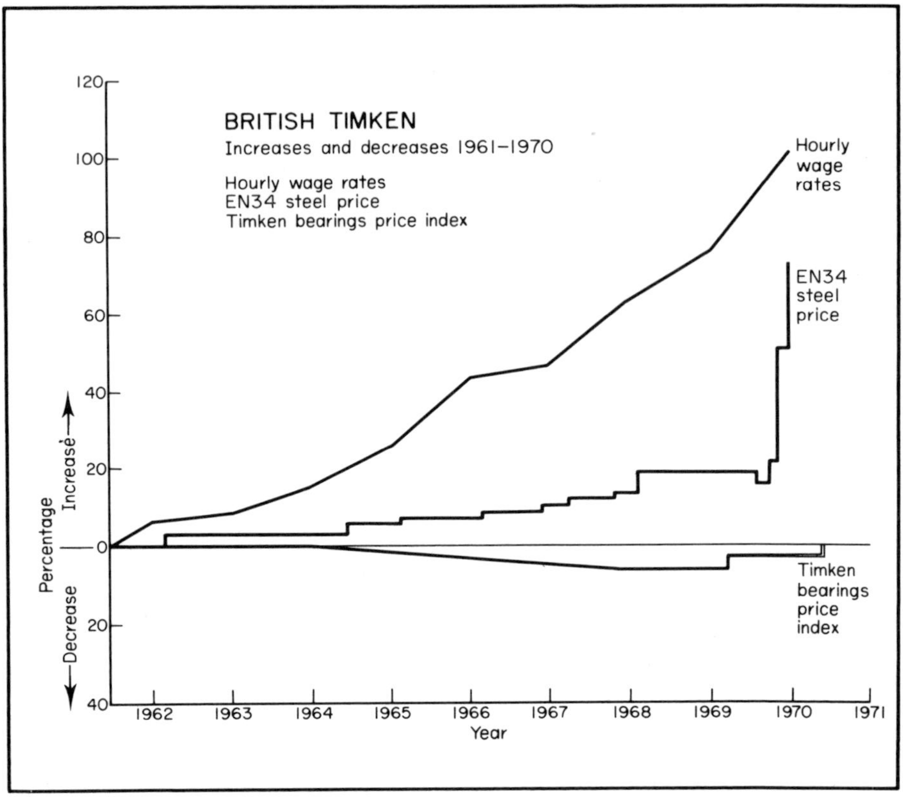

Figure 13:5 The 'actual cost' index. This graph illustrates the way in which the selling price of bearings has held steady over the years despite the escalation in the cost of both raw materials and labour.

in recent years and ratios have been established. The reasons for the difference are various, but the ratio is usually described as a productivity ratio[1] because the major reason for the difference is the improvements in productivity which have taken place over the years. Once again, there can be a variety of reasons for the improvement in productivity, but the end result is that manufacturing prices are kept down in the face of rising costs, as illustrated in Figure 13:5.

Of the various factors which result in this improvement in productivity, the most significant is that of *learning.* That is, learning plays a very significant role in the overall improvement. As time passes, more and more is known and everyone, from senior management to the workmen on the shop floor, grows in experience and skill in relation to the specific applications which confront them.

This learning factor applies not only to individual items of plant or equipment, such as that illustrated by Figure 13:5 but also to complete plants, and a 'learning curve' can be developed in that connection.

The validity of such an approach was first established in the aircraft industry: each subsequent batch of aeroplanes cost less, per machine, than the earlier batch, and it was found possible to calculate empirically the cost of the *mass produced* machine from the cost of the first prototypes, by using a 'learning factor'. In the aircraft industry, the factor found by experience has been of the order of 80 per cent—that is, each batch costs 80 per cent of the cost of the previous batch, assuming the same number of machines per batch.

The same principle can be applied to the building of production units. Two examples are shown in Figure 13:6. These originate from two different companies, so the process development organisation involved was completely different for both. Yet there is a close correspondence in the slope of the learning curve and it would appear that improvements of the order of 65 per cent, rather than 80 per cent, are possible in capital investment for this cause. The improvement occurs as the project develops from the initial process concept to the final process design. The data presented actually shows an improvement of 55 per cent over the periods of time indicated. This is, therefore, a factor which cannot be ignored and should be taken into account when assessing the investment that is to be anticipated, in the early stages of development of a project.

The significance of this factor was discussed in Chapter 4 when dealing with the fundamentals of project evaluation, since it has a bearing on the potential profitability of the plant. In the context of capital cost estimating, however, it still needs to be seen as a statistical probability. It is interesting to note, for instance, that considerable research has gone into this aspect of cost estimating in the USA, where the volume of data available for analysis is much greater, since plants are repeated more often. An improvement of some 75 per cent was noted over a period of four years (1962 to 1966), with plants already in commercial production. In plants, that is, where the process had already been fully developed. The potential is, therefore, much greater in plants which are still under study and in the process of development.

Validity and the Use of Contingency

From time to time reference has been made to *reasonable* limits of accuracy, and a degree of latitude in the approach to certain figures and data has been suggested on the basis that the validity of the estimate prepared from that data will not be materially affected. It is inevitable that phrases, such as this, bring to the fore a debatable question. What is the margin of error likely, or reasonable, in capital cost estimating?

Much depends upon the size of the project under consideration. The smaller the total estimated cost, the more difficult it appears to be to make a close estimate. Therefore, a larger margin of error should be provided. With a project costing £100 000 or less, it will be good fortune, rather than good estimating, if the actual cost is withing 20 per cent of the first estimate, assuming this to have been prepared on the lines indicated in this book, and without a very detailed use of

PLANT A

			RATIO
(1)	Estimated cost: 1964:	£1 350 000	–
(2)	Estimated cost: 1965:	£ 900 000	67%
(3)	Estimated cost: 1966:	£ 750 000	83%
(4)	Overall ratio, from cases 1 to 3 Project built after a delay of 2½ years		55%

PLANT B

(5)	Estimated cost:	mid 1967	£390 000	–
(6)	Estimated cost:	early 1968	£290 000	74%
(7)	Estimated cost:	mid 1968	£219 000	72%
(8)	Overall ratio, from cases 5 to 7 Project built after a delay of one year			54%

ANALYSIS OF THE ESTIMATES FOR PLANT B

ESTIMATE	5 £	6 £	7 £
Building and civil engineering works	50 000	80 000	50 000
Plant, equipment and pipework	155 000	85 000	70 000
Electrical works	23 000	12 000	10 000
Services	56 000	28 000	13 000
Instrumentation	20 000	9 000	9 000
Design and on-costs	66 000	56 000	43 000
Contingency	20 000	20 000	15 000
Totals	£390 000	£290 000	£210 000

Figure 13:6 Influence of 'learning' on estimates for projects in the course of process development.

quotations secured from suppliers and contractors for specific parts of the proposed project. It is usual, therefore, in preparing such estimates, to reduce the potential margin of error by securing quotations for major items of equipment and work, and perhaps spending more time on certain details. With projects totalling £200 000 or more it should be possible, by using the graphical and statistical method of approach, to prepare an estimate within plus or minus 15 per cent, whilst, by the time the overall estimated cost reaches one million pounds, plus or minus 10 per cent is a reasonable expectation. With very large estimates (£5 000 000 or more) it is remarkable how near to the final figures the first approximate figures can be, sometimes within plus or minus 2 per cent of the final cost. The factor of variability is so great, that provided the estimate has been prepared in detail on a consistent basis, errors in assessment tend to cancel one another out. It must not be forgotten, however, that an error of two per cent is a finite sum of at least £100 000 with estimates of this magnitude.

There is a definite psychological approach to estimating, in which this problem of the margin of error plays a large part. Not only should the estimator have a philosophy of approach to the problem, but management, to whom he is responsible, should also appreciate that philosophy, and recognise the limitations under which the estimator works. Attempts have been made to classify estimates in terms of margin of error, with a view to defining this major limitation, but the wisdom is doubtful. The continuing objective should be to prepare the best possible estimate in the given circumstances: target in terms of margin of error may well result in less than the best effort being put into the preparation of the estimate.

Contingency

The other major philosophy in this context is contingency. The more people contribute to an estimate, the more contingency grows and multiplies, since it is a common failing to 'play safe'. The danger is, of course, that high unrealistic figures can doom a project before it starts. The purpose of contingency should be clearly defined and its use limited to the purpose as defined. The purpose of contingency is to allow for unforeseen increases in cost that are statistically likely to occur. The major factor of this type is escalation. Then there are the errors and omissions of both the estimator and the engineers who provided the data from which the estimate was developed. But all this relates to a scope of work as defined. Contingency should *never* be provided to cover potential changes in scope. These changes, it is true, are also likely to occur, indeed, they are inevitable. Changes in scope, however, should be treated as variations, separately measured, and then added or deleted from the original estimated cost. A change in scope can never be defined until it is proposed. How then, can contingency provide for such possibilities?

Cost Indices

Mention has been made of escalation in relation to the provision of contingency. It has to be recognised that none of the prices and other cost data used in the preparation of an estimate can be of continuing value unless it is possible to relate them to present-day costs and prices. So far as the United Kingdom is concerned, the appropriate government departments record costs and publish data which can be of material assistance in this connection in the short term. By short term is meant: over a two to three year period. Over a longer period increasing caution has to be exercised because of the possible influence of 'learning', as discussed earlier. At the time of writing, the relevant data is published monthly in the *Monthly Digest of Statistics* (obtained from H.M. Stationery Office).

The first statistic of interest is the *Wholesale Price Index*. Details of the commodities used in the compilation of the various sub-indices are available, from which it can be seen that only the raw materials of manufacture and building have been taken into account. This can be used as an index for materials, if the total estimate is considered to be divided into three basic groups of materials as follows:

		Percentage
1	Building and civil engineering materials	10
2	Materials used in the mechanical engineering industries	55
3	Materials used in the electrical industry	5

The percentages suggested above are typical, but if information is available they can be adjusted to suit the particular type of installation normally built. They total 70 per cent—the balance, 30 per cent, is deemed to be for *erection costs*. For this element an index directly related to wages is better.

The *Digest* quotes an index for *all workers*—this is probably the most appropriate for the purpose in view. A weighted combination of these several indices, as indicated, gives an overall index which is a fair reflection of the probabilities. Care must be taken to ensure that the indices all relate to the same *base year.* If an adjustment has to be made, this can be done by relating the several indices being employed to the *latest* base year amongst the group chosen for integration. The others can then be adjusted, one by one, to that particular base year (Y) by multiplying by a factor F derived as follows:

$$F = \frac{\text{average index for category in year } Y}{100}$$

The foregoing is an independent approach to this particular problem. In the United Kingdom there are at least two published indices developed and maintained from the official statistics, but of a more complex character than the one that would result from the above approach. One of these was developed by a joint technical committee of the *Association of Cost Engineers* in 1964. The other has been published periodically by *Chemical and Process Engineering* since 1957. Both these indices have been designed to reflect escalation in relation to chemical plants and petrochemical plants, but they can be used quite generally with very little error. In fact, a very simple index, such as that published by *Engineering News Record* in the USA, and based on a few cost items, is almost equally effective within the limits of accuracy that can be expected, or required, in this context.

A simple index, such as the *ENR* index, has the definite advantage that it is available very quickly and, hence, is much more 'up-to-date' than the average run of published indices. Indices that wait upon government statistics will inevitably be at least two months out of date by the time that they become available, and their value is thereby much diminished.

The use of such indices for cost adjustments over periods of not more than five years is sensible. Over longer periods their use can be very misleading, because of the changes in technology that will inevitably have occurred over that time.

Location Factors

Another factor of interest, as more and more firms in the UK establish overseas branches and subsidiary companies, is the relationship between costs abroad to those obtaining in the United Kingdom. There is no easy answer to this question and intensive research is usually necessary to establish a sensible relationship between material and labour costs at home and overseas, and as between one country and another. It is important to recognise, when comparing material costs, that differences seen in the cost of basic materials, such as steel plate, will not necessarily be reflected in the manufactured equipment, or the completed building. Similarly, a direct comparison of published labour rates, when considering erection costs, is not necessarily the answer. Account has to be taken of the differences in production efficiency and working methods.

Another point that always has to be borne in mind, is the difference between the standard specifications of one country and another. The differences occasioned by climate and custom should also be considered. An outstanding example is found in the field of electrical equipment. The flameproofing regulations for electric motors vary considerably from one country to another, British regulations being far more stringent than most. Boiler and pressure vessel codes also vary, and here, the reverse is often found; overseas regulations tend to be wider in scope. Indeed, the differences are such that it is usually impracticable to use equipment other than that manufactured in the country where the plant is to be built. All these factors affect design, and hence cost, apart from the intrinsic cost differentials that will in any event exist from country to country.

Climatic considerations tend to be overlooked in the UK because the climate is temperate, with no greate extremes of hot or cold, or specific natural phenomena. But other countries can experience great differences between summer and winter conditions, earthquakes may be a distinct probability, cyclones may be common. Not all these factors tend to increase costs as such. Some are favourable, and will decrease costs as compared with the UK. But the most important point of all, perhaps, is to recognise that the location factor is not constant. It will depend upon the type of plant or factory installation that is to be built.

	HOLLAND	UNITED KINGDOM
Open structures	100	90
Warehouses	125	130
Manufacturing	215	250
Laboratories	310	400

Figure 13:7 Comparison of the cost of various types of buildings in Holland and the UK. It will be noted that the 'curve' is not so steep in Holland as in the UK.

So, once again, no reliance can be placed upon data provided by others, unless they are very much in the same business. Reference has already been made to the way in which building costs vary, being dependent upon the type of building (Figure 12:12). If a comparison is now made between two different countries, say, the United Kingdom and Holland, we find that the 'curve' for each country is different, as illustrated here by Figure 13:7.

The influence of 'mix' on the cost relationship can be demonstrated by comparing the cost of building two different plants in the USA. This is illustrated in Figure 13:8, from which it will be seen that despite the fact that the cost ratios are both the same, the difference in final erected cost from the one country to the other varies from 80 to 95 per cent. The controlling factor here, is the percentage of building work relative to the total cost of the project.

These several examples of relationships are cited by way of illustration only, as a guide to the type of problem that has to be met and overcome. They demonstrate that the estimating methods already discussed can continue to be applied with some success, and the type of relationship which can be anticipated is clearly seen. But the figures presented are no substitute for the patient work that will have to be carried out if such factors are to be used for a specific project. Those engaged in preparing estimates of cost for overseas projects are well advised to secure the maximum possible amount of local data.

The changing scene

It has to be recognised that there is nothing static about any of these relationships between costs in various countries. The data presented here are already several years old, and appreciable changes in the relationships discussed will already have occurred. The economic situation follows a different pattern in different countries, government policy having a profound influence on the situation. Prosperity in one country, as opposed to under-employment in another, will also influence the ratios. Political decisions also play their part, of which the recent decision by the UK to enter the Common Market is a typical example. To keep the data 'up-to-date' in such circumstances is most difficult—one must be alive to trends.

To illustrate the way in which a degree of 'awareness' in relation to this subject can be developed, the *Cost of Living Index,* as it is called in the UK, may be considered to be a useful pointer, when compared with the similar index as published in other countries. Most countries publish such an index. If the cost of living is rising, then costs in general

	RATIO OF COST U.S./U.K.	PLANT A		PLANT B	
		U.S.	U.K.	U.S.	U.K.
		%	Ratio	%	Ratio
Buildings and civil engineering	100 : 70	30	21	6	4
Plant and equipment, piping	100 : 110	40	44	66	73
Mechanical erection	100 : 50	21	10	21	10
Design and miscellaneous	not applicable	9	3	7	7
TOTAL	—	100	78	100	94

Figure 13:8 The influence of 'build-up' on the ultimate construction cost ratio. Plant A is a discontinuous liquids/solids process plant almost completely housed in air conditioned buildings. Plant B is a continuous 'outdoor' liquids/gases plant.

will rise sooner or later. The trend—that is, the direction and the rate of change—is far more important than the magnitude of the change. Nor need one be concerned with absolute values. That is, when comparing the index in one country with that for another, the relationship between the two—which is higher or lower—is of no interest. In comparing the cost of living between one country and another, one has to compare the *rate* of change. It is the difference in the rate of change that will increase or reduce the disparity accordingly.

Note

1 See, for instance, a paper by a consultant, Wilbur L. Nelson entitled 'Cost indexes without productivity means little', presented to the Association of Cost Engineers 12th National Meeting, Houston, Texas, June 17-19, 1968.

14

Getting Down to Detail

The cost of construction in the field always represents a very significant proportion of the total installed cost and is almost inevitably the most difficult aspect of the total erected cost to evaluate. Expressed as a factor, the ultimate relationship will depend very much upon the relative proportions within the total project of plant and equipment, pipework, electrical work, civil work and so on. If erection manhours are measured against material cost, which is, in effect, the intention when speaking of construction as a percentage of the value of the materials in the project, or elements thereof, a very wide range of ratios must inevitably be encountered. Bulky materials having a low intrinsic cost, such as pipe and fittings, will rate high in terms of erection manhours as compared, for instance, with instruments, where a very expensive item can be installed in a few hours. Ratios of this type can in fact vary from 0.1 to 3.0 manhours per £ value and a sound assessment of manhours can only result from experience.

Construction Factors

As design develops, once a project is approved, it will be necessary to improve the original estimate on which authorisation was based, and the main area for improvement will always be the estimated cost of construction. The first point to emphasise when considering construction costs is that an estimate of the number of hours that may be required to perform a certain operation is only the first stage in developing erection manhours. It is one thing to contemplate an operation in the office and quite another to see the work proceeding in the field. It is not the big items so much as the small that consume time and money. How often does one trade have to wait upon another? The fitter waits for a tool from the store, the riggers wait while the crane moves from the other side of the plot, the whole site waits on a telephone call for a missing bolt and nut. As has been said more than once to students[1] of engineering:

'The provision of a bag of nuts and bolts at the right time and place—especially if they are of the right length and diameter—may well bring its due reward. If you cannot manipulate Reynolds numbers and differential equations, you can at least be sure about engineering stores.'

Sundry materials and supplies for incorporation in the plant.

Subcontracts for specialist erection or supervision of erection of individual plant units carrying performance guarantees.

Hand tools and small tools by purchase and hire.

Protective clothing.

Provision of site offices, prefabrication shop with plant as appropriate and heating, lighting, etc., to such temporary buildings.

Stores, warehouse, etc., for materials being received, with binnage, handling equipment, etc.

Transport, around site, for personnel to local facilities, nearest town, etc., with purchase or hire of vehicles, fuel, etc.

Construction plant and equipment by purchase or rental, with loading, unloading and transportation charges.

Repairs and maintenance of vehicles and plant at site during course of construction.

Power, water, fuel and other consumables required.

Temporary facilities, such as scaffolding, piping for water, etc., possibly with storage, electric power and lighting cables, temporary roads, lighting and watching of works, telephone, fire and first aid precautions.

Site drawing office, with furnishing and supplies.

Land or use of land for construction force.

Erection labour payroll including travelling and subsistence allowances, abnormal condition money, provision for holidays with pay, paid holidays.

Supervision to erection labour, including site engineers, administration staff for payroll, stores, material handling, progressing of construction, bonus schemes, sundry purchasing, etc.

In large contracts, possibly temporary housing, site camp, etc., for part of erection force.

If construction is subcontracted, head office overheads and profit to the construction subcontractor.

Figure 14:1 Construction costs. Details of the type of expenses that are incurred during the course of construction at site.

But erection manhours are only the beginning, even when soundly established and with all contingencies allowed for. It is not always realised that the 'overheads' on the direct labour employed on construction practically doubles its initial cost. Some indication of the extent and scope of the facilities involved in the deployment of a construction force for a major project, and which lead to this drastic increase, are presented in Figure 14:1.

Another aspect of erection, often overlooked, is that there is a vast difference between doing a job on the ground and doing the same operation more than 100 feet up in the air. A consideration of the problems associated with the cost of 'traying' distillation columns gives a graphic illustration of the type of problem involved.

When the column has been set on its foundations and the work of traying commences, all the necessary materials, including the trays and bubble caps are assembled adjacent to the column. This work is seen proceeding in Figure 14:2. Each tray has to be levelled and fitted with caps. But, as the work proceeds, each tray is further and further away, with all that this implies in terms of 'fetching and carrying'. The work of fitting the trays and caps inside the column itself is shown in Figure 14:3.

Figure 14:2 Assembling tray material ready for installation in a distillation column. (Photograph by courtesy of Matthew Hall Engineering Limited, London).

Figure 14:3 Traying up a column. A view taken inside a distillation column in the course of erection, showing one tray, which is usually only a single dotted line on the flowsheet, as shown in Figure 7:3. (Photograph by courtesy of Matthew Hall Engineering Limited, London)

It is not practical to measure the time taken per tray, but work has been done on the time taken to tray columns of varying heights and diameters. Height and diameter are the main factors affecting the average time taken per tray and factors of up to ten have been noted for an increase in height from 20 to 120 feet. As a rule of thumb, it can be said in relation to working at a height, whether on, or in, columns, or on any other similar equipment, that by the time the height at which the work is being carried out has doubled, the cost of doing that work will have trebled.

Erection Costs

One of the major factors affecting the validity of an estimate is the actual circumstances relating to the construction site. For instance, the following questions are always immediately relevant:

1 Is it a 'green site, or in the midst of existing facilities? (the problem of 'live site' working)

2 Is it in the UK or overseas? (the problem of learning local regulations and facilities)
3 Will it be built in the winter or in the summer? (the problem of the weather, even in the UK)

The influence on cost of working in the midst of existing facilities can be considerable. Throughout this chapter, the distillation column has been taken as an example. If that example is taken yet once again to illustrate the significance of this further cost factor, consider first setting up a column on prepared foundations, on a new site, as part of a major development. The site is clear and level. A large construction force is being built up and mechanical handling equipment of a wide variety of types is to hand. Skilled supervisory staff are organised on the site and construction is proceeding, so that the erection of the column occupies a planned position within an overall programme. A careful study has been made of the problems likely to be encountered and 'dead men' have been set out at strategic points.

The cost of erecting a single tower under such conditions is not usually segregated but, if an assessment is made of the number of hours taken by the erection crew, adding plant hire as applicable, and a percentage for all incidental overheads, it might be found that the total cost for setting up one column was around £500. But consider the same column installed within an existing works, as part of an extension wherein that column is the only major item of plant to be erected. Access is restricted and all the equipment for handling the column has to be brought on site for the one specific operation. This means that transit and waiting time are no longer spread over a large number of plant units, but concentrated on one. The skilled supervision is still required, but has to visit the site specially, and so becomes a major overhead, seeing that the erection force is now small. In such circumstances the cost of erection for this single column could quite easily soar to some £3 000. This is only an example, but it does serve to emphasise the problems likely to be met in the field, and the fact that each circumstance must be assessed, for costs, upon its own merits. There can be no table of factors to serve as a substitute for experience.

Labour Rates

The basic problem relating to construction overseas has already been outlined. This is, in part, a recognition of the fact that a change in location will affect costs. To go overseas is an evident and drastic

BASIC DATA

No. hours worked per week		hours
Non-productive hours		hours
Distance of site from London		miles
Periodic return home allowed		weeks
Cost of return fare	£	
Estimated travel time		hours
Ratio, imported to local		%
Subsistence paid, per week	£	

	LABOUR	
	IMPORTED	LOCAL
Basic rate		
N.P.T.		
Subsistence		
Return fares		
Travel time		
Daily fares		
Allowances		
H.W.P.		
Paid holidays		
N.I.P. payments		
Totals		

TYPICAL QUALIFYING CLAUSES

1. The above rates are based on today's costs of labour and an average working week, excluding nightwork.
2. Premium time for hours worked over 50 hours per week, would be charged at cost plus.——
3. Our normal insurance payment, including employer's liability, third party and National Insurance, is included in the rates detailed above: any other insurances, etc., taken out in agreement with you or at your request would be reimbursable.
4. The above rates are based on today's costs of labour and an average working week, excluding nightwork. In the event of any increases, the rates will be adjusted accordingly.

Figure 14:4 *Calculating labour rates.* This form illustrates the information that is required to calculate the potential cost rate for each trade on site, including unskilled labour. The average rate will be a weighted *mean* of the various individual rates.

change in location, but even in the United Kingdom costs will vary from location to location, and due consideration must be given to this point. The cost of erection labour at the 'home' location is normally known in great detail and very accurately. The cost of labour in the new and different location can be calculated in relation to these known facts. A typical calculation sheet is presented as Figure 14:4. This illustrates the data that has to be ascertained. The factor that is usually unknown and will have to be estimated–and which has a very substantial influence on the final cost rate–is the relationship between 'imported' and 'local' labour on the site. This will be a matter of judgement. If very little major construction is going on in the area, the ratio of imported to local labour is likely to be low. If there is a high volume of industrial development taking place then the ratio will be high, local labour with the necessary skills having already been absorbed.

Conclusions

This part has been, and can only be, a very brief survey of the fundamental principles governing the estimating of the capital cost of production units. Such a survey is of necessity, very selective and much has been left unsaid.

In developing capital cost estimates, the objective will always be to attain the desired degree of accuracy with the minimum of information (and hence for minimum cost) in the shortest possible time. But let it be said once again–estimating is still an art, rather than a science. One must not be misled by the apparent wealth of data, the formulae and the computer program. We are still left with an *estimate*, and any and every estimate is subject to a margin of error. The objective of the estimator will be to keep that margin of error within the limits appropriate for the use to which the estimate is to be put.

Note

1 Dr W. Preston, in a lecture to engineering students, as later published in *Trans. Inst. Chem. Eng.* **35**, Nos 2/3.

PART FOUR

COST CONTROL IMPLEMENTATION

15

Cost Analysis

The basic concept of cost analysis is well known and the average company will employ cost analysis both in relation to its production activities and to its capital assets. The governing factor determining the nature of the analysis made, particularly in relation to capital assets, is usually the requirement of the accountant. This is why the listing of the several groups into which capital costs are sub-divided, is generally referred to as a 'code of accounts'. A typical analysis of this type is presented as Figure 15:1 and the various items in the list are often given a numeric or alphabetic identification to facilitate quick reference. This is the *code.*

Such a listing divides the costs into a number of distinct and different categories. The heading 'engineering' is usually for those costs which cannot be specifically allocated, such as the time spent on overall planning, the preparation of schedules, progress reports, and cost control reports. If, however, the organisation has a design team available, or if we are to consider the value of such an analysis to an integrated project organisation such as illustrated in Figure 8:2, then it becomes apparent that there are certain shortcomings in this particular system. Whilst one objective has been achieved, in that the costs have been analysed and are all in recognisable 'pockets', another, that of control, is not really facilitated. For proper control, the costs need to be divided into two basic groups: those incurred internally and those incurred externally. There is also a need, for instance, to sub-divide an item such as 'buildings' into categories of a different sort to those illustrated in Figure 15:1.

MAIN GROUPS

General
Site
Services
Buildings
Piping
Equipment
Electrical
Instrumentation
Engineering

Illustrative analysis of one of the above groups:

BUILDINGS

Design calculations
Specifications
Correspondence with suppliers

Operating data
Layout
Grading
Excavation
Formwork
Reinforcing

Concrete
Structural steel
Cladding
Heating and ventilation
Lighting
Sprinkler systems

Figure 15:1 A typical cost analysis, or 'code of accounts'.

The nature and scope of this particular sub-division is illustrated by the need to be able to recognise and assess separately the process unit or units (that is, the plant concerned directly with the manufacture of the product) and the various supporting units, often referred to as 'off-site facilities'. The term 'off-site' derives from the petroleum industry, where there are inevitably a series of refinery units through which the petroleum is processed and a series of services necessary for the proper operation of the plant. But any manufacturing installation will contain elements of this character, sometimes considerable, sometimes insignificant. In a completely new works, or 'green site' development, the off-site facilities are usually substantial. A general indication of the scope of off-site facilities is given in Figure 7:8. The important thing to recognise at this stage is that the same type of materials and work, in engineering terms, can be found both in process units and in off-site facilities. For instance, lighting appears on the process units, on the roads, in the warehouse, and so on. A form of analysis which recognises this is very important if the collected costs are to be meaningful at a later date.

Another aspect which needs consideration in relation to the structuring of a code of accounts, is its value to the various interested parties. The accountant can well be satisfied with an analysis as given in Figure 15:1, but the project engineer and, more particularly, the estimator, have very differing requirements. The coding system should be designed in such a way that it serves the best interests of all parties, insofar as that is possible. This requires that it has a certain structure whereby sections of the code are grouped. If a system of grouping is adopted, which is appropriate to the type and style of installation normally being built, then it will be found that analysis and comparison of costs can be achieved with a substantial degree of consistency. At the same time, data can be readily transferred from existing costs to facilitate the evaluation of proposed new projects. This requires that the coding system must be motivated by and generated from experience of capital cost estimating needs.

It is also important to remember that, whilst a lot of detail is theoretically available in the files of the company relating to past capital investment, analysis of such data after the event, and usually long after the event, is not only difficult, but extremely unreliable. There is no time like the present to analyse costs, when everyone involved is still available and the details can be remembered. If the costs are put into known, clearly defined categories at the time they are incurred, then at a later date there is no need to rely on memory. Indeed, the data is readily available to those who had nothing to do with the original project.

Another danger in dealing with historic costs which have not been collated to an agreed pattern, is their source. The accountant will have an analysis, but will find it difficult to define in acceptable terms, the precise content of each cost figure. Accounting procedures vary from one company to another so that another pitfall is the possibility that the figure provided may not be the initial installed cost. It may well be the depreciated cost, written down over the years. Such misleading data should not be presented, but it often is.

Cost Coding as a Management Tool

The ideal system of cost coding will be that which it is possible to use at all stages in the development of a project, not that which only serves a purpose at the end. In terms of an integrated organisation (See Figure 8:2) such a system would be adopted in the estimate, used for the identification of equipment in the process of drafting, quoted on the requisition and consequent order, and would finally appear on the supplier's invoice. Thus, at all stages, from design through the stages of creating the commitment to the final collection of the cost, a common system of cost allocation and identification is being used. This integration of the coding system adopted in the estimate at the beginning, into all the administrative procedures through to final accounting, is not only, or not merely, an estimating 'tool'—it is also a basic system for the provision of information to management for the purposes of control.

A variety of systems can be adopted which will achieve this end, but a numeric system is probably the best if there is a possibility that the resultant data will be processed by computer. A typical coding system could be:

1 Code identification: 10398/06/16/03

where:

2 10398—is the project identification number

3 06 —is the department or discipline responsible for initiating the particular element of work. (for instance, a building)

4 16 —is a sub-group number identifying the particular aspect of the work. (such as structural steel)

5 03 —is the specific area of operation to which the work relates. (For example, an off-site facility such as a warehouse)

A developed system applying this particular approach to cost coding is presented as Appendix A, whilst Appendix B gives a detailed description of each of the nominated sub-groups. This detailed description is very important, since if the system is to be of continuing use, there must be consistency of analysis. Only in this way will comparable data ever result. It will be noticed that the sub-groups all describe groups of materials, the erection of materials, or the costs relating to the movement of materials, their repair or replacement.

In the context of a manufacturing company lacking the resources for the building of a new facility, all these materials and their erection would be purchased from sources external to the company, such as suppliers and contractors. The orders placed and the invoices received can then be analysed in accordance with the coding system. In the

CODE	DESCRIPTION
01	Salaries. The salaries of personnel directly engaged on the project, of which the following are typical: Process engineers Project engineers Electrical engineers Structural engineers Architects Mechanical engineers Specialist engineers Quantity surveyors Drafting and design personnel
02	Out-of-pocket expenses. The following are typical: Travelling and living expenses The cost of prints and reproduceables Telephone, telex and cable costs Materials for scale models
03	Overhead costs. Rent Lighting, heating, water etc. Depreciation on office furniture and equipment Proratable costs, such as general administration, legal, library, and similar expenses. Office supplies Social taxes and insurance, vacation, leave, sickness and pension provision.
04	Fees. Fees paid to other engineering firms or consultants.

Figure 15:2 A typical analysis of design costs.

event that certain of the materials and the related work can be provided from within the company, perhaps via a maintenance department, the same principle of coding and cost collection should be applied. Under no circumstances should such costs be allocated elsewhere: it is in this manner that posterity is deceived into thinking that the plant can be built much more cheaply than is, in fact, the case.

The company itself could, perhaps, be carrying out all or part of the detailed design, planning and supervision of the project, depending upon the resources available within its own organisation. This internal activity is equally subject to analysis, and control will be better if this is done. If a project team is an established part of the management organisation, and a number of projects of varying size are being handled at the same time, analysis and control in this area becomes very important. The analysis can take various forms. For instance, there is the relationship between salaries paid and the related overheads and other costs. Figure 15:2 illustrates and describes the several cost areas which could be established. In general, however, such an analysis is most interesting to the accountant. The estimator is more concerned with the overall cost by manhour of the design effort. That is, the totals of the cost of the items grouped under sections 01, 02 and 03 in Figure 15:2, divided by the number of manhours to which those costs relate.

An alternative approach to the analysis of the cost of the engineering function as a whole is by discipline. This is illustrated in Appendix A, where ten different disciplines are described, 01 to 10, as the basic analysis by 'main groups'. The intention, in relation to Appendix A, is the breakdown of the material costs and erection costs. Thus, in general, the building and civil engineering department would be writing the requisitions resulting in orders relevant to the classes of work described in subgroups 10 to 19. This particular analytical approach will be used throughout this book in the presentation of estimates, cost data and the other illustrations of the techniques being discussed. The analysis of design, beyond this basic division into discipline, can be developed in a number of different ways. Appendix C illustrates a somewhat different approach, giving a typical analysis of the design function, together with a brief outline of the duties and responsibilities of the several design groups. The important thing to recognise is the need to keep such costs separate from the material and erection costs dealt with under Appendices A and B. That is, this analysis must be parallel to, and not integrated with, the analysis of materials and services.

The Degree of Analysis is Important

It is possible to analyse costs, including design costs, in ever increasing detail. Further detail is possible, for instance, in relation to the several design functions set out in Appendix C. One such possibility is illustrated by Figure 15:3, where piping engineering is further sub-divided into fourteen separate activities. Such an approach may be used and found useful for a large design organisation employing several hundred engineers and draughtsmen, but it is hardly of value in the type of design organisation associated with a manufacturing facility. Consideration of such an analysis can, however, be a positive discipline

PIPING ENGINEERING
SECTION 10

1000 Piping Engineering, general and unallocable.
1001 Supervision, general.
1002 Supervision of contract engineers and liaison with other departments.
1003 Preparation of basic specifications.
1004 Writing requisitions and related work.
1005 Preparation of spares list.
1006 Layout drawings.
1007 Installation and fabrication drawings.
1008 Checking
1009 Piping support and bracket design.
1010 Mode part manufacture.
1011 Model assembly.
1012 Material take-off schedules.
1013 As-built drawing work.
1014 Site Survey.

Figure 15:3 A typical analysis of one activity in the design function.

in assessing the scope of the work to be done by the smaller organisation.

The important principle to be appreciated at this point is that this analysis, or system of cost coding, is not to be pursued as a matter of intellectual satisfaction. It can and should only be pursued because it has value as a management tool. Only if found to be valuable and to have real purpose should it be used. This implies that the analysis should only be developed to that degree of detail that is strictly necessary, not merely from the viewpoint of one particular department, but also from a general, managerial point of view. To illustrate this point, it will be seen that Appendix A lists a sub-group analysis enumerating some seventy categories out of the ninetynine available within the coding system adopted. An alternative system could be adopted affording much greater scope, but its value is questionable. Care must be exercised if the system is not to negate its usefulness by its very complexity. It is not unknown for a coding system to be of such detail and complexity that it took three weeks to prepare each monthly report. This made the report up to six weeks behind the state of affairs it portrayed, since the monthly accounting figures had to be assessed

ESTIMATE

Client ______ Location ______ Project number ______

Description ______ Estimate number ______

______ Type of estimate ______

Department responsible ______ Sheet number ______ of ______

Area ______ Sub-group ______ Date ______

Item number	Description	Number off	Unit price	Unit rate	Estimated cost	Erection man hours
			£		£	

Prepared by ______ Approved by ______ Totals

To be retained by ______

Figure 15:4 Estimate detail sheet. This form is suitable for use by either client or contractor.

before the report could be prepared. When a project is in progress on the site, such delays make the report worthless to the project engineer controlling site costs, assuming he had the time to study the report in all its detail when it became available. In addition, the detail in a coding system must be associated with realism. There is no merit, for instance, in analysing an estimate of electrical work between the cost of the cable and the cost of laying that cable on site, if in practice a contract exists which embraces these two items in one lump sum, or a combined rate in a schedule of rates. The separate costs *cannot* be analysed, so why break down the estimate?—the system must be the slave, not the master.

Typical Forms

As stated previously the first and continual standard of reference is the estimate. Assuming a specific sub-group analysis of that estimate is to be adopted then the estimator should develop and present the estimate to the agreed pattern. This is facilitated if a suitable form is available. A typical *estimate detail sheet* is presented as Figure 15:4. All the immediately relevant data is presented in the heading, including the basic elements of the costing data—project number, area and sub-group. The total estimate for each sub-group will then be available and two forms of summation are possible—by area and by design discipline. Both can be useful. The summary by design discipline can be carried to an *estimate summary sheet* generally as illustrated in Figure 15:5. The *general* section will include design costs and other charges specific to the project, such as insurance premiums, import duties and the like. General overheads which cannot be directly allocated to any specific project should be included under 'contribution'. A typical list of these is given in Figure 15:6, as an *aide-mémoire*, but where costs such as sick leave, and holiday expenses relate to design staff, they should be a part of the design overhead.

Assuming that estimates were prepared in this format for projects under consideration, then when the project has been approved the commitments and finally the costs should be analysed to the same pattern. As has been said earlier, orders and invoices should be analysed in precisely the same way as the estimate, and the first step in the cost control procedure is then to record the orders as issued. This can be done on a form similar to the *estimate detail sheet* (Figure 15:4), thus enabling a direct comparison to be made between estimate and commitment. A typical form for this purpose is presented as Figure

ESTIMATE SUMMARY

Client ______________ Location ______________ Project number ______________

Description ______________________________ Estimate number ______________

______________________________ Type of estimate ______________

______________________________ Sheet ________ of ________

Area ______________________________ Date ______________

Description	Estimate sum	
02 Material handling		
03 Technical		
05 Plant		
06 Building and civil engineering		
07 Site construction		
08 Electrical		
09 Instruments		
10 Services		
Sub-total £		
General, including design		
Sub-total £		
Contingency		
Basic estimated cost £		
Contribution		
Total £		

Approved by ______________

Date ______________

Figure 15:5 Estimate summary sheet. As with Figure 15:4, the format is appropriate to both client and contractor. 'Contribution' can be the contractor's overhead and profit, or an overhead allocation in the manufacturing organisation.

INDIRECT OFFICE COSTS AND GENERAL
ADMINISTRATIVE OVERHEADS

1. Sales personnel
2. Legal personnel
3. Public relations personnel
4. Administative staff, including managers and directors
5. Messenger services, gateman and watchmen
6. Medical and first aid staff and facilities
7. Filing, mailing, library personnel
8. Indirect labour, such as typists and clerks in direct charge departments, such as design
9. Stand-by time for employees on military or jury service
10. Costs of preparing engineering standards and procedures
11. Sick leave and holiday expenses (salary burden)
12. Travelling and out-of-pocket expenses incurred by employees engaged on the above activities
13. Maintenance and repair of buildings and equipment related to the above activities
14. Advertising and entertainment expenses
15. Bad debts
16. Contributions to charity
17. Service and rental for telephones, office machinery and data processing equipment
18. Legal fees
19. Income tax
20. Company tax and other burdens, such as dividend payments.

Figure 15:6 Indirect office costs and administrative overheads. This schedule is typical and is in no sense comprehensive. Profit is the final overhead when a contractor is being employed.

15:7, which is described as the *cost control sheet.* This form parallels the estimate detail by project area and sub-group, thus providing a clear record of the original orders and the amendments thereto sub-group by sub-group. Totals per order are recorded throughout, not incremental differences. As and when the order is completed and all the invoices relevant to that order are in, the final value invoiced against the order is recorded in the end column. Scrutiny of the record, item by item, then gives a direct indication of outstanding commitments in terms of incomplete orders and the summation of the final values will be the final total cost per sub-group. The cost control sheet thus becomes a record of *total* commitment: that is, both the outstanding commitment and the money already paid are handled as totals per order. The

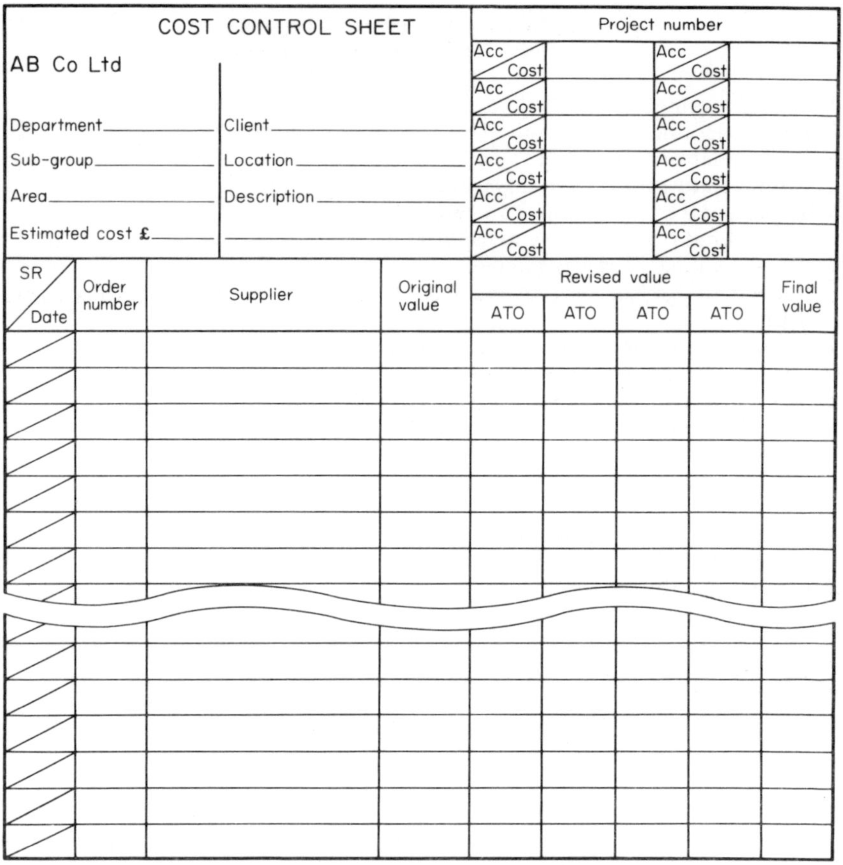

Figure 15:7 Cost control sheet. The detailed record of orders placed and invoices received.

final total commitment thus becomes the total project cost. This cost control sheet is fundamental, whether used manually or as a basis for computer input data, as discussed later.

The other aspect of every project requiring vigorous, detailed control, and hence careful recording, is the changes made in the project following its initial authorisation. These are usually described as 'variations', and a typical *variation control sheet* is presented as Figure 15:8. This control is applied to the total approved project cost. Every technical change in the scope of the work, as originally agreed and estimated, should be recorded and a detailed estimate (by sub-group) prepared of the cost of the change, or variation. The detailed estimate

VARIATION CONTROL SHEET

A B Company Limited

Project number ______
Estimate number ______

Client ______ Location ______ Sheet number ______ of ______
Description ______ Date ______

1 Code	2 Section	3 Original estimated price £	Revised price									13 Final allowed price £
			4 Variation to price £	5 Latest allowed price £	6 Variation to price £	7 Latest allowed price £	8 Variation to price £	9 Latest allowed price £	10 Variation to price £	11 Latest allowed price £	12 Variation to price £	
02	Material handling											
03	Technical											
05	Plant											
06	Building and civil engineering											
07	Site construction											
08	Electrical											
09	Instruments											
10	Services											
	GENERAL—Staff time											
	Travel expenses											
	Miscellaneous											
	SUB-TOTALS											
	Contingency											
	SUB-TOTALS											
	Contribution											
	TOTALS											

Figure 15:8 Variation control sheet. This relates to commitments and gives a detailed record, department by department, of each change made in the financial status of the project.

of the variation is summarised as shown on the form, and a running total maintained of the *estimated* cost of the project. This maintains the estimate as a basis for comparison with the the actual cost which is being recorded in parallel on the cost control sheet. Differences can then be noted and acted upon. This 'action' is discussed later. The first consideration is that the procedures established must be set up in such a manner that the necessary data is available to serve as a basis for action.

16

Cost Control Procedures

As has already been demonstrated in Chapter 15 (Cost Analysis) the basic requirement in any system of control for a new project is a close adherence to a *code of accounts*, so that the project in all its aspects can be analysed on a consistent, detailed basis. It has also been said earlier, in Part 1, Chapter 3, that the only way in which construction projects can be controlled is by measuring and comparing planned effort with actual performance. This measurement and comparision requires a set of procedures if it is to be effective. The planning of any project takes place in two basic fields:

1 Time—the scheduling of the performance of the work that has to be done
2 Cost—the scheduling of the expenditure which will be incurred

These two factors are of course interrelated. Reference was made right at the beginning to the fact that 'time is money'. So true is this that the two fields mentioned above are closely interrelated, indeed, they integrate the one with the other and become inseparable. If this interrelationship is disregarded for a moment, it is possible to effectively segregate and process four basic elements in every project:

1 Planned or scheduled progress
2 Actual progress
3 Planned, or budgeted expenditure
4 Actual expenditure

All these four elements are dynamic throughout the life of the project, for a variety of reasons. Actual progress and expenditure can easily be seen to be variable over time, but it is equally true that the plan also changes over time. Thus the *planning* needs control just as much as does the actual achievement. Indeed, when all these four elements are truly under control, the whole project is under control.

Cost Reporting is Not Cost Control

It is all too easy to establish a system of project organisation and administration, with a regular flow of reports, and then believe that costs are under control. The greater the detail in which the reporting is done, the stronger is the impression that everything is under control, but beyond a certain optimum point the reverse is almost invariably true. The fundamental difference between *cost reporting* and *cost control* is illustrated by Figure 16:1. With Case A, the project is reviewed at intervals and revised estimates of costs are then prepared. To prepare these estimates, an appraisal must be made of the time that is still required to complete the project, so that both cost and time are under surveillance at the point in time when the estimate is being prepared. If successive estimates indicate that costs are rising, or that the project is taking longer to complete than was at first anticipated, then steps will be taken in an endeavour to improve the situation. But such corrective action can only be minimal in its effect, since it comes very much 'after the event'. The decisions or circumstances which have given rise to the new situation reflected in the revised estimate will already be very largely a matter of history. The estimate reflects the situation as seen at that particular moment in time. The situation therefore already exists as reflected in the estimate, and can hardly be altered.

Case B, however, illustrates a process of evaluation, followed by corrective action as indicated. In order to evaluate a trend, a forecast has to be made not merely of the anticipated end result, but also of the route by which that end result is expected to be reached. Comparison of the route actually being followed with that forecast allows the trend, either along the route or away from it, to be seen. Any divergence can be studied before it becomes too significant and the appropriate action taken. The result of the action taken has also to be ascertained if the system of control is to be effective, thus we have a cycle:

1 Evaluate

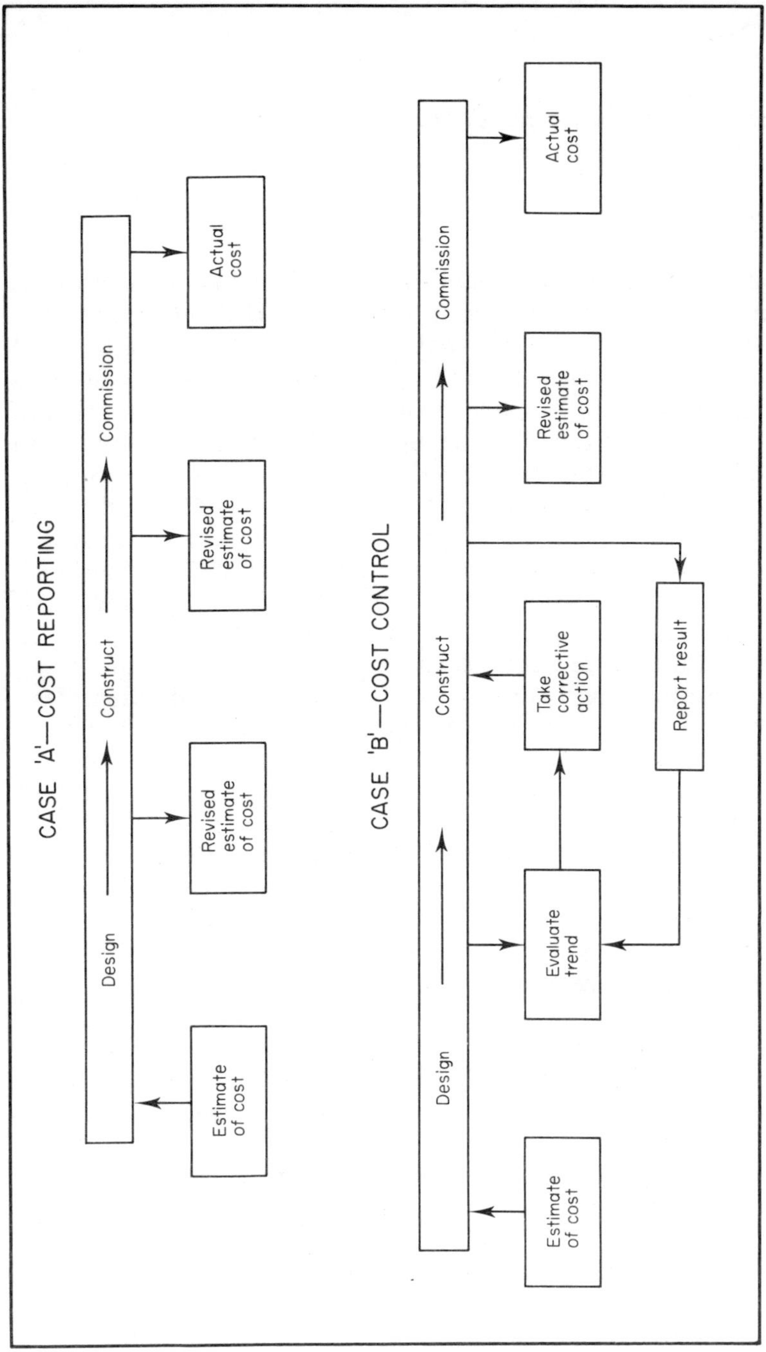

Figure 16:1 *Cost reporting versus cost control.* Reporting is the comment on the activity which is proceeding. Control must influence as well as comment.

2 Correct
3 Report

This cycle of events is fundamental to effective cost control.

Forecasting

The capital cost estimate provides a forecast of the cost of the project, whilst there will also be available an estimate of the time required to complete the project. The precise way in which this estimated cost and time data will be analysed will be dependent on the internal resources of the company that can be made available for the implementation of the project, as compared with the resources which will be utilised from outside the company. If complete reliance is placed upon a consultant and contractors, then the problems of forecasting will, effectively, have been delegated to others. In order, however, to demonstrate the principles involved, the fairly common situation can be examined, where the basic design work is carried out by a project managment team maintained within the company. This team will usually deal with a number of different projects of varying size, all at the same time, engaging a consultant, perhaps, for specific areas of specialised interest. The project team would purchase equipment and employ a number of separate contractors for construction.

This particular organisational approach is only one of a number of alternative management situations to which the concepts established in this book are relevant, as discussed in Part 1. However, the specific concept of employing a project team will be adopted throughout this chapter, as being a very common situation that will serve to illustrate the proposed techniques adequately. In this context, then, forecasting is required in the following areas:

1 Manpower. This is the project team or manpower resource within the company that can, or will be, allocated to the project. It can be expressed and measured in manhours, although it ultimately becomes a cost.
2 External commitments. These are the orders placed for materials or services with suppliers and contractors.
3 External expenditure. This is the sum of the invoices received in respect of the orders placed under (2) above.

When the growth of these three components is plotted over time, a

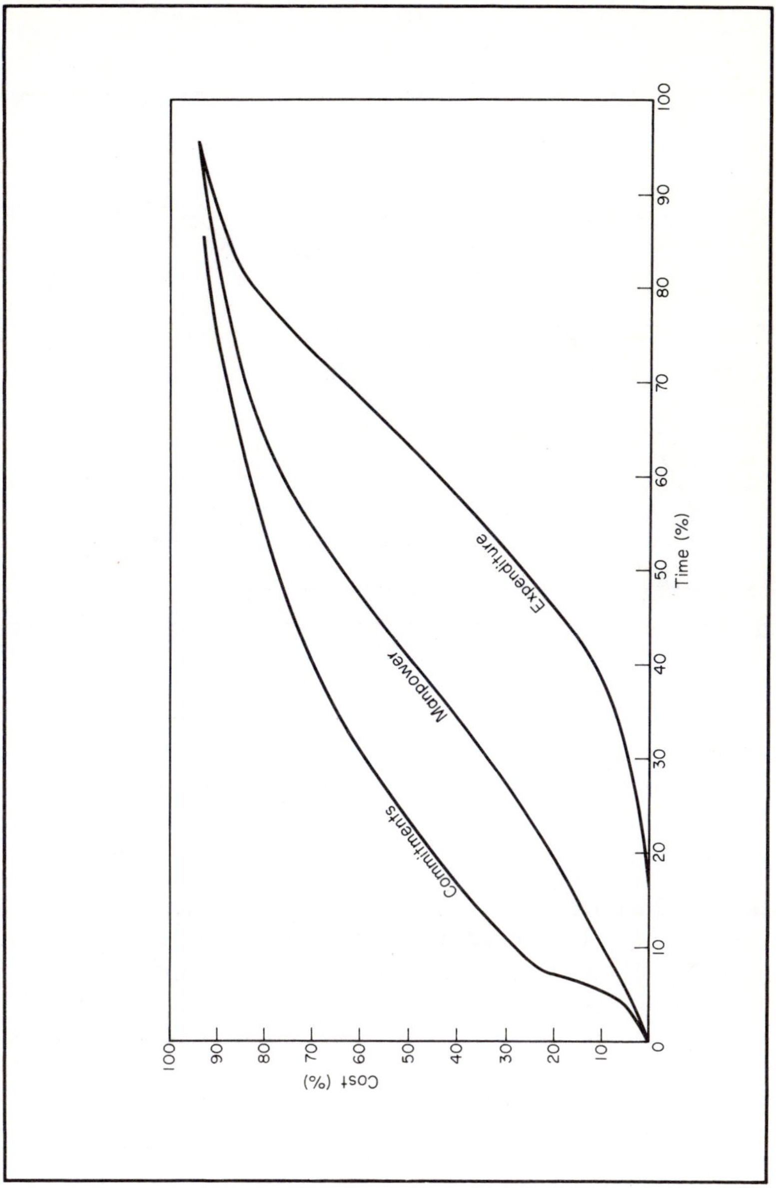

Figure 16:2 **Commitments and expenditure:** *the characteristic 'S' curves.*

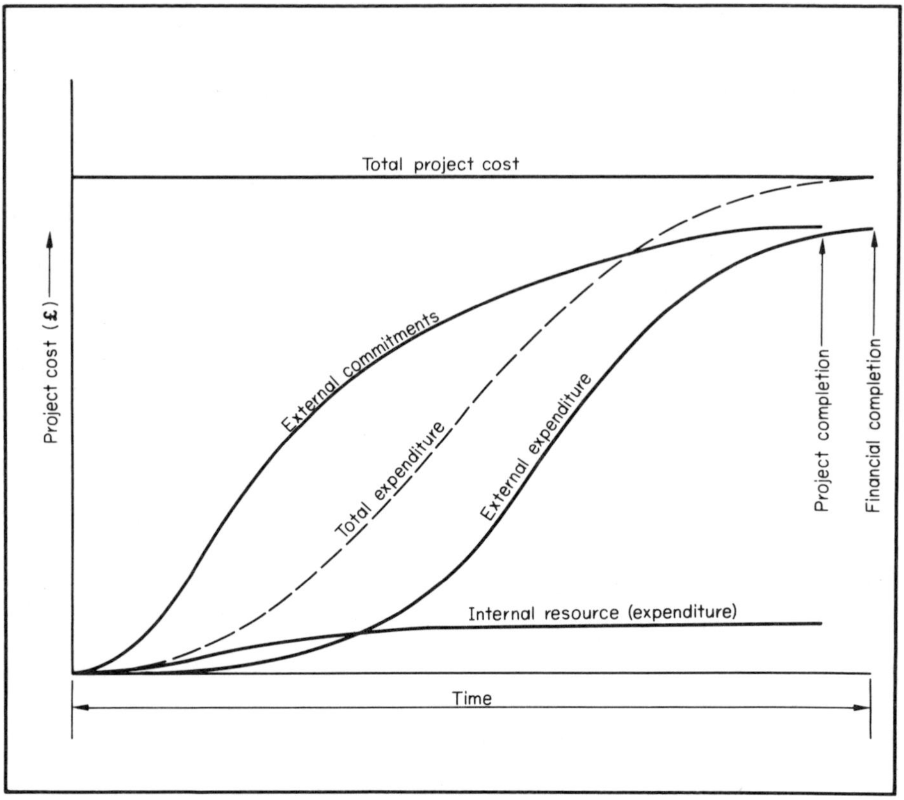

Figure 16:3 Commitments and expenditure: a specific project.

characteristic curve results, usually referred to as the 'S-curve' because of its shape, as illustrated in Figure 16:2. Here, the relative values of the several componenets have been disregarded. For any specific project, the relationship when expressed, relative to total project cost, would take the form shown in Figure 16:3. Assuming that the detail is available, curves as illustrated in Figure 16:3 could be plotted for each element of each project in hand. Once drawn, we have through the medium of these curves, a forecast of the correlation in the project between cost and time. The curve illustrates the forecast trend, and the result, as it occurs, can be plotted and compared with this indicated trend. Any discrepancy can then be seen and acted upon. As the project proceeds, it is possible that the forecasts for both cost and time will be revised. This would require that the forecast curves are redrawn to take account of these revised predictions, and the process of comparison continued against the new curves that will have been developed. This is cost control in action.

With further reference to Figure 16:3 it is also possible, assuming the relevant detail to be available, to plot the curves which are specific to any one particular project as targets. Once the targets have been established, it is then possible to plot the actual results being achieved and compare these with the targets. This will allow the trend referred to above to be discerned. Such a detailed procedure for comparison between targets and results is quite effective when only one project is involved of limited size. Once, however, the size of the project is such that a number of separate units are involved, or a number of separate projects are on hand at the same time, then the comparison procedure becomes extremely tedious and time consuming.

Experience has shown, however, that the progress made, as reflected in the shape of the S-curve is very similar between projects of the same type. It is then far quicker to plot the actual situation against a standard curve and proceed to query manifest departures from the norm. If, at the same time, the cost and time relationships are expressed as percentages, rather than as finite numbers, or absolute values, then the standard curve becomes the same in every case, irrespective of the total cost of the project or the time taken.

This is illustrated by reference to Figures 16:4 and 16:5 and making a comparison. The two plants A and B are different in size, their project duration is different, they will have been started at different times, and therefore, will be at different stages of project development. Plant A has been in hand for some ten months (52 per cent time elapsed), whilst Plant B has been in progress for six months (28 per cent time elapsed). Comment is given on the progress seen, but it has to be remembered that, apart from the fact that no project is going to follow the standard curve precisely, deviation will also result from under, or over, estimation of, either total commitment or, total design hours required on the project. Yet again, a poor estimate of the duration of the project will also affect the conclusions. That is, poor estimates will result in deviations being indicated which are not, in fact, real.

Manpower

There is a crucial difference between resources drawn from within a company and those drawn from outside the company, for the purpose of completing a project. Relative to the project, it may be said that the

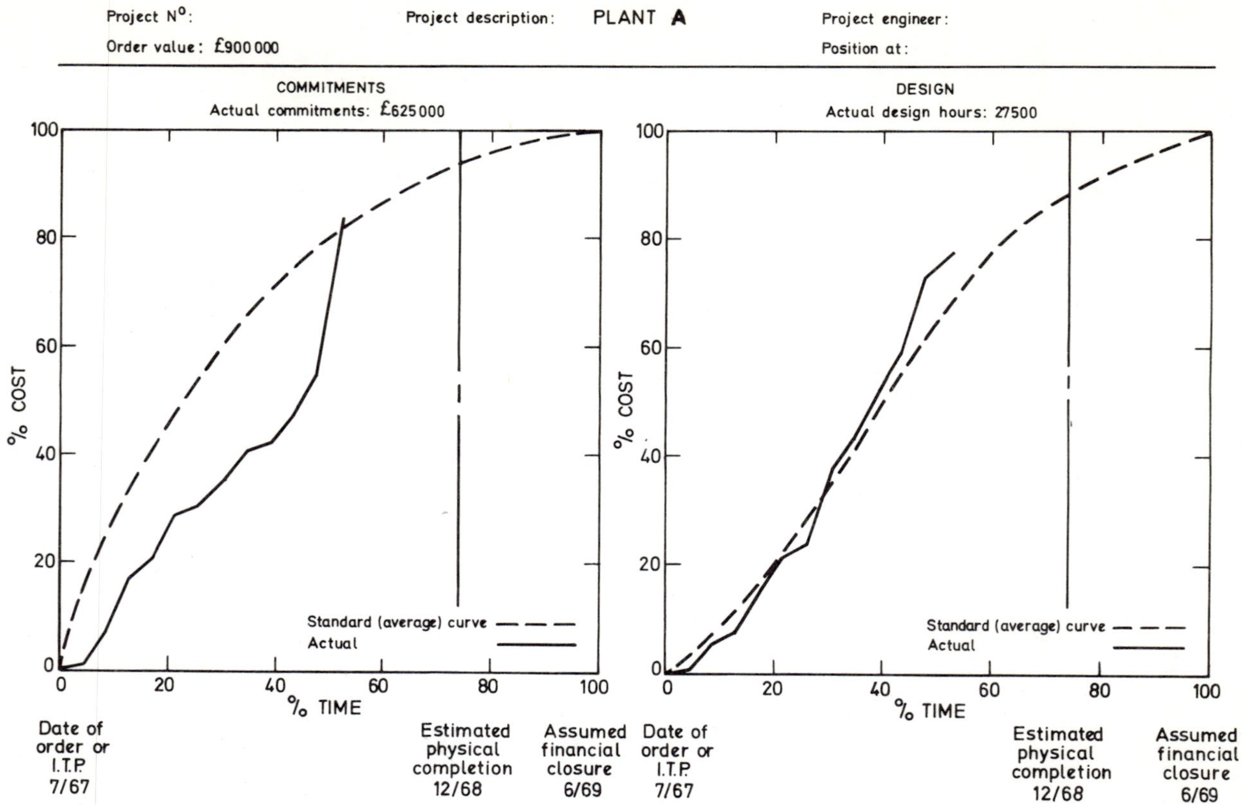

Figure 16:4 Progress report, Plant A. Whilst design is well up to programme, the placing of commitments was lagging for a while, although the position has now been redeemed. This was due to a delay in full financial approval, resulting in certain major orders being held back.

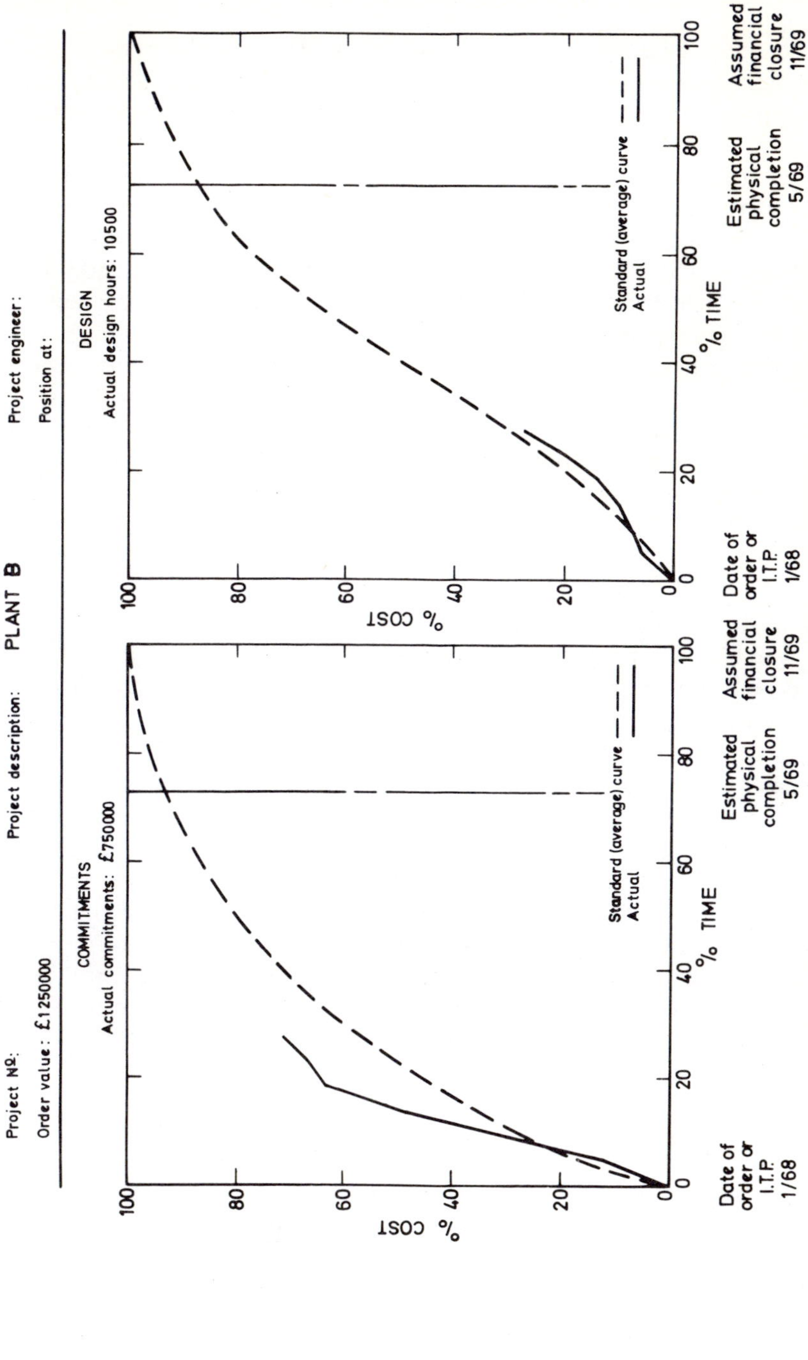

Figure 16:5 Progress report, Plant B. The graphs indicate that progress on design is satisfactory and that commitments are being placed well. There is, therefore, no need for concern.

external resources are limitless: they are there to be drawn upon and used as required. There can be, and often are, specific limitations in relation to the availability over time, but they are normally very large. The internal resources, however, are strictly limited. The ability to work on a project has then to be considered, not only in relation to the project itself but also, in relation to any other projects also being handled at the same time, and a comparison made with the total resources of the company allocated or available for project implementation.

This consideration is demonstrated by Figure 16:6. The available staff stays relatively constant. People on the permanent staff may leave and others be engaged; it is possible to hire temporary staff, such as 'contract draughtsmen'; but these fluctuations are normally minor over the period through which it is possible to make any sensible forecast. The graph illustrates the characteristic situation in relation to current work. If no more new projects are contemplated, then the work in hand will be progressively completed and the workload falls, eventually, to about zero. The graph also illustrates another very common situation: that of overload. The work in hand at the beginning of the period surveyed (July, 1971) is more than the available staff can cope with. Since it is not usually desirable as a matter of policy to meet such situations in the short term by increasing staff, the result must be that work will be delayed and the completion of a project, or projects, in all probability will also be delayed. The work delayed will be carried out at a later stage in time, as illustrated by the shaded area on the graph.

The effect of this delay on the projects being dealt with has then to be studied, perhaps progress on the most important can be maintained at the expense of others. This consideration demonstrates the interplay between a number of projects and the resources available when those resources are limited. Consideration must also be given to new projects, perhaps in the course of study or development, that are going to be put in hand in the future: 'contemplated projects' is the term which will be used here. A live, growing organisation always has a number of contemplated projects in the 'pipeline'.

External Commitments

The initial result of the purchasing activity described earlier, (see Chapter 9) is that orders are placed external to the project organisation. Orders are of two basic types. There is the order for a specific item of equipment or a defined volume of work, or services, which has a fixed

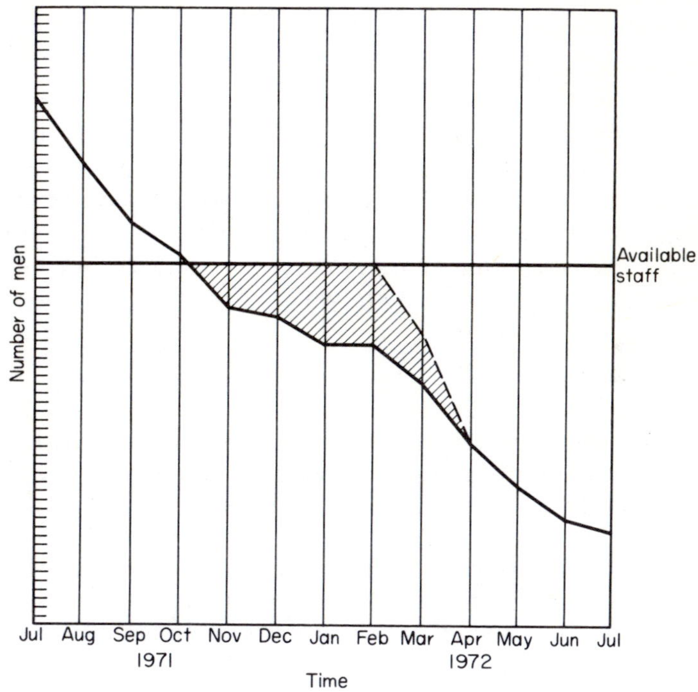

NOTES:

1 Hours have been converted to numbers of men at the rate of 125 hours per month. This then allows for the hours spent on education, holidays, sickness and office routine

2 The workload includes, in addition to current projects, a provision for work in relation to standards, and so on

Figure 16:6 Projects Group workload forecast.

price. There is also, what the writer is determined to describe as the 'open order', despite constant criticism from purchasing officers, who are of course doing their best at all times to 'close all doors'.

The fixed price order

The term *fixed* is relative in this context. Apart from the fact that the terms of the order may contain provisions varying the price if material or labour costs change, the instructions to the supplier may well be changed whilst manufacture is in progress. It is usually possible, however, to value such changes fairly precisely as they occur, so that the total value of the order is known.

The open order

It is often necessary to place orders where the rate which will be paid for the materials and services provided is specified, but the volume of such materials and services is only known in 'order of magnitude' terms. Typical of such orders are those placed on the basis of a *schedule of rates,* or *daywork rates,* or a combination of both. The commitment established by such orders can only be an estimate, but every attempt should be made to keep that estimate realistic and up-to-date.

The sum of all such orders represents the total commitment at any one time. In this sense, the commitment represents an express intention, and not the absolute commitment, since orders can be cancelled. The final cost in such circumstances will often be materially less than the face value of the order. It should also be remembered that purchasing policy can materially influence the rate at which commitments (as just defined) are created. For instance, if the policy is to maximise the orders placed on a lump sum basis, then the rate will be slower than if open orders are placed, since time will be required to allow for the necessary design and specification work, and then for the supplier to calculate the price of the tender. The commitment curve in Figure 16:2 represents a situation where the need for initiating site works at an early stage has resulted in an order being placed for the building and civil engineering works on a schedule of rates basis, long before the design of the works has been completed. In the illustration the average situation is reflected, such building works representing some twenty to thirty per cent of the total value of the project. Where such works are minimal (for example, on an 'outdoor' plant), or where the order was delayed until a detailed specification had been prepared, then the curve would not rise so sharply at the beginning of the project for this particular cause.

This comment makes it appropriate to state at this point, that all the S-curves presented here are typical, reflecting certain specific relationships between the various elements of project cost, applicable only in a specific context. It is necessary for any project team proposing to utilise such techniques as these, to establish its own data by a study of the historical data relevant to its own field.

Time Factor

To forecast, it is necessary to contemplate the future, and in connection with the placement of orders, this implies that 'time' has to be considered as well as cost. Time in this context is usually interpreted as the time required by the supplier to make the delivery, but this is only one facet of the subject. One objective of placing an order is to contribute to the control of cost and it has to be remembered that cost is more than money. A supply source cannot, therefore, be selected on price alone; such a basis of selection will, more often than not, add to cost and reduce ultimate profit. The constituent parts that go to make up the overall cost in relation to an order are time, quality, source, quantity, place and price. All these must receive proper consideration when the source of supply is being selected.

The delivery date is, of course, important. Suppliers are often bitterly criticised for their failures in this direction, but, the delivery period follows from, and starts from, order placement. Order placement is, itself, the consequence of an enquiry process. Look at it from the point of view of the supplier, as illustrated in Figure 16:7. It will be seen that the average time taken to prepare the tender in response to the enquiry is about four weeks. The order will be received, on average, up to ten weeks later, making a total elapsed time of fourteen weeks between enquiry and order.

The graph also illustrates possible extremes in this situation: the minimum period is of the order of four weeks and the maximum twenty weeks. Put this concept of possible time periods, into the context of the delivery period that can be expected for the equipment to be supplied. With specially fabricated equipment it could be as short as three months, perhaps as long as twelve months. So the period from enquiry to order is almost always a very significant proportion of the total time taken from enquiry to delivery. The supplier does not know,

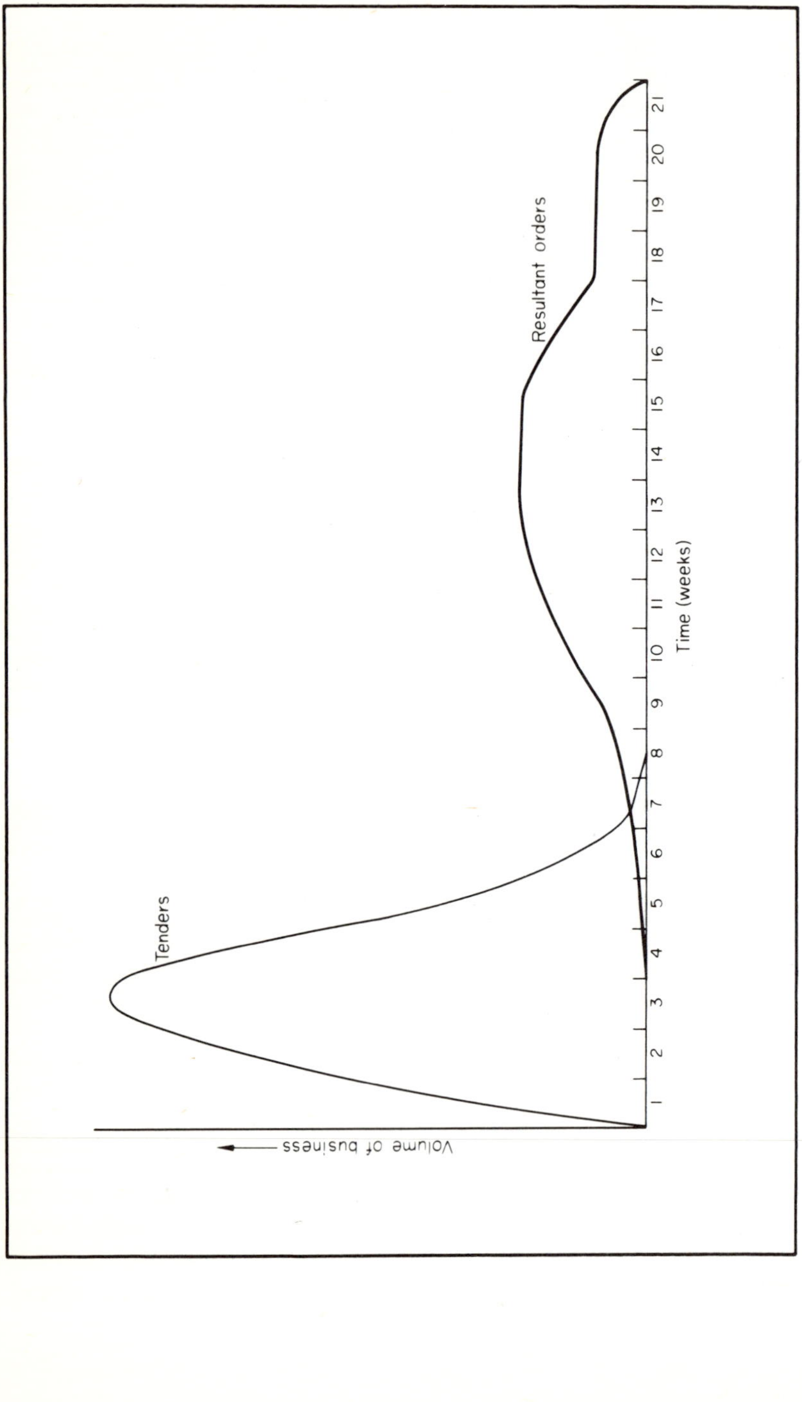

Figure 16:7 Order placement—the time lag.

of course, how long the buyer has taken to prepare the enquiry. That is the missing dimension so far as he is concerned.

Expenditure

This is the end of the road. The materials have been supplied, the work has been done, but it is *not* all over. Control is still necessary–very necessary. And, perhaps surprisingly, time is still money. Poor invoice clearance procedures can still cost money, not only in the sense that more is paid to a supplier than is deserved, but also, if payment is unjustly delayed, the progress of the project can suffer.

In relation to the requirements of cost control, it is important that invoices are not paid unless they are fully covered by the order, or amendments thereto. There is usually a practical 'tolerance' in this connection which should be adopted in order to minimise paperwork. Apart from such a working tolerance, the *final invoice price* should agree with the price on the order. In order to ensure that the total commitment, as recorded from the orders, agrees with the total paid, it is necessary, where a tolerance is allowed, to ensure that the final invoice price is recorded as the final commitment in relation to any specific order. The manner in which this is done in practice can be seen by reference to the cost control sheet in Figure 15:7. The final invoice price, in total, appears in the end right hand column, replacing the previous order value. Invoice processing and clearance procedures are usually well established within any particular company, so that principles, rather than practices, are all that it is necessary to discuss here. Payment in relation to goods and services falls into two basic categories:

1 Payment when the goods or services have been delivered and completed
2 Progress payments related to materials supplied, or work done

Most companies will be fully familiar with the first category but not necessarily familiar with the latter. It is essential to maintain a historical record in relation to invoices received under the latter, since a number of payments, instead of one single payment, are going to be made against one order. This can be done by authorising payment by means of a payment slip, as shown by Figure 16:8. The details on the form illustrate the aspects which need control. The preparation of the form will usually be the responsibility of the accounts department,

Supplier's account number	PAYMENT SLIP (PROGRESS CLAIMS)	Accounts department serial number

Supplier:	To: (Project engineer) Date:

Supplier's:

Invoice number ________ Value ________ Date ________

Allocation:	Order number	Instalment number

Type of contract Lump sum Day work Schedule of rates Other	Description

Contract value	£		£		Claims
Original					Total claimed
Approved variations					Less retention
Other variations claimed					Payment due Previous claims Present application
Latest (including claims)					Total payments
Previous claims	Claim number				Dated
Outstanding	Claim number				Dated

IF APPROVED, sign this form, and return to ⎤
IF NOT APPROVED, refer details of query to ⎦ — ACCOUNTS DEPARTMENT

Notes:

Signature for approval ________ Date ________

Figure 16:8 Payment slip. This is appropriate where progress payments have to be made against an order.

who will seek authorisation for payment from the project engineer in control of the project. The form maintains a record of the total claim made by the supplier: this is the potential contract value, although subject to negotiation, and is the figure maintained as the commitment. This total commitment can be directly compared with the total payment agreed to be due, including retention and the immediate payment being processed.

17

Effective Cost Control

It has already been demonstrated that anticipation is the key to effective cost control. Lack of anticipation occurs even when the principle—that it is needed—is recognised. Over-expenditure, all too often, seems to take the participants in a project by surprise. When the over-expenditure is of such a magnitude as to threaten the economics of the project, a feeling of frustration develops—management finding itself trapped into completing a project they wish that they had never started.

This feeling of frustration leads to what are commonly known as 'inquests'. Considerable effort is put into analysing the costs, sorting out coding errors, appraising the cost of variations, assessing the real impact of escalation. Explanations are developed, which go through the various levels of management, and wrath is appeased. But this careful documentation is, in fact, just the solemn authentication of a reality, and the formal background to an application for additional funds.

This is not to imply that one is absolutely helpless at this stage, or that such analyses make no contribution at all to the control of costs. Analysis can disclose areas where suppliers or contractors are making unjustified claims, and such claims can then be resisted. The point that has to be made, emphasised and continually borne in mind is that cost control can only be achieved by *management,* and this means management of the entire project. Successful management in any sphere demands intelligent anticipation.

The various functions which have been discussed, such as estimating, cost reporting and cost analysis are the tools of management, but they cannot replace management. Part of the problem lies in the fact that the project team is involved in a management situation where the basic concern, in relation to a new project, is the contribution to be made to profit when it has been completed. The tendency is, therefore, to look at the end, when all the attention should be focussed on the *beginning.* As a result, problems in the development of the project are dealt with as individual crises when they arise, expedients are developed to solve the problem and the solutions found reflect emergency decisions made by the persons who happened to be in a position to take action at the time.

It has already been demonstrated, however, that the effort to control cost must be exerted throughout the life of the project and that this effort will be most effective during the early stages. There is every justification, therefore, as has been seen, for treating the project cost, as reflected in the control estimate, as a target to be beaten. There is a challenge to make a profit on the project itself. This is the impelling motive in a contracting organisation. The same motive also exists in the manufacturing organisation, but it is often lost sight of because of the attention paid to the profit coming at the *end* of the project from the operation of the facility. There is a profit to be made *by* the project—so make it!

The Role of the Control Estimate

The control estimate, initially the basis for an application for company funds, will be available in the relevant detail, analysed in accordance with an agreed code of accounts. For details of possible codes of account, reference can be made to Chapter 15 and, Appendices A and B. This basic tool, in conjunction with the parallel analysis of all the project functions, such as design, procurement and construction, provides:

1 A check on the cost trend
2 A check on the time trend
3 Localisation of the areas calling for corrective action
4 An estimate of additional funds required (if any)
5 A check on suppliers' and contractors' tenders

The control estimate, which in the first instance, is the estimate representing the capital cost of the project for authorisation, is not a static document. It is subject to both review and to development, in detail, in the course of review. Review, in essence, is ascertaining what has happened to date, and then estimating what has still to happen, in order to complete the project. These principles of approach are clearly presented in the proposed format for the preparation of a review estimate, as given in Figure 17:1. The estimate is seen to be varying on the background of changes made in the project. There are four major reasons for such alterations:

1 Change in scope
2 Changes in programme
3 Changes on site
4 Escalation

Changes in scope fall into two basic categories, additions or deletions to the project, and variations within the project consequent upon design development. Changes in programme follow upon delay (rarely improvement) in delivery schedules related to the late development or finalisation of design. Escalation costs are forecast and included in contingency, but there is a steady movement of values from contingency to direct estimated cost during the life of a project on this account.

The predicted final cost is the sum of all the foregoing influences, representing the sum of the situation then existing (expenditure and commitments to date) and an estimate of what has still to be done in order to complete the project. There is also the basic division, referred to above, between internal expenditure, expressed in manhours, and external expenditure, actual and potential, expressed in money.

On a project of any magnitude, the preparation of a review estimate is a time-consuming process and it can, therefore, only be carried out at intervals during the life of the project. The usual sort of interval is every three or four months. Changes will arise that are going to vary the cost more or less continuously, but continuous revision is neither necessary nor economic. The changes have to be consolidated at intervals, and the intervals can be established either on a chronological basis, or in relation to significant stages in the completion of the project. The latter is preferred, and typical 'milestones' are finalisation of process design, commencement of work on site, completion of delivery of major equipment, completion of erection and completion of commissioning. But scrutiny at such intervals of time is not effective, in itself, for the purposes of cost control, even if carried out very thoroughly. A more

REVIEW ESTIMATE SUMMARY	Customer	Project number
R Project	Site	Project manager/engineer
	Order value (T.5): £	Position at

1 Code	2 Section	3 Original estimated price £	4 Authorised variations to contract £	5 Latest allowed price columns 3+4 £	6 Expenditure and commitments to £	7 Estimated to complete £	8 Predicted final cost columns 6+7 £	9 Estimated under/over-expenditure columns 5–8 £
02	Material handling							
03	Technical							
05	Plant							
06	Building and civil engineering							
07	Site construction							
08	Electrical							
09	Instruments							
10	Services							
	GENERAL—Staff time							
	Travel expenses							
	Miscellaneous							
	SUB-TOTALS							
	Contingency							
	SUB-TOTALS							
	Contribution				Revised contribution (T.5–ST.8)			

Staff time hours				
Code	Hours originally estimated	Actual to	Estimated to complete	Total
02				
03				
05				
06				
07				
08				
09				
10				

Notes

Design start date:

Review history: First review______ Last review______ Next review______

Target completion date

Prepared by		Approved				
Initials	Date		Original predicted contribution	%	£	Figures in brackets denote over-expenditure
			Previous predicted contribution	%	£	
			Latest predicted contribution	%	£	

Original:
Previous:
Latest:

Figure 17:1 The review estimate. The form shown is 'contractor' orientated, to illustrate the desire to make a 'contribution' to profit. The same philosophy must be present in a manufacturing organisation, namely the urge to beat a target.

systematic and frequent scrutiny of a different type is needed for this purpose.

The generally accepted interval for reporting is monthly, since this can be aligned with the accounting periods. This makes it not only a convenient interval, but has the further benefit that some of the necessary data is readily available from the accounting records. Once the various estimates have been made, either initially or on review of the project, movement is reflected under the heading of 'expenditure and commitments' (column 6 in Figure 17:1). This can be re-evaluated at monthly intervals and the results of that re-evaluation given in the form of a cost control report, as shown by Figure 17:2.

The review estimate, together with the cost control report, are the means of checking directly on the cost trend and, indirectly, on the time trend. Since the estimate is in detail and the commitments/expenditure are analysed in similar detail (see Figures 15:5 and 15:7) it is possible to localise the area in the project where corrective action is needed. The details provide the analysis, but it is the action taken that is the contribution to cost control. As soon as an unfavourable trend is discovered, management should act. If action is delayed, it will always be too little and too late. The action to be taken usually involves:

1 Revising design
2 Changing personnel
3 Revising schedules
4 Changing suppliers

The result of these actions will not necessarily reduce costs. They could, indeed, involve an increase in the capital cost of the project. There is a correlation between time and money and if, for instance, the product has to be on the market by a certain date, then extra expenditure, to reduce the time taken to complete the project, may more than offset the possible loss due to the delay that would occur in marketing the product.

When the project is seen to be costing more than was originally anticipated, whether this is involuntary or by design, additional funds are required, and an estimate is therefore required to indicate the magnitude of these requirements. For the situation to be redeemed, the funds have to be available. It is not always recognised by project groups that the extra funds are not necessarily available. The potential overrun could, therefore, lead to drastic curtailment of the project, with the result that a useless installation is provided. Alternatively, if the

COST CONTROL REPORT		Customer	Project number
C	Project	Site	Project manager/engineer
			Position at

1 Code	2 Section	3 Original estimated cost £	4 Authorised variations to contract £	5 Latest allowed cost columns 3+4 £	6 Expenditure and commitments to £	7 Estimated to complete £	8 Predicted final cost columns 6+7 £	9 Estimated under/over-expenditure columns 5–8 £
02	Material handling							
03	Technical							
05	Plant							
06	Building and civil engineering							
07	Site construction							
08	Electrical							
09	Instruments							
10	Services							
	GENERAL—Staff time							
	Travel expenses							
	Miscellaneous							
	SUB-TOTALS							
	Contingency							
	TOTALS							

Notes:

Figure 17:2 The cost control report. This report is normally issued monthly. Column 6 will vary each month and hence column 7, which becomes at this stage the arithmetical difference between columns 8 and 6.

commitment was unavoidable, the bankruptcy of the company could be the end result. These possible consequences *must* be appreciated—overrun is always serious and can be catastrophic.

It may be more economical to stop a project and resume at a later date than continue. To make a realistic appraisal of the situation, a sound valuation of the project at the stage then reached *must* be available. If the cost control systems described here have been implemented, such data will be immediately to hand.

The last point to be mentioned, with regard to the role of the control estimate, is the facility which it offers to check on tenders submitted by potential suppliers and contractors. Whilst competitive tenders can usually be secured, and comparison of these tenders is a basic means of ensuring value for money, equitable bargains are essential to the successful completion of projects of the nature under discussion. A one-sided bargain always leads to trouble. Whilst, at the commencement of the negotiations, the one-sidedness may not be apparent, it always becomes apparent as the work progresses, creating dissatisfaction and resentment. The availability of a relatively disinterested assessment of the cost of the proposed order is, therefore, valuable and is an essential part of proper bid analysis. (see Figure 9:2)

Programming the Project

So far, consideration has been given, primarily, to the *money* aspect of cost control, but as mentioned previously, time *is* money. This means that consideration must also be given to the review of time in relation to the project. Programming is project time review and is an integral part of project planning. Planning is the managerial process of deciding the way in which the project should be implemented. The subsequent programme reflects the planning decisions and forms the basis of physical progress reviews.

Project Planning

In the many and diverse activities involved in the design, engineering, and construction, of a typical production facility, the critical path technique is a powerful management tool. It integrates certain relevant factors, such as materials deliveries, with the passing of time, and allows the planning engineer to develop a balanced optimum schedule relating the various events that will occur as the project is built. The critical path technique is so widely known and accepted that it no longer seems to need justification, but its value for a particular project should always be assessed. The technique differs from the simpler approach in two fundamentals:

1 It separates planning from scheduling

Planning consists of determining what events must occur, and in what order. Scheduling translates those events into a list with a timetable

2 Time and cost can be directly related

This means that once an activity has been valued, the direct cost of moving it can be established.

A typical critical path diagram has been presented in Chapter 2 (Figure 2:3). It is not the intention to elaborate on the techniques of critical path scheduling, but the principle needs to be well understood. This is, that the diagram establishes the precedence relationship between the various elements of the project, and so provides:

1 A disciplined approach to the project
2 A clear picture of the total scope
3 A method of evaluating objectives
4 A means of preventing the omission of work that is an essential part of the project
5 An aid in planning the project

Once the diagram has been developed, the critical elements in the project can be seen and given particular attention. It has to be remembered that the timing presented is usually on an optimum basis. It is always possible to depart from this optimum and so shorten the time taken, at a cost.

In the example given in Figure 2:3, the critical activities have been identified and it will be seen that these particular activities have only one start and finish time. This means that any delay along this path will delay completion of the total project. The critical path is, therefore, the longest (in time) connected sequence of events throughout the life of the project.

The introduction of this particular planning technique has established a vocabulary which is not necessarily clearly understood by those not in regular contact with this particular approach. The term 'critical path' is one of these, but probably, readily understood.

Another term also in constant use is 'float' and perhaps this might require some explanation. Float is the amount of time by which the particular activity can be delayed without affecting the overall completion of the project. There are three different types of float, namely:

1 Total float. This is the spare time available when *all* the preceeding activities occur at the earliest possible time, and all later activities occur at the latest possible time.
2 Free float. This is the spare time available when all the preceeding activities start at the earliest possible time and all the later activities also begin at the earliest possible time.
3 Independent float. This is the spare time available when all the preceeding activities occur at the latest possible time, and all the succeeding activities occur at the earliest possible times.

The whole purpose of the exercise, which must never be forgotten, is to assist the project engineer in his control of the project. Only then does planning contribute to cost control. The benefit is that the project engineer can concentrate his efforts on the actual jobs in hand, with the assurance that he knows the critical activities and has full knowledge of the effects in time of the actions it might be proposed to take. This is the measure of the value of the exercise, not the detail in the diagram.

Problems

The introduction of the critical path technique brings problems which sometimes lead to a reluctance to use it. The technique has certain implications, namely:

1 Failures are emphasised
2 It demands rigourous scheduling
3 Inadequacies are disclosed

Failures in project planning are seen in all their foolishness, whilst inadequacies in methods, management skills, supervisory control, manpower balance, equipment selection, choice of supplier, are all highlighted in their turn. As a result, the use of the technique brings a certain discipline which is very desirable, although sometimes accepted with reluctance. But, it is still true that the technique is no panacea, and remains only as good as the effort which is put into it.

18

Use of the Computer

There is no doubt that the automatic processing of data is here to stay and will play an ever-increasing part in management activities. Cost control is just one area where, when used properly, real advantages may be gained. It is no longer necessary to 'own' a computer in order to enjoy its facilities, and the use of data terminals, coupled to a central computer, via the telephone network, will undoubtedly grow. This means that the smaller manufacturing units will increasingly find such facilities both valuable, and economic, in use. But the relationship between the project group and the computer must be clearly understood. Simply expressed, it is the relationship between man and machine. The project group has resources completely lacking in a computer, namely:

1 Initiative
2 Originality and creative ability
3 Judgement

By contrast, the capabilities and facilities inherent in a digital computer are:

1 Rapidity
2 Accuracy
3 Memory capacity (for storage and processing)
4 Reliability
5 Data reproduction

The objective of the project group, therefore, is to delegate to the computer those tasks which the computer can perform better than the group. It is very necessary for this relationship to be appreciated and the myth and fantasy which still seems to surround computers stripped away. Because a machine has capabilities whereby it appears, very nearly, to think does not constitute proof that it does in fact think. It is still a mechanism, designed and built by someone who *can* think and has built into the machine the implications of his thinking. This demonstrates a further objective of the projects group in relation to the computer—to make the machine process data in appropriate fashion. It is, therefore, essential that the systems adopted (reflected in the 'software', or program) are designed by people who know and understand the problems. Only then, will the computer be an effective management tool.

Speed of Response

An outstanding characteristic of the computer is its speed of response. Once data has been fed in, the answers to problems can be obtained almost instantaneously. It is possible to arrange for a continuous flow of data to the computer, resulting in a continuous flow of answers back from the computer. The computer is then operating in *real time* and information can be had by 'pressing a button'. But for the purposes of cost control, such an approach is completely unnecessary, and to the extent that such facilities obviously cost more money, the additional expense is not wholly justified. Truly, cost control information must be available—must be readily available, but only in relation to time cycles appropriate to the context. The normal time cycle in relation to project management is one month, and things rarely happen so fast that even fortnightly reporting is an urgent necessity. Information, particularly from the construction site itself, is almost invariably marshalled on a weekly basis, but it is quite acceptable to consolidate such data on a monthly basis for reporting purposes. The usual practice, where daily access to the computer is available, is to feed input data on a daily basis, but call for reports either weekly or monthly, as may be appropriate in the circumstances. The prime consideration governing timing in this context is the volume of the work. The larger the volume, the more necessary it becomes to have weekly, as opposed to monthly reporting in certain areas. This can be illustrated by comparing the commitment record with the erection labour record. Even on major projects, orders are rarely placed at such a rate that monthly reporting is not adequate for the purposes of control or commitments placed. On the other hand, the labour force on site on a major project will be such that a weekly report of hours worked on site will be essential to properly appraise progress.

The speed of response in relation to data presented by the computer is especially valuable once its resources are really brought to bear upon project control. It is not merely a glorified adding machine—it can also sort, summarise and compare. These facilities make it possible to prepare *summaries* and *exception reports*, which highlight for management the specific areas where consideration is necessary, as a prelude to possible action.

Computer Returns

What are the possible reports from a computer, relevant to project cost control? The reporting facilities available can be summarised as:

1 Reports on the present situation
2 Exception reports, stating the deviation, if any, from the present situation.
3 Forecasts of the future situation, based on the present situation.
4 Exception reports, stating the deviation, if any, of the forecast made in 3 above from the predicted future situation. The term 'predicted' in this context is equivalent to 'planned'.

Action is expected to be the direct consequence of exception reports. The action will be designed, in the first instance, to correct the situations seen, in order to bring events back into line with the plan, or programme. Where this is not possible, the plan itself will require revision. Once the plan has been revised, then the exception reports will be made against the new plan. There is no merit at all in making comparisons with something known to be unreliable, or impractical. Plans, or targets, are only of value if they are realistic. Reports on the present situation are generally referred to as 'status reports' and a typical example of a status report in relation to current projects is shown in Figure 18:1.

The report shown in Figure 18:1 lists all 'current' projects and gives immediately relevant data on such projects. A current project is a project still in progress, and not yet physically completed. Once a project has been physically completed, it would be deleted from such a list. The departments involved on each project are listed, together with

CURRENT PROJECTS

PROJ.NO	DESCRIPTION	DEPARTMENTS INVOLVED						D.S.D	P.C.D
10062			B & CE	CONST	ELECT			08/67	11/69
10084		PLANT	B & CE	CONST	ELECT	INSTR	SERV	06/67	12/69
10107			B & CE		ELECT		SERV	07/67	10/69
10123		PLANT			ELECT	INSTR	SERV	02/67	10/69
10130		PLANT	B & CE		ELECT			03/68	12/69
10158		PLANT	B & CE	CONST	ELECT	INSTR	SERV	11/67	12/69
10235			B & CE	CONST	ELECT	INSTR	SERV	10/67	10/69
10298			B & CE	CONST	ELECT	INSTR	SERV	01/68	01/70
10300		PLANT	B & CE	CONST	ELECT	INSTR	SERV	12/67	01/70
10320			B & CE	CONST	ELECT	INSTR	SERV	08/68	10/69
10328		PLANT	B & CE	CONST	ELECT	INSTR	SERV	11/68	11/70
10330			B & CE	CONST	ELECT	INSTR		03/68	12/69
10333					ELECT			04/68	12/69
10334					ELECT			01/68	11/69
10338		PLANT	B & CE	CONST	ELECT	INSTR	SERV	05/68	04/70
10342		PLANT	B & CE		ELECT	INSTR	SERV	03/68	12/69
10358		PLANT	B & CE	CONST	ELECT	INSTR	SERV	04/68	01/70
10368			B & CE	CONST	ELECT		SERV	06/68	01/70
10378		PLANT	B & CE	CONST	ELECT	INSTR	SERV	07/68	12/69
10388		PLANT	B & CE	CONST	ELECT	INSTR	SERV	08/69	10/70
10394			B & CE		ELECT	INSTR	SERV	04/68	11/69
10397		PLANT	B & CE	CONST	ELECT	INSTR	SERV	07/68	01/70
10403			B & CE	CONST	ELECT			10/68	10/69
10419		PLANT	B & CE	CONST	ELECT	INSTR		10/68	01/70

Figure 18:1 Status report serving as a check on current projects. 'D.S.D.' is design start date and 'P.C.D.' is physical completion date.

the start date and the estimated completion date. Reference here is to physical completion only: that is the point at which the plant is handed over, mechanically tested, for the production staff to commission. Financial completion will follow much later, when all accounts have been cleared and all retentions paid. This could easily be as much as a year later in certain circumstances.

Another type of status report is that illustrated by Figure 18:2. This reports on commitments and introduces comparison between the commitments actually being incurred and the various estimates which have been made of these commitments. From this report it is possible to compare the total commitment which has been incurred to date (shown as 'cumulative') with the latest prediction of the total commitment (shown as 'adjusted'). As a matter of interest, the initial estimate, which would have served as a basis for approval of the project, is also shown, and described as the 'target'. It is usual to adjust this target for authorised variations to the original scheme as approved.

A third type of status report is shown by Figure 18:3. Here a look is being taken into the future, but it is still *status* which is being reported upon. This is a summary report and the outstanding work in the organisation is analysed by departments and spread over time in accordance with the appropriate S-curves (see Figure 16:2) which have been incorporated into the computer program. Knowledge of the existing staff levels (or available staff) would enable some appraisal to be made of the significance of this report. It is a very necessary document and becomes a basis for action if used in conjunction with other information of the type just mentioned.

Exception reports

As has been implied, a status report is all very well, but study of such a report will show that it is not particularly helpful unless it is referred in some way to the plan. Here the exception report has a role to play. Exception reports can take a variety of forms, typical of which are:

1 Projects overspent
2 Projects ahead or lagging in cost compared with the forecast
3 Projects due for completion
4 Projects which have overrun duration

A typical exception report is presented in Figure 18:4. The forecast having been made, as summarised in Figure 18:3, it becomes possible to

REPORT FOR 1 WEEK(S) ENDING 07 FEB
(COMMITMENT)

		1 6/0	2	3 TECH	5 PLANT	6 B&CE	7 CONST	8 ELECT	9 INSTR	10 SERV	COST TOTALS
EXTND SPARES	FACTORY										
10610 00 00	TARGET		18025		129000	1033410		298000	5000	328000	1811435
	WEEK										
	PERIOD										
	CUMULATIVE		53			1033410		60147		51353	1144963
	ADJEST		18025		129000	1033410		298000	5000	328000	1811435
SPRINKLER INSTALL'N											
10613 00 00	TARGET					16690				28125	44815
	WEEK										
	PERIOD										
	CUMULATIVE										
	ADJEST					16690				28125	44815
W/HSE EXT & LOAD BAY.											
10615 00 00	TARGET					11100					11100
	WEEK										
	PERIOD										
	CUMULATIVE					10600					10600
	ADJEST					11100					11100
FNDTN WRK. EFFLUENT PLT.											
10616 00 00	TARGET					35820					35820
	WEEK										
	PERIOD										
	CUMULATIVE					33320		163			33483
	ADJEST					35620					35820
4 LINE MOULD PLANT											
10617 00 00	TARGET	352432	31330		36285			46400	87038		553455
	WEEK	3007							1342		4349
	PERIOD	3007							1342		4349
	***CUMULATIVE	328920	7244		137			42456	80292		459049
	ADJEST	352432	31330		30285			46400	87036		553485

Figure 18:2 Status report on commitments. This is one page of a computer print-out, summarising commitments placed on a series of projects by departments. The movement in the period is shown, and the totals (cumulative) compared both with the orginal estimate (the budget) and the latest estimate (adjusted).

DEPARTMENTAL WORKLOAD FORECAST

CURRENT PROJECTS FINAL TOTALS AS AT 1.07.70 Q = CONVERSION RATE (HRS/MAN MONTHS)

	5		6		7		8		9		10			
	PLANT		B & CE		CONST		ELECT		INSTR		SERV		TOTALS	
	Q=135		Q=125		Q=175		Q=120		Q=130		Q=127		TOTALS	
MONTH	HOURS	STAFF	HOURS	STAFF	HOURS	STAFF	HOURS	STAFF	HOURS	STAFF	HOURS	STAFF	HOURS	STAFF
07/70	2944	22	10032	87	7214	45	3074	33	2064	16	4340	35	31688	238
08/70	2090	22	8312	67	7068	41	3615	31	1574	13	3736	30	27201	204
09/70	2623	22	6050	55	5647	33	3185	27	1562	13	3295	26	23162	174
10/70	2519	19	5913	46	5445	32	2996	25	1547	12	3039	24	21459	160
11/70	2443	14	5623	41	5158	30	2714	23	1504	12	2593	21	19435	146
12/70	2246	19	4475	38	4963	29	2343	20	1030	8	2344	19	17341	129
01/71	1874	14	2761	23	3431	20	1730	15	859	7	1648	13	12303	92
02/71	1380	11	2160	17	1979	12	1289	11	615	5	1502	12	8865	68
03/71	1381	11	2024	17	2476	15	1279	11	591	5	1426	12	9171	71
04/71	1156	9	1373	11	1703	10	840	7	531	5	929	8	6532	50
05/71	1104	9	1369	11	1131	7	739	7	534	5	718	6	5595	45
06/71	919	7	1089	9	781	5	591	5	382	3	518	5	4260	34
07/71	919	7	871	7	551	4	463	4	349	3	270	3	3423	28
08/71	921	7	112	1	467	3	112	1	350	3	66	1	2028	16
REMDR	0		0	0	9369	54	0	0	0	0	0	0	9369	54
TOTAL	25325	188	53084	425	57917	331	25770	215	13492	104	26424	209	202012	1472

Figure 18:3 Forecast of outstanding work, analysed by departments, and spread over time in accordance with a pre-arranged programme.

PROJECTS WHOSE RATE OF PROGRESS SIGNIFICANTLY DIFFERENT FROM STANDARD

PROJ. NO	DESCRIPTION			
10062	ELECT	SIGNIFICANTLY ABOVE	STANDARD.	83 PER CENT TIME FLAPSED
10084	CONST	SIGNIFICANTLY ABOVE	STANDARD.	83 PER CENT TIME FLAPSED
10084	ELECT	SIGNIFICANTLY ABOVE	STANDARD.	83 PER CENT TIME FLAPSED
10084	INSTR	SIGNIFICANTLY ABOVE	STANDARD.	83 PER CENT TIME FLAPSED
10084	SERV	SIGNIFICANTLY ABOVE	STANDARD.	83 PER CENT TIME FLAPSED
10158	CONST	SIGNIFICANTLY ABOVE	STANDARD.	83 PER CENT TIME FLAPSED
10158	SERV	SIGNIFICANTLY ABOVE	STANDARD.	83 PER CENT TIME FLAPSED
10235	B & CE	SIGNIFICANTLY ABOVE	STANDARD.	83 PER CENT TIME FLAPSED
10235	CONST	SIGNIFICANTLY ABOVE	STANDARD.	89 PER CENT TIME FLAPSED
10298	B & CE	SIGNIFICANTLY BELOW	STANDARD.	79 PER CENT TIME FLAPSED
10320	CONST	SIGNIFICANTLY ABOVE	STANDARD.	94 PER CENT TIME FLAPSED
10320	ELECT	SIGNIFICANTLY ABOVE	STANDARD.	94 PER CENT TIME FLAPSED
10328	PLANT	SIGNIFICANTLY ABOVE	STANDARD.	44 PER CENT TIME FLAPSED
10328	B & CE	SIGNIFICANTLY ABOVE	STANDARD.	44 PER CENT TIME FLAPSED
10328	INSTR	SIGNIFICANTLY ABOVE	STANDARD.	44 PER CENT TIME FLAPSED
10330	B & CE	SIGNIFICANTLY BELOW	STANDARD.	84 PER CENT TIME FLAPSED
10330	CONST	SINGIFICANTLY BELOW	STANDARD.	84 PER CENT TIME FLAPSED
10330	ELECT	SIGNIFICANTLY BELOW	STANDARD.	84 PER CENT TIME FLAPSED
10330	INSTR	SIGNIFICANTLY BELOW	STANDARD.	84 PER CENT TIME FLAPSED
10338	PLANT	SIGNIFICANTLY ABOVE	STANDARD.	67 PER CENT TIME FLAPSED
10338	SERV	SIGNIFICANTLY ABOVE	STANDARD.	67 PER CENT TIME FLAPSED
10358	PLANT	SIGNIFICANTLY ABOVE	STANDARD.	80 PER CENT TIME FLAPSED
10358	INSTR	SIGNIFICANTLY ABOVE	STANDARD.	80 PER CENT TIME FLAPSED
10368	B & CE	SIGNIFICANTLY BELOW	STANDARD.	78 PER CENT TIME FLAPSED
10368	CONST	SIGNIFICENTLY ABOVE	STANDARD.	78 PER CENT TIME FLAPSED
10368	SERV	SIGNIFICANTLY BELOW	STANDARD.	78 PER CENT TIME FLAPSED

Figure 18:4 Exception report (project progress)

compare progress, project by project, with that forecast. If the result of the comparison shows a deviation from the forecast, then that is a matter for report. In order to limit the number of projects that will be the subject of report, it is sensible to set certain limits between which deviation is considered to be insignificant in relation to the nature and accuracy of the data involved.

It has to be remembered that the concept, assumed to have been adopted in the computer program for ease of application, is that of *standardised* S-curves, rather than S-curves which are specific to the particular project. A degree of tolerance must therefore be allowed—plus or minus 15 per cent is sensible in this context. Significant variations, therefore, as enumerated on the print-out, given as in Figure 18:4, are therefore variations *outside* this previously established limit. It will also be noticed that the time which has elapsed from the start date is also given for each project, as well as the progress related to the standard set. This is very relevant. The data becomes significant over the period from 30 to 75 per cent of the life of the project, since it is here that effective action can be taken. It has to be remembered that a report of this nature is an indication that action *may* have to be taken: not that action *must* be taken. A case for investigation has been made: no more. The variation from the standard may be quite acceptable for the specific project.

There is also the possibility that the deviations from the standard are due to poor data rather than poor progress on the project. For instance, if the report shows that the placing of the commitments is significantly below standard it may be that design is delayed and hence, orders cannot be placed when they should be. It could however be that the total cost of commitments is grossly over-estimated, so that comparison is being made with an over-stated target. These comments make it apparent that the first step to be taken, following upon the report, is to investigate, in order to determine whether action is, in fact, appropriate. The investigation will also disclose the nature of the action that should be taken, if any.

Another type of exception report is that shown by Figure 18:5. The computer can be programmed to list all projects due for completion two or three months ahead. This is still an exception report, since it is a selective list developed on the basis of one specific characteristic in the project, and its relationship to a standard. The standard here is the point in time when the report is made. A list of this nature is very valuable for overall project control, where a number of projects are in hand at the same time. Here *movement* can also be of both interest and significance. The number of projects on such a list can be an indicator

PROJECTS DUE FOR PHYSICAL COMPLETION IN 2 MONTHS

PROJ.NO	DESCRIPTION
10613	SPRINKLER INSTALL/N
10662	SITE DEV.
10682	YARN WAREHOUSE
10686	MODS. TO SRVC. RQRMNTS
10721	UNIT 7 CONVERSION
10744	CHIP BLENDING SILO
10773	GENERAL FACILITIES
10788	STEAM TRAPS

Figure 18:5 *Report on projects due for physical completion in two months.*

of the way in which the volume of work is varying from month to month.

Management Information

Consideration must be given, first of all, to the objective of providing management with information. The primary objective of management is to establish policy and make decisions within that policy framework that will conform to the agreed policy. Hence, the purpose of management information is to assist and promote the taking of decisions, either to establish policy or to implement it. In the specific context now being dealt with—project cost control—it has been seen that cost control is, in effect, the making of a series of decisions. The project is to be considered, for the sake of illustration, to be the responsibility of a project team within a manufacturing organisation. The team will, therefore, require information to assist their decisions in relation to their prime objective which is to build the project as defined for the estimated cost, within the estimated time. The project team is, therefore, the first level of management and the various members of the team may require different information to enable them to perform the functions allotted, relative to the administration of the project as a whole.

The project team itself is carrying out an assignment at the behest of *its* management. This is the second level of management. At that level, a decision was made to build on the basis of certain data presented to it. (See Chapter 5—The Report to the Board) The project team, therefore, have to report to this second level of management and its report will have to have relevance, to the decision made at that level and, with the reasons for which it was made. From time to time a great deal of criticism is levelled at management information systems and, indirectly, at managers, since they are responsible for the systems they use. Almost every seminar on management these days includes a quotation from an article by R.L. Ackoff (*Management Science* 14 No. 4, Dec. 1967) entitled 'Management Information Systems', in which five common erroneous assumptions on management information systems were highlighted, namely:

1 The critical deficiency under which most managers operate is the lack of relevant information
2 The manager needs the information he wants
3 If a manager has the information he needs his decision making will improve

4 Better communication between managers improves organisational performance
5 A manager does not have to understand how his information system works, only how to use it

Recognition of these potential failings in management should lead to the development of a positive approach. This positive approach lies in establishing the basic principles relating to management information and then applying these principles to the specific situation, the project team, its duties and responsibilities.

The basic principles that must be considered in relation to the provision of information to management may be summarised as:

1 Need
2 Usage
3 Simplicity
4 Consistency and accuracy
5 Speed of response
6 Presentation

First and foremost, the need has to be established and it will be seen from Ackoff's comments that those using the information cannot be relied upon to establish the need. The best indication of need is usage: the use made of the information provided. But here caution should be exercised; it could be that the information is not used because, although relevant and needed, it is presented in a form which makes it unintelligible. So the third principle is also integral in this consideration. Simplicity and clarity of presentation is essential. The remaining three principles relate to the information itself. It must be both consistent and accurate. If it is not, and the recipient discerns an error, or gets two different statements from two different sources about the same thing, the information is returned, with a request for clarification.

With regard to the particular purpose for which the information is being provided, the discrepancy might be irrelevant or unimportant, but the question will still be asked. Why? Because this is a 'management' device to escape decision. Although the prime function of managers is to make decisions, most managers seem to display a curious reluctance to do so. Part of the function of those providing management with information is, therefore, to minimise the opportunity for deferring a decision. For effective cost control, prompt and early decisions are vital—delay in making decisions once the appropriate information is available will only cost money.

The purpose of management information, therefore, is to assist and promote the formulation of decisions. This leads to the speed of response. How soon after the events depicted should information be available? The computer, in a certain context, offers an instantaneous response by providing instant data at the press of a button. This instant availability at the end of a telephone line is referred to as *real time.* But what is 'real time'? Consideration ought to be given to the difference between instantaneous availability and relevant availability—there is a difference. In the specific context of project cost control it is common, and normally adequate, to operate on a monthly cycle and this matches accounting procedures quite conveniently. Rarely do events move so fast that even a fortnightly appraisal is really justified. On a large project the preparation of the reports, when done manually, can take up to three weeks, and this means an overall lag of up to five weeks in relation to the events portrayed. Use of computer techniques can make the data available a few days after the end of the period, and this is a very material and significant improvement. It brings the information very close to the event.

Accepting, then, that the use of computer techniques has value where, either the size of the project or, the number of projects to be controlled at any one time provide a basis for justification, the final point to be considered is 'presentation'. The data must be presented to management in 'usable' form. The computer fan-fold print-out looks very impressive, but nothing is more exasperating than to have such a bundle of paper cascade on to the floor. Reforming can be quite a chore.

Management Reports

Consideration has now to be given both to the nature of the information to be provided and the degree of detail it is necessary to provide in reporting procedures of this nature. There are two basic rules in this context:

1 That the same information is not provided twice
2 That if detailed information is provided, then summarised information, or abstracted information will not be provided as well, even if such summarised or abstracted information, is being prepared for others

A typical reporting system is illustrated in Figure 18:6, as applied to an organisation set up for the implementation of capital works projects in

	Review estimates	Review estimates summary	Cost control reports on projects	Cost control summary: departments	Staff time return	Workload re-forecast	Project sales report	Projects over £250,000: summary	Financial closure statement
Chairman	—	x	—	—	—	x	—	x	—
Managing Director	—	x	—	—	—	x	—	x	—
Projects Director	x	x	—	x	—	x	x	x	x
Financial Director	—	x	—	—	—	x	x	x	x
Heads of departments	—	—	—	x	x	x	—	—	—
Project manager/engineer	x	—	x	—	—	—	—	—	—
Company accountant.	—	—	—	—	—	x	x	—	—

Figure 18:6 Management reports—distribution.

relation to a group of companies. In a smaller organisation, where the project team requires the information, the reporting would be more limited, but it should still have the same general characteristics.

Conclusion

Underlying the approach to project cost control that has now been presented, is the continuing need for estimates. Estimating and cost control have been linked closely together and good estimating is fundamental to good cost control. There are some who say that estimates are not required to control costs, but this is a delusion. Without a standard—and the estimate provides the standard of reference—no-one will ever know whether the cost control was effective or not.

The distinction between estimating and cost control has also to be clearly seen. Estimating involves appraisal and the expression of opinions on probable costs, whilst control involves management and the appraisal of results. But if control is limited to checking results against estimates, then once again it is not really control. It is only an accounting procedure, the comparision of actuals with the budget. Effective cost control has to go well beyond this.

Another aspect which should by now have become apparent, is that neither estimating nor cost control are exact sciences. The techniques can be highly sophisticated and many detailed calculations made, but personal judgement remains a vital ingredient throughout.

The whole activity of cost control can be compared to painting a picture. The project engineer, the design engineers, the purchasing and construction personnel are the ones who actually paint the picture, or achieve the result. The estimating engineers, the cost control engineers and the accountants only provide the frame which enables the picture to be seen clearly. So then, if the project engineer and his team do not think and practise cost control, then costs will not be controlled, however elegant the frame. However sophisticated the cost control techniques are, that is, and regardless of the number of cost control engineers employed.

The next point which has to be clearly seen, is that the picture has been drawn in outline, and its size set, at a very early stage in the project. This occurs sometimes long before any detailed estimates are made and long before the cost control engineer starts his work. In other words, it is often the basic engineering concepts which determine the ultimate cost of a project, and good basic engineering, supported by attention to detail as the design develops, is the secret of the successful control of costs.

Problems

Discussions on project cost control are often fruitless because all that is actually discussed are the various problems that have been encountered on the project. But these problems, burdensome though they may have been to the project engineer, have little or nothing to do with cost control. To take an example, a strike could occur in a basic industry such as steel manufacturing, which would affect all the suppliers to a particular project, delaying completion and causing costs to escalate. Management would be concerned at the increases in cost but, nevertheless, the project staff could have done an excellent job so far as cost control was concerned. The project engineer and his staff should not be criticised, or allow themselves to be criticised, for not controlling costs when the real fault lies elsewhere. One merit of a good system of cost control would be that the project team could defend themselves by pinpointing the increase in cost due to causes outside their control.

On the other hand, an underrun is not necessarily a cause for pride. An underrun can give a great deal of satisfaction to both management and the project team, but the cost control could still have been extremely inefficient. Better control would have resulted in even greater savings.

All this leads to the conclusion that the basis for appraisal is the estimate. For better or worse, it becomes the standard of comparison from the moment that it has been made and accepted. But any estimate is no better than the project information that was made available when the estimate was prepared. Often the cost of the project is compared with the original estimate and conclusions drawn, when, in effect, the final cost cannot be directly related to the original estimate. This is not because of changes in scope. These are usually seen, recognised and evaluated.

The difference actually lies in the changes that take place *within* the scope as described, because that description lacked definition. In addition, over the life of the project, conditions change. Deliveries are late, the weather does not perform to pattern, the results of strikes have to be offset. Cost control cannot stop or alter the differences in scope definition that occur or the changing conditions over the life of the project. But what it *can* do is to monitor, evaluate and record them. If this work is carried out patiently and accurately, then the combined estimating and cost control facility becomes a valuable tool for the project engineer. It enables him to establish an economical design, to set proper budgets and guide the project to a successful completion.

The estimator highlights the areas of importance from a cost point of view, whilst the cost control engineer analyses the potential and actual costs to date and indicates the trend. But none of these activities is truly control. Control is the result of the technical decisions that are taken by the project engineer, or under his guidance.

All the aspects of the financial control of projects have now been concluded but, the real *conclusion* is the completed plant, built within the budget and making a profit. This is the objective to which one, and all, should be striving. If that end result is, in fact, achieved, it should not be seen as a matter for pride. Rather should it have been a humbling experience. So much could have gone wrong, and did not. Many things did go wrong, largely due to ignorance, but sometimes due to bad luck. The end result would never have been achieved but for the co-operation of the foreman, the tradesmen and the labourers. All played their part.

APPENDICES

A

Numbering System for the Administration and Control of Engineering Projects

A *Reference system for the departments responsible for initiating the requisition for materials or work:*

01 Bought out design work
02 Materials handling
03 Technical development
04 Project management
05 Plant and equipment (mechanical)
06 Building and civil engineering
07 Construction (site)
08 Electrical
09 Instrumentation
10 Services

B *Numbering for sub-groups:*

10 Building and civil engineering works (general)
11 Site preparation and development
12 Roads and railways
13 Piling
14 Foundations and concrete sub-structures
15 Buildings
16 Steel structures
17 Storm and water drainage

18	Effluent drainage
19	Arboricultural works
20	Columns
21	Unfired heat transfer equipment
22	Tanks and vessels, mild steel
23	Tanks and vessels, alloy, non-ferrous
24	Tanks and vessels, lined
25	General plant and equipment
26	Pumps, compressors, fans, blowers
27	Mixers, stirrers, agitators
28	Site erection of plant and equipment
29	Fixed inventory (workshops, etc.)
30	Process pipe and fittings
31/32	Unused
33	Offsite fabrication (process pipe and fittings)
34	Process valves
35/37	Unused
38	Site erection of process pipework and valves
39	Site erection, general
40	Electrical equipment (general)
41	Unused
42	Transformers
43	Switchgear, starters, controllers
44	Power wiring
45	Lighting systems
46	Motors
47	Instrument wiring
48	Site erection of electrical equipment and cabling
49	Unused
50	Instruments (general)
51	Control Valves (instrumentation)
52	Instrument installation materials
53	Site erection of instrumentation
54/55	Unused
56	Services pipes and fittings (supply only)
57	Services valves
58	Offsite fabrication of services pipework
59	Site erection, services pipework
60	Compressed air service equipment
61	Instrument air service equipment
62	Vacuum services equipment
63	General services plant and equipment

64	Sprinklers, hydrant systems, etc.
65	Water treatment and purification equipment
66	Cooling towers
67	Fired steam generators
68	Electrical generating equipment
69	Air conditioning and heating installations
70	Refrigeration plants
71/74	Unused
75	Acid and effluent services
76	External insulation
77	Painting
78	Yarn manufacturing and processing machinery
79	Spinnerettes
80	Laboratory requisites and apparatus
81	Miscellaneous fire fighting and safety equipment
82	Fasteners
83/86	Unused
87	Catalysts and chemicals (initial supply)
88	Initial maintenance spare parts
89	Miscellaneous supplies
90	Unused
91	Remedial site work
92	Rectification work (maintenance period)
93	Travelling expenses
94	F.O.B. costs
95	Materials (bulk orders)
96	Packing and miscellaneous costs
97	Carriage
98	Unused
99	Revenue items

C *Numbering for plant areas:*

00	Use when no plant areas have been allocated
01/99	For allocation of plant areas as required

B

Description of Sub-Groups for Engineering Projects

Civil Engineering

10 *Building and Civil Engineering Works*

The costs, including materials, labour, supervision, preliminaries and similar expenses (including contractors overheads and profit) for the construction of building and civil engineering works, as described in detail under sub-group 11-19.

11 *Site Preparation and Development, including Fencing*

The cost of developing the site, including levelling, removal and supply of soil, soil investigations, reclamation of land, dredging and fencing, with gates and the like.

12 *Roads and Railways*

Roads (including trenching, cleaning, scrubbing, scraping and topping), dykes, railroads, bridges, parking places.

13 *Piling*

Piling for foundations, tanks, retaining walls, channels, including sheet piling, including the provision of all the necessary pile driving equipment and piles (but not pile-capping).

14 *Foundations and Concrete Sub-Structures*

Foundations, pump blocks, footings, supports, sleepers, ground floors, pipe trenches, cable trenches, sumps, oil catchers (including skimming devices, but excluding pumps, drives and pipelines): paving, gutters, trench covers, curbs, angles, including excavation, backfill, gravel, sand, cement, timber, reinforcing rod and fabric, trench covers and the like embedded in concrete.

15 *Buildings (above DPC Level)*

Concrete, brick, masonry and steel framed buildings, houses, main offices, churches, clubs, schools, hospitals, clinics, gate houses, fire stations, canteens, control houses, switch houses, pump houses, including natural ventilating systems, windows, doors, gutters, down pipes, sanitary equipment and plumbing, and chimneys in these materials.

16 *Steel Structures*

All steel structures other than those forming part of a building, for the support of, or access to columns, vessels, and other plant and equipment, including pipebridges, supports, masts, platforms, railings, staircases, grating, hoisting beams, (travelling cranes, hoist blocks are included in sub-group 25).

17 *Storm and Water Drainage*

Storm and water drainage system for the discharge of rain water, domestic water and other waste water (other than chemical effluents), excluding purely mechanical work such as steel pipelines, pumps, including gutters, sumps, channels, trenches, weirs, culverts.

18 *Effluent Drainage*

Chemical and other process effluent drainage systems, including separating, purification, clarification and filtering equipment, with gutters, sumps, channels, trenches.

19 *Arboricultural Works*

Architectural and aesthetic treatment of site, with landscaping, provision of trees, shrubberies, grass areas and the like.

Mechanical Engineering

20 *Columns*

Strippers, absorbers, fractionators, scrubbers, evaporator columns, extraction columns, including all internals, manhole covers, davits, linings, trays, bubble caps, raschig rings and anchor bolts.

21 *Unfired Heat Transfer Equipment*

Reboilers, coolers, condensers, heat exchangers, chillers, scraper type exchangers (including drives), condenser and cooling boxes (including coils and supports) barometric condensers (including ejectors), evaporators, suction heaters, preheaters, and waste heat boilers, including all accessories such as gaskets, bolts, linings, test rings.

22 *Tanks and Vessels, MS*

Vessels operating at atmospheric pressure and those operating above or below atmospheric pressure, with all internals such as blades, partitions, heating or cooling coils and jackets, fabricated from mild steel materials (including nickel steels for low temperature applications).

23 *Tanks and Vessels, Alloy*

Vessels operating at atmospheric pressure and those operating above or below atmospheric pressure, with all internals, such as blades, partitions, heating or cooling coils and jackets, fabricated from alloy steels and non-ferrous metals, and synthetic materials such as glass, celmar, keebush and the like.

24 *Tanks and Vessels Lined*

Vessels operating at atmospheric pressure and those operated above or below atmospheric pressure, with all internals, such as blades, partitions, heating or cooling coils and jackets, fabricated from steel and lined (for example with rubber, pentaphane, glass, teflon or special paints).

25 *General Plant and Equipment*

Furnaces, heaters, ovens, kilns, incinerators, including related stacks, flues, ducting, tubes, air heaters, induced and forced draught fans (including drives), soot blowers, burners, vacuum filters, filter presses, centrifuges, cyclones, extruders, mills, kneaders, driers, screens, crystallisers. Mechanical handling equipment, including equipment for the transport of materials or personnel, including elevators, conveyors, hoisting and lifting equipment, stackers and lift trucks, trucks, tractors and trailers; locomotives, marine small craft, miscellaneous vehicles; packing plant. Lifts are included in sub-group 40.

26 *Pumps, Compressors, Fans, Blowers*

Reciprocating, centrifugal, rotary and miscellaneous pumps, including bedplates, couplings, gearboxes, and reciprocating steam engine, turbine or electric motor drives to such pumps, when integral with pumps. Reciprocating, centrifugal, screw and other compressors, vacuum pumps, induced and forced draught fans and blowers, including bedplates, couplings, gearboxes, and reciprocating steam, gas or oil engines, turbine or electric motor drives to such units when integral with equipment. Electric motors purchased separately and delivered to the manufacturer for mounting are allocated to sub-group 46.

27 *Mixers, Stirrers, Agitators*

Mixing, stirring, agitating and scraper devices, including gearboxes and also including drive if integral with device. Electric motors purchased separately and delivered to the manufacturer for mounting are allocated to subgroup 46.

28 *Erection*

All site costs related to the erection of the plant and equipment included in sub-group 20-27, including the provision of all necessary temporary facilities, construction plant and equipment, including scaffolding required for electrical and instrumentation erection work, supervisory, skilled and unskilled labour.

Attendance by building contractor is allocated to subgroup 10.

29 *Fixed Inventory*

Portable machinery and tools for workshops and stores, consisting of small tools, pneumatic tools, welding equipment and the like, and fixed plant and machinery for mechanical, electrical, carpentry, instrument and other workshops; storage and bins; machine tools. (Note: This sub-group also includes such equipment when requisitioned in the first place for construction purposes, and retained on the project, credit being given for all such equipment ultimately returned to general construction stores.)

30 *Process Pipe and Fittings*

Screwed, welded, socketed, pipe in mild steel or alloy, or non-ferrous materials, including all linings, coatings, C.I. fittings and ductwork. Flanges, weld fittings such as tees, elbows, bends, reducers; screwed fittings, gaskets, bolts, nuts, expansion fittings; steam traps, strainers, filters, hoses, pipe support brackets.

33 *Offsite Fabrication of Pipework and Fittings*

The fabrication by a manufacturer in his shops of pipework, utilising pipe and fittings requisitioned under sub-group 30, or including the value of the pipe materials when requisitioned from the fabricator.

34 *Process Valves*

Gate, globe, check, plug, butterfly valves and dampers in mild steel, stainless steel, copper, metal and other alloys, lined valves and valves fabricated from synthetic materials.

38 *Site Erection of Pipework*

The fabrication and erection on site of the pipe, fittings, valves, is included in sub-group 30, 33 and 34.

39 *Site Erection, General*

The site erection of plant, equipment, pipework on process units. This sub-group covers the erection of all materials requisitioned under sub-group 20-27 and 30-37, but is only to be used when it is not possible to requisition separately the work covered by sub-group 28 and 38.

Electrical Engineering

40 *Electrical Equipment (General)*

Electrical equipment, materials and supplies. This sub-group number is only to be used when analysis under sub-groups 42-48 is not possible. Electrical work covered by sub-groups 42-48, which will be carried out as a sub-contract shall be requisitioned here under, although it may have been included in the estimate under the appropriate sub-group. Telecommunication, radio, special electronic equipment, lifts, fire alarm systems, low voltage circuit materials and so on can be requisitioned in this sub-group.

42 *Transformers*

Transformers, batteries, rectifiers and protective apparatus (capacitors, reactors, resistors).

43 *Switchgear, Starters and Controllers*

HV (over 650 V) switchboard, busbar chambers, isolating switches, switches (air break and oil immersed), with related metering and control devices. MV (250-650 V) switchboards, busbar chambers, isolating switches, switches (air-break or oil immersed), with related metering and control devices. Motor starters and controllers, push-button stations.

44 *Power Wiring*

HT and LT wires, cables, distribution boxes, channels, rails and racks, connectors, earthing rods, cable markers, insulation materials (tapes, liquids, compounds), insulators, poles and lightening conductors.

45 *Lighting Systems*

Lamps, lamp fittings and accessories, lighting cable and conduit, switchboard, switches, fuse, distribution and cable boxes, socket outlets.

46 *Motors*

Motors, where purchased separately, are to be requisitioned under this sub-group. Where the motor is an integral part of the equipment to which it relates, or is purchased from the supplier of the equipment, then the motor is requisitioned together with the equipment in the appropriate sub-group.

47 *Instrument Wiring*

Electric wiring to instruments and instrument panels, including all related switches, isolating, fuse, distribution, cable and sealing boxes, sockets.

48 *Site Erection of Electrical Equipment*

The site erection of electric equipment materials and supplies requisitioned under sub-groups 40-47.

Instrumentation Engineering

50 *Instruments (General)*

Instruments, including flow, level pressure and temperature instruments, analytical instruments, switches actuated by a hydraulic, pneumatic or electric impulse, pneumatic or electric relays, thermocouple assemblies, and thermocouple extension cable, instrument panels.

51 *Control Valves (Instrumentation)*

Instrumentation valves only, such as control valves (pneumatically, electrically or hydraulically operated) solenoid valves, control valves with integrally mounted controllers, air reducing valves, valve positioners, actuating cylinders.

52 *Instrument Installation Materials*

Instrument installation materials, such as name-plates, instrument air piping (including copper tubing, fittings and so on, but excluding main headers and main branches), air headers behind panels, air valves, conduit and conduit fittings for instrument cables, flexible metallic tubing, cable channels (solid or perforated), instrument pressure piping. Equipment for instrument air supply, such as instrument air compressors (including drives, coolers) air vessels, air dryers and so on are included in sub-group 61.

53 *Site Erection Instrumentation*

Installation on site of instrumentation materials as included under sub-groups 50-52 including calibration.

Services Engineering

56 *Services Pipe and Fittings (Supply Only)*

Screwed, welded, socketed, MS, CI, alloy or plastic (resin bonded and polythene, for example), pipe, including all linings and coatings: pipe fittings, pipe support brackets, expansion fittings, steam traps, strainers, filters.

57 *Services Valves*

Gate, globe, check, plug, butterfly valves and dampers in mild steel, stainless steel, copper, metal and other alloys, lined valves and valves manufactured from synthetic materials.

58 *Offsite Fabrication of Services Pipework and Fittings*

The fabrication by a manufacturer in his shops of pipework, utilising pipe and fittings requisitioned under sub-group 56, or including the value of the pipe materials when requisitioned from the fabricator.

59 *Site Erection, Services Pipework*

The fabrication and erection on site of the pipe, fittings, valves, included in sub-groups 56, 57 and 58.

60 *Service Equipment*

Plant and equipment as required for compressed air services.

61 *Service Equipment*

Instrument air compressors, air dryers and related equipment for instrument air services.

62 *Service Equipment*

Vacuum pumps and related equipment for vacuum services.

63 *Service Plant and Equipment*

Plant and equipment as required for general services, including oil storage tanks, pumps, heaters, for oil services, loading and unloading facilities and storage for nitrogen and similar gases, brine.

64 *Sprinklers, Hydrant Systems*

Sprinkler systems, hydrant and other similar piped systems for fire protection purposes, hose reels. Note: Fire doors, whilst specified as to need by the Services Department, will be requisitioned by the Building and Civil Engineering Department under sub-group 10. Miscellaneous fire fighting equipment, when ordered direct and not by the client, are to be requisitioned under sub-group 81.

65 *Water Treating and Purification Equipment*

Treaters, softeners, chlorinators, filters, screens, rotating screens (including drives).

66 *Cooling Towers*

Forced or induced draught cooling tower, including fans and drives, spraying equipment.

67 *Fired Steam Generators*

Fired steam generators, including waste heat boilers, flue gas boilers, with all auxiliary equipment and accessories, such as superheaters, desuperheaters, dampers, air heaters, induced and forced draught fans (including drives) soot blowers, flue stack (excluding those in brick, stone or cement), burners, tubes, insulation, platforms, steel structures, instrumentation, pipework, ducting, roofing, feed water deaerators, fuel handling and ash disposal plant.

68 *Electrical Generating Equipment (Turbine Driven)*

AC and DC generators including related drives and all accessories such as metering, lubricating oil installations, related HP and LP piping, circulating pumps.

69 *Air Conditioning and Heating Installation*

Air conditioning and heating installations, including plant for heating and domestic water services, ventilation fans (with drives) heaters and filters; air filters and washers, automatic louvre and shutter systems, heating and chilled water piping systems, lagging, steel structures, ducting and instrumentation. Refrigeration plant if required solely for HV & C duties.

70 *Refrigeration Plant*

Refrigeration plant units, with pumps and compressors, and including local pipework, valves and fittings, instrumentation, metering, storage equipment, anti-freeze systems, lagging, steel-structures.

75 *Acid and Effluent Services*

Acid storage and handling facilities (where not treated as part of the process plant) effluent settling and disposal systems, effluent purification and processing (both liquid and gaseous) where not treated as part of the process, or as a civil engineering work.

Preservation

76 *External Insulation*

External heat and cold insulation for columns, vessels, pipelines, pumps, tanks, heat transfer equipment (excluding oil furnaces and steam generating equipment), including all materials (wire mesh, sheet covering, scaffolding) tools for the application thereof, and installation. Include painting when carried out by the contractor responsible for insulation.

77 *Painting*

Paint, varnish, and the application thereof to plant, equipment, pipework, including the provision of any necessary scaffolding or other access facilities, where not available (painting to buildings is included in sub-groups 10 and 15).

Production Machinery

78 *Yarn Manufacturing and Processing Machinery*

Spinning machines, washing machines, drying machines for yarn manufacture, twisting, warping, coning, cheesing machines, knitting machines, weaving machines.

79 *Spinnerettes*

Spinnerettes as required to clothe the spinning machines.

Miscellaneous

80 *Laboratory Requisitions and Apparatus*

Equipment, glassware, experimental apparatus for use in laboratories.

81 *Miscellaneous Fire Fighting and Safety Equipment*

Trucks, trailers, foamite, extinguishers, crash tenders, safety supplies (clothing, booths, goggles, masks, respirators) and similar loose equipment.

82 *Fasteners*

Nuts, bolts, screws, washers, spring clips and similar fasteners (where not ordered as an integral part of another sub-group).

86 *Testing and Initial Start-Up*

Provision of engineers and supervisory staff for initial testing and start-up of plant prior to commissioning.

87 *Catalyst and Chemicals*

The initial supply of fresh or used catalyst, acids, soda.

88 *Initial Maintenance Spare Parts*

Spare parts (for one years' operation) for a new construction project. (does not include installed spares).

89 *Miscellaneous Supplies*

Medical equipment and supplies, first aid equipment, and supplies, warehouse equipment and supplies, water, electricity, fuel, for construction purposes (where charged to project) and other items not specified elsewhere.

91 *Remedial Site Work*

Expenses involved in repairs or alterations to the plant in course of construction, occasioned by the restitution of items subject to damage or replacement due to theft, fire, accident, wilful damage, and the like.

92 *Rectification Work*

Expenses involved in repairs or alterations to the plant on setting to work, to achieve guarantees or other commitments, or during the maintenance period. (These expenses could arise after the job has been physically closed).

93 *Travelling Expenses*

All expenses incurred in the sending out of engineers, specialists, supervisors, such as board, lodging, travelling expenses, allowances and the like.

94 F.O.B. Expenses

Packing, transport costs, dock charges and dues on items for shipment abroad, where charged as a separate expense. Note that insurance ex works to f.o.b. is covered on a group basis, so that there will not be a separate charge for this.

95 *Materials (Bulk Orders)*

Pipe, plate and similar materials when ordered from 'stock', or in bulk prior to allocation to a specific use within the project.

96 *Packing and Miscellaneous Costs*

Packing and related costs for plant and equipment when not incorporated in the cost of the equipment, for shipment in Great Britain and Northern Ireland.

97 *Carriage*

Carriage and trans-shipment costs, when not incorporated in the cost of the equipment, or when dealt with on a 'group' or 'bulk' transport basis, for shipment in Great Britain and Northern Ireland.

99 *Revenue Items*

All items of a revenue nature

This appendix appears by kind permission of Courtaulds Engineering Lt

C

Typical Analysis of the Design Function

1 *Process Engineering*

Process evaluation, selection and the preparation of process data and engineering flow diagrams. Integration of process facilities and liaison with other departments, and process design of off-site facilities and utilities.

2 *Project Engineering*

Co-ordination and overall supervision of the engineering design and construction activities, liaising with the client's representatives as necessary.

3 *Electrical Engineering*

Design work associated with the electrical power and lighting facilities within the site, including the preparation of general arrangement and detailed drawings, with the writing of requisitions and material schedules as required for procurement and installation.

4 *Structural Engineering*

All calculations and design work for steel framed buildings, process plant steelwork and supporting structures. General arrangement drawings are prepared and the vendor's detailed drawings and specifications-checked.

5 *Architectural and Civil Works*

The design and specification of all civil and building works, including site preparation, access roads, drainage and effluent disposal, plant and building foundations.

6 *Mechanical Engineering*

Preparation of specifications and requisitions for all mechanical equipment, with the subsequent approval of vendor's drawings and specifications.

7 *Heating, Ventilating and Conditioning*

The basic design and specification of heating, air conditioning and associated facilities for buildings, with the issue of requisitions to specialist manufacturers and subsequent approval of suppliers' proposals.

8 *Vessel Design*

Stress calculations and design work on pressure vessels, heat exchangers and furnaces to a degree sufficient to enable competitive tenders to be invited from specialist suppliers, with subsequent approval of drawings and specifications submitted by suppliers.

9 *Instrumentation Engineering*

The specification of instrumentation in accordance with the process requirements, with the preparation of the relevant drawings and requisitions. Drawings and other data submitted by specialist vendors are subject to approval.

10 *Piping Engineering*

Design work and stress calculations for pipework throughout the installation, with the preparation of plot plans, detail drawings, piping layouts, piping isometrics, specifications, material schedules and requisitions. Where appropriate, block and detailed models would be prepared to facilitate design.

11 *Materials Handling*

Preparation of integrated schemes, with the relevant layouts and general arrangement drawings together with subsequent approval of the suppliers' proposals in relation thereto.

Index